The Geography of Travel and Tourism

BRIAN G. BONIFACE

BA, MA, (University of Georgia), MTS
*Lecturer in Geography, Bournemouth
and Poole College of Further Education*

CHRISTOPHER P. COOPER

BSc., Ph.D, MTS
Lecturer in Tourism, University of Surrey

HEINEMANN PROFESSIONAL PUBLISHING

Heinemann Professional Publishing Ltd
Halley Court, Jordan Hill, Oxford OX2 8EJ

OXFORD   LONDON   MELBOURNE   AUCKLAND   SINGAPORE
IBADAN   NAIROBI   GABORONE   KINGSTON

First published 1987
Reprinted 1988, 1990

British Library Cataloguing in Publication Data
Boniface, Brian G.
  The geography of travel and tourism.
  1. Tourist trade
  I. Title   II. Cooper, Christopher P.
  338.4'791   G155.A1

ISBN 0 434 90166 0

Printed and bound in Great Britain by
Butler & Tanner Ltd, Frome and London

The Geography of Travel
and Tourism

WITHDRAWN

97

Contents

Preface   xi

Acknowledgements   xv

1 An introduction to the geography of tourism   1
   Learning objectives   1
   Leisure, recreation, and tourism   1
   Geography and tourism   3
   Summary   7

2 The geography of demand for tourism   8
   Learning objectives   8
   Leisure, recreation, and tourism: a basic human right?   8
   The demand for tourism: concepts and definitions   8
   Effective demand   9
   Suppressed demand   14
   Summary   15

3 The geography of resources for tourism   17
   Learning objectives   17
   Introduction   17
   Resources for tourism   17
   The world scale   18
   The national scale   26
   The local scale   27
   The pleasure periphery   29
   Summary   29

4 The elements of transport for tourism   30
    Learning objectives   30
    Introduction   30
    Principles of interaction   30
    The elements of transport   31
    Transport costs and pricing   32
    Transport modes   33
    Transport routes and networks   35
    Summary   36

5 The geography of transport for tourism   37
    Learning objectives   37
    Air transport   37
    Surface transport   40
    Summary   42

6 The demand for tourism in the British Isles   44
    Learning objectives   44
    Introduction   44
    Changes in post-war British society   44
    British residents' demand for tourism   46
    Demand for tourism in the British Isles from overseas   50
    Summary   51

7 The supply of tourism in the British Isles   52
    Learning objectives   52
    The physical setting for tourism   52
    The components of tourism   53
    The regional setting for tourism   57
    Summary   61

8 Scandinavia   62
    Learning objectives   62
    Introduction   62
    Denmark   63
    Norway   64
    Sweden   66
    Finland   67
    Iceland   68
    Summary   69

9 Central Europe: Austria, Switzerland, and West Germany   70
    Learning objectives   70
    Introduction   70
    Austria   71
    Switzerland   74
    West Germany   75
    Summary   77

10   The Benelux countries   79
Learning objectives   79
Introduction   79
The Netherlands   80
Belgium   82
Luxembourg   83
Summary   84

11   France   85
Learning objectives   85
Introduction   85
The demand for tourism in France   86
The organization of tourism in France   87
Tourist resources and planning in France   88
Summary   92

12   The Iberian Peninsula   94
Learning objectives   94
Introduction   94
Spain   95
Gibraltar   101
Portugal   101
Summary   103

13   Italy, Malta, Greece, and Yugoslavia   104
Learning objectives   104
Introduction   104
Italy   104
Malta   108
Greece   109
Yugoslavia   111
Summary   114

14   Eastern Europe and the USSR   115
Learning objectives   115
Introduction   115
Hungary   116
Czechoslovakia   118
Rumania   119
Bulgaria   119
Poland   120
The German Democratic Republic   120
Albania   121
The USSR   121
Summary   124

15   Africa   125
   Learning objectives   125
   Introduction   125
   North West Africa   126
   East Africa   131
   Southern Africa   134
   The islands of the Indian Ocean   136
   West Africa   137
   Central Africa   138
   Summary   139

16   The Levant and the Middle East   140
   Learning objectives   140
   Introduction   140
   The Levant   141
   The Middle East   145
   Summary   147

17   Asia   148
   Learning objectives   148
   Introduction   148
   The Indian subcontinent   149
   Southeast Asia   152
   The Far East   155
   Summary   158

18   Australasia   160
   Learning objectives   160
   Introduction   160
   Australia   161
   New Zealand   165
   The Pacific Islands   166
   Summary   167

19   North America   169
   Learning objectives   169
   Introduction   169
   The United States   170
   Canada   178
   Summary   182

20   Latin America and the Caribbean   183
   Learning objectives   183
   Introduction   183
   The Caribbean Islands   184
   Mexico   188
   Central America   190

South America   191
Summary   196

Further reading   198

Selected bibliography   201

Appendices   203

Indexes   216

Preface

Tourism is a growing area of study in its own right, boasting its own journals and a small academic community. Although tourism is being increasingly taught at a variety of levels ranging from schools to university departments, it is often seen as providing good case study material which can be utilized by other disciplines, rather than as a separate subject.

The subject area of tourism is characterized by two main concerns. It is first and foremost multidisciplinary with the human dimensions of tourism attracting the attentions of geographers, historians, and behavioural scientists while the nature of tourism as a commercial activity appeals to those engaged in economics and business studies. Secondly it is a young area of study – at most fifty years old – without the antecedents of a mature subject. Indeed tourism, and leisure studies in general, have only recently been recognized as areas worthy of investigation.

However, the rapid growth of world tourism and its associated problems have prompted academics, governments, and businesses to take close interest. Yet there are signs that this growth of the subject area is too rapid. Not only has it spawned the proliferation of ideographic studies, but it has also encouraged an increasingly fragmented and specialized approach, accentuating lack of direction and threatening the coherence of the subject area.

The need to synthesize information from a variety of sources is a familiar one to geographers and one with which they are well equipped to deal. The geographer's contribution to tourism must focus around the spatial expression of tourism as a human activity. This involves the study of both tourist-generating areas and tourist-receiving areas, as well as the links between them. Geographers must also be aware of the economic, political, and cultural background to developments in tourism and be able to chart the place of tourism in the regional geography of the world, particularly as this branch of the subject is enjoying a revival.

However, there is evidence that geographers are failing in the task of training potential recruits for the travel and tourism industry effectively. There is a current concern among both representatives of the industry and tourism teachers that students often have a poor knowledge of basic geography. While most students have been taught the subject at school, few appear to be equipped with the practical stock of geographical knowledge required by the travel and tourism industry. They are not, in general, well informed on such facts as national capitals, frontiers, ports, rivers, mountain ranges, and climate; even more serious, they often have only a hazy notion of distance and the locations of tourist destinations. This information is both basic and mundane, yet it is weaknesses in these areas which have brought problems to students and teachers on tourism courses, and subsequently to employers in the industry.

It is possible to point to a number of factors

which have contributed to this situation. Firstly, the scope of geographical teaching in many British schools is restricted to the rigid elements of the syllabus laid down by the examining bodies. This can exclude from consideration many countries which are now becoming important tourist destinations, and increasingly a case study approach is used concentrating on agriculture and manufacturing while neglecting service industries such as tourism. Secondly, in many educational establishments geography has been neglected in favour of environmental studies which stress the home region rather than the wider world view. Finally, there is the attitude among many in academic circles that systematic learning about the location of places is somehow old-fashioned 'capes and bays' geography, descriptive rather than analytical.

There is then a gap in the available literature which this book seeks to fill, partly to satisfy the vocational needs of the travel and tourism industry mentioned above. The student is provided in this volume, if not with solutions to the usual questions about tourist destinations, at least with the necessary knowledge to point him/her in the right direction – for example we do not specifically address the issue of the impact of tourism as this is covered elsewhere. A twofold approach has been adopted; firstly outlining the basic principles underlying the geography of tourist demand, supply, and transportation, and secondly carrying out a broad regional survey of world tourism, drawing heavily on the principles laid down in the first section. Considerable space has been devoted to European tourism, including the British Isles, in view of Europe's pre-eminence as both a tourist-generating and receiving area, but other regions have not been neglected, including those areas with tourist potential as well as those already important as both destinations and generators. Particular attention has been given to regions such as Africa and Latin America as students may find it difficult to obtain information about the tourist geography of these regions elsewhere. Regional groupings of countries follow those of the International Air Transport Association where possible, but for some chapters geographical logic dictated otherwise – for example North Africa has been retained as part of

the African region for the purposes of this book. Again, to avoid confusion most place names have been anglicized.

It is hoped that this book will provide a way of thinking about the geography of world tourism and act as a handbook for further study. It is intended that the book should be used with a good atlas and that students will update their knowledge with an awareness of current affairs and news events. The bibliography and guide to further reading are selective, drawing on sources readily available to the student and avoiding citing less accessible works.

This book is designed primarily for students taking tourism courses at the level of the British Business and Technician Education Council and the Scottish Vocational Education Council diplomas in both business studies and in hotel and catering studies. By including chapter by chapter objectives the book will allow independent study. The book will also be valuable to students who study the geography of tourism in schools and those following vocational courses such as those provided by the British Institute of Travel and Tourism, City and Guilds, and the Association of British Travel Agents. While the book is written with a UK audience in mind, the approach can be readily adapted for the purposes of students and teachers of tourism in English-speaking countries throughout the world. Finally those employed in the tourism business whether they be in travel agencies, tour operations, airlines, or shipping will find this book a useful source of information.

Throughout, the guiding hand of Professor Medlik is evident, not only in terms of the overall inspiration and discipline he has encouraged in the book but also his encyclopaedic knowledge of tourism across the globe. His help with, and positive criticism of, our drafts are gratefully acknowledged. Many others have helped to produce this book, both wittingly and unwittingly – the staff in libraries of the Dorset Institute of Higher Education, the Bournemouth and Poole College of Further Education, and the British Tourist Authority/English Tourist Board have been invaluable in their cooperation and search for material, as have the national tourist organizations, embassies, and consulates of most of the world's countries. Last but not least our colleagues and families have been particularly forbearing given the time and effort that this book has involved, and Mrs Cooper Senior undertook the chore of producing the typescript with her characteristic enthusiasm and accuracy.

Acknowledgements

The authors and publisher gratefully acknowledge permission to use the following copyright material.

For Figure 1.1 reprinted by kind permission of Annals of Tourism Research; for Appendix 10 reproduced from *Recreational Geography* by Patrick Lavery (ed) in the Problems of Modern Geography Series by permission of David and Charles; for Figure 11.2 taken from *Modern France* by I. B. Thompson p. 444 (Butterworth 1970) and used by permission of the publisher, Butterworth and Co. (Publishers) Ltd. and H. D. Clout, *The Geography of Post-war France* (1972) reprinted with permission from Pergamon Press; for the map in Appendix 1 reproduced by kind permission of the International Air Transport Association.

ONE

An introduction to the geography of tourism

LEARNING OBJECTIVES

After reading this chapter, you should be able to:

1 *Define and use the terms leisure, recreation, and tourism and understand their inter-relationships.*
2 *Distinguish between the different forms of tourism – international and domestic, long and short haul, and holiday, common interest, and business tourism.*
3 *Appreciate the importance of scale in explaining patterns of tourism.*
4 *Identify the three major geographical components of tourism – tourist-generating areas, tourist-receiving areas, and transit routes.*
5 *Explain the push and pull factors which give rise to tourist flows.*
6 *Appreciate the main methods used to measure tourist flows and be aware of their problems.*
7 *Explain and use the term carrying capacity.*

Leisure, recreation, and tourism

What exactly is meant by the terms leisure, recreation, and tourism and how are they related?

Leisure is a measure of time and is usually used to mean the time left over after work, sleep, and personal and household chores have been completed (Figure 1.1). In other words, leisure is free for individuals to spend as they please. This does however introduce the problem of whether all free time is leisure. A good example of this dilemma is whether the unemployed feel that their free time is in fact 'enforced' leisure. This has led to the view that leisure is as much an attitude of mind as a measure of time.

Recreation is normally taken to mean the variety of activities undertaken during leisure time (Figure 1.1). Basically, recreation refreshes a person's strength and spirit and can include activities as diverse as watching television, or holidaying abroad.

If leisure is a measure of time, and recreation embraces the activities undertaken during that time, then *tourism* is simply one of those activities. It is however, more difficult to desentangle the meanings of the terms recreation and tourism in practice. Perhaps the most helpful way to think about the difference is to envisage a continuum with, at one end, recreation based either at home or close to home, and at the opposite extreme travel for tourism where some distance is involved and overnight accommodation may be needed. This continuum is based on the time needed for the activity and the distance travelled, and it places

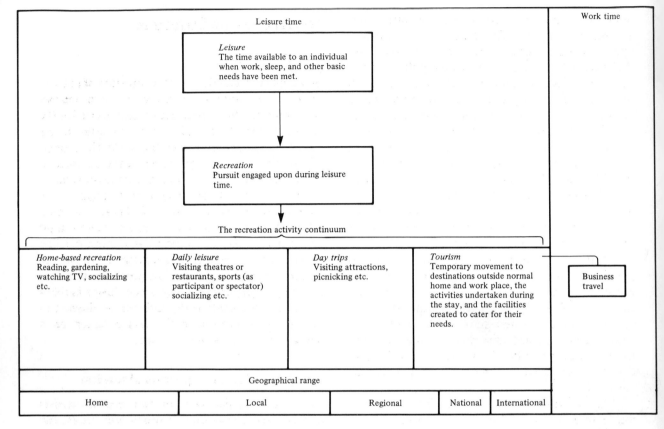

Figure 1.1   *Leisure, recreation, and tourism*

tourism firmly at one extreme of the recreational activity spectrum (Figure 1.1).

Clearly tourism is a distinctive form of recreation and demands separate consideration. Many different definitions of tourism exist and for the purposes of this book the definition of Mathieson and Wall (1982) has been adopted: 'Tourism is the temporary movement of people to destinations outside their normal place of work and residence, the activities undertaken during their stay in these destinations and the facilities created to cater for their needs'. Of course, tourism itself is only one part of the spectrum of travel which ranges from daily travel to work, or for shopping, to migration, where the traveller intends to take up permanent or long-term residence in another area.

Forms of tourism

Tourism can be divided into many different forms on the basis of length of stay, type of transport used, price paid or the number of travellers in the group. From a geographical point of view important distinctions are those between international and domestic tourism, and long and short haul tourism. *Domestic tourism* embraces those travelling within their own country, while *international tourism* comprises those who travel to a country other than that in which they normally live. International tourists invariably have to cross national frontiers and may well have to use another currency and encounter a different language. Clearly, the size of a country is important here. Larger countries are more likely to have a variety of tourist attractions and resorts and, quite simply, the greater physical distances which have to be overcome may deter international tourism. This is exemplified by the volumes of domestic tourism in the USA (almost 90 per cent of all tourism) and the Netherlands (around 50 per cent). Increasingly, too, the distinction between these two forms of tourism is diminishing as the facilitation of movement between countries is increased and barriers to travel lowered. *Long haul tourism* is generally taken to be journeys of over 3000 kilometres, while *short haul tourism* comprises journeys below that distance. The distinction is important in terms of aircraft operations and for marketing.

A further basic distinction in tourism relates to purpose of visit (again a marketing consideration). *Holiday tourism* is perhaps the most commonly understood form. It can be divided into the 'sun, sea and sand' type where good weather and beach-related activities are important or the 'touring, sight-seeing, and culture' type where new destinations, and different life styles, are sought (Holloway, 1983).

Common interest tourism comprises those travelling with a purpose common to visitor and visited (such as visiting friends and relatives, religion, health, or education reasons). Those visiting friends and relatives may make little or no demand upon accommodation or other tourist facilities at the destination.

Business tourism makes up the final purpose-of-visit category. Included among business tourists are those attending trade fairs and conferences, or participating in incentive travel schemes. The inclusion of business travel complicates the simple idea of tourism being just another recreational activity. Clearly business travel is not regarded as part of a person's leisure time and cannot be thought of as recreation. Yet, because business travellers do ·use the same facilities as those travelling for pleasure and they are not permanent employees or residents of the host destination, they must be included in any definition of 'tourists' (Figure 1.1).

Geography and tourism

The idea of scale

Geographers study the spatial expression of tourism as a human activity, focusing on both tourist-generating and tourist-receiving areas, as well as the links between. This study can be undertaken at a variety of *scales* ranging from the world distribution of climatic zones, through the regional assessment of tourist resources, to the local landscapes of resorts.

The idea of scale has been used to organize the material presented in this book because at each different scale, a distinctive perspective and insight on tourism is gained. Simply, as a more detailed explanation is required, attention is drawn to smaller and smaller parts of the problem. This idea of scale, or geographical magnitude, keeps in focus the area being dealt with, and can be likened to increasing or decreasing the magnification on a microscope or the scale of a map.

The geographical components of tourism

From a geographical point of view tourism consists of three major components which are: firstly, the countries of origin of tourists, or generating areas; secondly, the tourist destinations themselves; and finally, the routes travelled between these two sets of locations (Leiper, 1979). This simple model is illustrated in Figure 1.2 and the components form the basis for Chapters 2 to 5 in this book.

Taking each of these components in turn, *tourist-generating areas* represent the homes of tourists, where journeys begin and end. The key issues to examine in tourist-generating areas are the features which stimulate demand for tourism and will include the geographical location of an area as well as its socio-economic and demographic characteristics. These areas represent the main tourist markets in the world and naturally enough, the major marketing functions of the tourist industry are found here (tour operation, travel retailing, etc.). Tourist-generating areas are considered in Chapter 2.

Tourist-destination areas attract tourists to stay temporarily and will have features which may not be found in the generating areas. The tourist

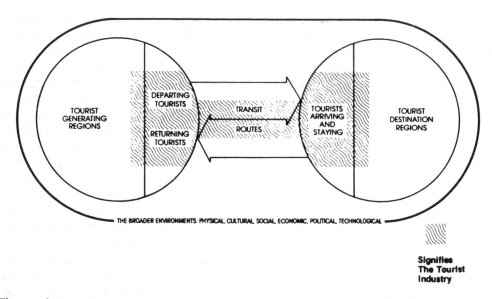

Figure 1.2 *The tourism system*
Source: Leiper, N., 'The Framework of Tourism', *Annals of Tourism Research*, vol. 6, no. 1., 1979, pp. 390–407.

industry located in this area will comprise the accommodation, retailing and service functions, entertainment, and recreation. Features of tourist-destination areas are examined in Chapter 3.

Transit routes link these two types of areas and are a key element in the system as their efficiency and characteristics shape the size and direction of tourist flows. Transit routes represent the location of the main transportation component of the tourist industry and are considered in Chapters 4 and 5.

Tourist flows

Introducing tourist flows

While the study of the geography of tourism should include the three components identified above, there is a danger that, in conveniently dissecting tourism into its component parts, the all important inter-relationships are lost. The consideration of *tourist flows* between regions is therefore fundamental to the geography of tourism and allows the components of tourism to be viewed as a total system, rather than a series of disconnected parts.

Tourist flows are a form of spatial interaction between two areas with the destination area con-taining a surplus of a commodity (tourist attrac-tions for example) and the generating area having a deficit, or demand for that commodity. In fact, it is possible to detect regular patterns of tourist flows. They do not occur randomly but follow certain rules and are influenced by a variety of push and pull factors.

Push factors are mainly concerned with the stage of economic development in the generating area and will include such factors as levels of affluence, mobility, and holiday entitlement. Often too, an advanced stage of economic development will not only give the population the means to engage in tourism but the pressures of life will provide the 'push' to do so. Pull factors include accessibility, and the attractions and amenities of the destination area. The relative cost of the visit is also important, as is the marketing and promotion of the receiving area.

Explaining tourist flows

The flows, or interaction, between places are highly complex and influenced by a wide variety of inter-related variables. A number of attempts have been made to explain the factors which affect tourist flows and to come up with rules governing the magnitude of flows between regions. Firstly, Williams and Zelinsky (1970) selected fourteen countries which had relatively stable tourist flows over a few years and accounted for the bulk of the world's tourist traffic. They identified a number of factors which helped to explain these flows. These factors included distances between countries (the greater the distance, the smaller the volume of flow); international connectivity (shared business or cultural ties between countries); and the general attractiveness of one country for another.

A second means of explaining tourist flows is offered by the gravity model, based on two main factors which influence flows. The first of these is the push and pull factors which generate flows and the gravity model states that the larger the 'mass' of the pushing or pulling regions, the greater the flow between them. The second factor is a restraining one, based on the distance between the origin and the destination of the flow. Here, the time and cost involved in travel act to reduce flows with distance. This is known as the friction of distance. The gravity model is explained in Appendix 1.

Measuring tourist flows

As tourist flows have grown in prominence, national governments and international organizations have introduced the measurement of both international and domestic flows. Burkart and Medlik (1981) have identified three main reasons why this statistical measurement of flows is important. Firstly, statistics are required to evaluate the magnitude of tourism flows and to monitor any change. This allows projections of future flows to be made and the identification of market trends. Secondly, statistics act as a base of hard fact to allow tourism planners and developers to operate effectively and plan for the future of tourism. Thirdly, the statistics are used by both the public and private sectors as a basis for their marketing.

Measurement of tourist flows can be divided into three main types. *Statistics of volume* give the number of tourists leaving an area or visiting a destination in a given period of time and provide a basic count of the volume of tourist traffic. Volume

statistics also include the length of stay of visitors at their destination. The second category of statistics is that of *tourist characteristics*. While statistics of volume are a measure of the quantity of tourist flows, this second category measures the quality of the flow and will include information on types of tourist (sex, age, socio-economic group, etc.) and their behaviour (structure of the trip, attitudes to the destination, etc.). It is not uncommon for statistics of tourist characteristics and volume to be collected together. The third type is *expenditure statistics*. Tourist flows are not simply movements of people but they also have an important economic significance for the destinations, the generating region, and the transport carriers.

A variety of methods are available to measure tourist flows. For volume statistics, tourists can be counted as 'they enter or leave an area and immigration figures will often provide this information. Obviously this is relatively straightforward for international flows, but much more problematical for domestic tourism. For destination areas, an alternative method is to enumerate tourists at their accommodation by the use of registration cards. This method is only effective with legal enforcement and normally omits visitors staying in private houses, or with friends or relatives.

Statistics of domestic tourism volume may be obtained by national travel surveys or destination surveys. National travel surveys involve interviewing a representative sample of the population in their own homes. Questions are asked on the nature and extent of travel over a past period (normally a year) and the results provide statistics not only on the volume of domestic tourism, but also may include expenditure and the character of the flows. Examples of national travel surveys include the British National Travel Survey, the new British Tourism Survey, and the German Reiseanalyse. In destination surveys visitors to a tourist area, specific site, or attraction are questioned to establish the volume, value, and characteristics of traffic to the area or site.

Surveys of tourist characteristics have evolved from straightforward questioning which gives basic factual information (for example the age profile of visitors) to surveys which now concentrate on questions designed to assist the marketing and management of a destination, or to solve a particular problem. Statistics of tourist characteristics are obtained in a variety of ways. Additional questions can be added to accommodation registration cards, or border checks, but more commonly a sample of travellers is asked a series of questions about themselves, their trip, opinions of the destination, etc. (An example of this approach is the UK International Passenger Survey (IPS) which measures the volume and value as well as the characteristics of UK inbound and outbound tourism.)

Measurement of tourist expenditure can be obtained by asking tourists directly how much they have spent on their holiday, or indirectly by asking hoteliers and other suppliers of tourist services for estimates of tourist spending. For international expenditure statistics, bank records of foreign currency exchange may be used as another indirect method.

Despite the variety of methods available to measure tourist flows, it is not easy to produce accurate tourist statistics. In the first place, the tourist has to be distinguished from other travellers (e.g. returning residents) and, while internationally agreed definitions of tourists do exist, they are not yet consistently applied throughout the world. At the same time, there is no real attempt to co-ordinate international surveys. To add to these problems, survey methods change over the years, even within single countries, and comparison of results from year to year is difficult. A further problem is that surveys count 'events' not people so that a tourist who visits a country twice in a year will be counted as two arrivals. Those on touring holidays may be counted as separate arrivals in various countries or areas and will inflate the overall visitor arrival figures. The relaxation of border controls, especially within groups of trading countries (such as the European Economic Community (EEC), aggravates the statistician's problem making it difficult to enumerate tourists.

Capacity to accommodate tourist flows

One result of tourist flows may be that the pressures of demand on a destination become too great and begin to threaten the existence and quality of the very features that tourists have come to see. Therefore, before flows are encouraged, a destination must be assessed for its capacity to absorb tourists.

A useful rule of thumb here is *Defert's Tourist Function Index* which compares the number of tourist beds available in a destination to the total number of residents, or hosts, in the region (see Appendix 2). The index is a useful guide to the relative magnitude of tourism in a region but does underestimate the important impact of tourism in major cities where the resident population is large.

A second approach is to look at *carrying capacity*. Carrying capacity can be defined as 'the maximum number of people who can use a destination without an unacceptable alteration in the physical environment and without an unacceptable decline in the quality of the experience gained by visitors' (Mathieson and Wall, 1982). Although the emphasis is on the destination area, carrying capacity problems can arise in each of the three component areas of tourism. In tourist-generating areas problems may arise from a failure to stagger holiday periods leading to a concentration of demand at particular times. On the transit routes bottlenecks and delays may occur if the system cannot cope with demand, and in the tourist-receiving areas the tourist resources may be at risk. Carrying capacity depends on two sets of factors; the physical/environmental, and the psychological.

Firstly, there are the basic physical and environmental characteristics of a destination which will influence the number of tourists that can be absorbed. The *physical capacity* of a destination relates to the amount of suitable land available for accommodation, tourist facilities, and services such as roads and water supply. It also includes the finite capacity of facilities such as car parking spaces, seats in theatres or restaurants, and also the capacity of local transport systems. Physical capacity is a relatively straightforward concept and is useful in planning resorts and destinations.

Environmental carrying capacity is the most commonly used, although more difficult to measure. Most tourist destinations suffer some form of environmental wear and tear, whether it be the trampling away of grassy swards at picnic sites, disturbance of wildlife, or the physical erosion of important historic monuments by visitors' feet. However, while it is very clear at some destinations that environmental capacity has been exceeded, it is difficult to judge the point at which this 'wear' becomes 'unacceptable' rather than simply a necessary but harmless effect of visitors enjoying themselves. The carrying capacity of an area may be altered by careful management. For example parts of the Appalachian Trail in the USA and the Pennine Way in England have been given an artificial surface to absorb the impact of visitors.

The second set of factors influencing carrying capacity is even more complex to assess. The psychological or *perceptual capacity* of a destination is exceeded when the visitor's experience is significantly impaired. This depends on visitors' attitudes to both the number and behaviour of other users, and also their tolerance of the physical wear and tear or pollution at the destination. Again, psychological capacity can be manipulated by managers of a destination. For example, vegetation may be used as screening to reduce feelings of crowding, or to separate conflicting activities (such as sports and picnicking).

Summary

Leisure has come to be accepted as a measure of free time, while recreation is seen as the activity undertaken during that time. Tourism is a distinctive form of recreation including a stay away from home, often involving long-distance travel, and encompassing travel for business or vocational purposes. Different types of tourism can be distinguished including domestic and international tourism and a variety of purpose-of-travel markets.

From a geographical point of view, tourism can be considered from a number of scales from the world scale, to the regional, and local scales, depending upon the level of detail required. Tourism consists of three main geographical components; the tourist-generating areas, the tourist-receiving areas, and transit routes. The study of tourist flows through this system is fundamental to the geography of tourism and can be achieved by considering the push and pull factors which give rise to these flows.

As tourist flows have grown in importance, two issues have arisen. The first is the need to measure these flows, and the statistics which result can be conveniently classified into statistics of volume, expenditure, and tourist characteristics. The second issue is that of the capacity of the destination to absorb flows.

The geography of demand for tourism

After reading this chapter, you should be able to:

1 Explain the term *tourist demand* and distinguish between its components.
2 Understand the concepts of travel propensity and frequency.
3 Identify the determinants of demand for tourism.
4 Explain the influence of stage in economic development, population factors, and political regimes on demand for tourism.
5 Understand the influence of personal variables on the demand for tourism.
6 Appreciate the main barriers to travel which lead to suppressed demand.

Leisure, recreation, and tourism: a basic human right?

Leisure, recreation, and tourism are of benefit to both individuals and societies. The United Nations (UN) recognized this as early as 1948 by adopting its Universal Declaration of Human Rights which states that everyone 'has the right to rest and leisure including . . . periodic holidays with pay'. More specifically in 1980 the World Tourism Organization declared the ultimate aim of tourism to be 'the improvement of the quality of life and the creation of better living conditions for all peoples'.

This chapter examines how participation in tourism differs between both nations and individuals and explains why, despite declarations to the contrary, tourism is an activity highly concentrated among the affluent, industrialized nations. For much of the rest of the world, and indeed many disadvantaged groups in industrialized nations, participation in tourism remains an unobtainable luxury.

The demand for tourism: concepts and definitions

Geographers define *tourist demand* as 'the total number of persons who travel, or wish to travel, to use tourist facilities and services at places away from their places of work and residence' (Mathieson and Wall, 1982). This definition implies a wide range of influences, in addition to price and income, as determinants of demand and includes not only those who actually participate in tourism, but also those who wish to, but for some reason, do not.

Demand for tourism consists of a number of components. *Effective or actual demand* comprises the actual numbers of participants in tourism. This is the component of demand most commonly and easily measured and the bulk of tourist statistics refer to effective demand. *Suppressed demand* is made up of that section of the population who do not travel for some reason.

Two elements of suppressed demand can be distinguished. Firstly, potential demand refers to those who will travel at some future date if, for example, purchasing power increases or other relevant social changes take place. Deferred demand is a demand postponed because of the scarcity of a good or service (e.g. travel opportunities). In other words, both deferred and potential demand may be converted into effective demand at some future date. Finally there will always be those who simply do not wish to travel, constituting a category of *no demand*.

Effective demand

Travel propensity

In tourism, a useful measure of effective demand is *travel propensity*, meaning the percentage of a population who actually engage in tourism. *Net travel propensity* refers to the percentage of the population who take at least one tourism trip in a given period of time, while *gross travel propensity* gives the total number of tourism trips taken as a percentage of the population. Clearly, as second and third holidays increase in importance, so gross travel propensity becomes more relevant. Simply dividing gross travel propensity by net will give the *travel frequency*, in other words the average number of trips taken by those participating in tourism during the period in question (see Appendix 3).

The suppressed and no demand components will ensure that net travel propensity never approaches 100 per cent and a figure of 70 per cent or 80 per cent is likely to be the maximum. Gross travel propensity however, can exceed 100 per cent and often approaches 200 per cent in some Western European countries where those participating in tourism take more than one trip away from home annually.

Travel propensity is determined by a variety of factors which, for the purposes of this chapter, can be divided into two broad groups. Firstly, there are the influences that lie at the national level of generalization and comprise the world view of travel propensity including economic development, population characteristics, and political regimes. Secondly, a personal view of variations in travel propensity can be envisaged in such terms as life style, life cycle, and personality factors. In fact, a third group of factors relating to the supply of tourist services is also important. This group encompasses the price, frequency, and speed of transport, as well as the characteristics of accommodation, facilities, and travel organizers. These factors are dealt with in Chapters 3 to 5.

The world view

(i) Stage in economic development

A society's *level of economic development* is a major determinant of the magnitude of tourist demand because the economy influences so many critical, and inter-related, factors. The economic development of nations can be divided into a number of stages, as outlined in Table 2.1.

As a society moves towards a developed economy a number of important processes occur. The nature of employment changes from work in the primary sector (agriculture, fishing, forestry) to work in the secondary sector (manufacturing goods) and the tertiary sector (services such as tourism). As this process unfolds an affluent society usually emerges and numbers of the economically active increase from around 30 per cent or less of the total population in the developing world to 50 per cent or more in the high mass consumption stage of Western Europe or the USA. With progression to the drive to maturity, discretionary incomes increase and create demand for consumer goods and leisure pursuits such as tourism.

Other developments parallel the changing nature of employment. The population is healthier and has time for recreation and tourism (including paid holiday entitlement). Improving educational standards and media channels boost awareness of tourism opportunities, and transportation and

Table 2.1 Economic development and tourism

Economic stage	Some characteristics	Examples
Traditional society Long-established land-owning aristocracy, traditional customs, majority employed in agriculture. Very low output per capita, impossible to improve without changing system. Poor health levels, high poverty levels.	**The undeveloped world** Economic and social conditions deny most forms of tourism.	Much of Africa; Southern Asia.
Pre-conditions for take-off Innovation of ideas from out-side the system. Leaders recognize the desirability of change. **Take-off** Leaders in favour of change gain power and alter production methods and economic structure. Manufacturing and services expand.	**The developing world** From the take-off stage, economic and social conditions allow increasing amounts of domestic tourism (mainly visiting friends and relatives). International tourism is also possible in the drive to maturity.	South and Central America[+]; parts of the Middle East[+] and Asia.
Drive to maturity[++] Industrialization continues in all economic sectors with a switch from heavy manufacturing to sophisticated and diversified products.		Iberian Peninsula; Mexico; parts of South America.
High mass consumption Economy now at full potential, producing large numbers of consumer goods and services. New emphasis on satisfying cultural needs.	**The developed world** Major generators of international and domestic tourism.	North America; Western Europe; Japan; Australia; New Zealand.

+ Countries which are members of the Organization of Petroleum Exporting Countries (OPEC) are a notable exception in these regions; examples include Algeria, Libya, Nigeria, Iran, Iraq, Kuwait, Saudi Arabia, Ecuador, and Venezuela.

++ Centrally planned economies merit a special classification, although most are at the drive to maturity stage; examples include China, Mongolia, North Korea, Vietnam, the USSR, Bulgaria, Czechoslovakia, East Germany, Hungary, Poland, and Romania.

Adapted from: Chubb, M. and Chubb, H. R., *One Third of Our Time*, Wiley, New York, 1981; Cleverdon, R., *The Economic and Social Impact of Tourism on Developing Countries*, Economist Intelligence Unit, 1979; Rostow, W. W., *The Stages of Economic Growth*, Cambridge University Press, 1959.

mobility rise in line with these changes. Institutions respond to this increased demand by developing a range of leisure products and services. These developments occur in conjunction with each other until, at the high mass consumption stage, all the economic indicators encourage high levels of travel propensity. Clearly, tourism is a result of industrialization and, quite simply, the more highly developed an economy, the greater the levels of tourist demand.

As more countries reach the drive to maturity or high mass consumption stage, so the volume of trade and foreign investment increases and business travel develops. Business travel is sensitive to economic activity, and although it could be argued that increasingly sophisticated communication systems may render business travel unnecessary, the very development of global markets and the constant need for face-to-face contact should ensure a continuing demand for business travel.

(ii) *Population factors*

Levels of population growth, its development, distribution, and density affect travel propensity. *Population growth and development* can be closely linked to the stages of economic growth outlined in Table 2.1 by considering the demographic transition where population growth and development is seen in terms of four connected phases.

Firstly, the high stationary phase corresponds to many undeveloped countries with high birth and death rates keeping the population at a fluctuating, but low level. Secondly, the early expanding phase sees high birth rates but a fall in death rates due to improved health, sanitation, and social stability leading to population expansion characterized by young, large families. These countries are often unable to provide for their growing populations and are gradually becoming poorer. Clearly tourism is a luxury that cannot be afforded, although some nations are developing an inbound tourism industry to earn foreign exchange. The late expanding phase sees a fall in the birth rate rooted in the growth of an industrial society and birth control technology. Most developing countries fit into these two categories with a transition to the late expanding phase paralleling the drive to

maturity. Finally, the low stationary phase corresponds to the high mass consumption stage of economic development. Here, birth and death rates have stabilized to a low level.

Population density has a less important influence on travel propensity than has the *distribution of population* between urban and rural areas. The densely populated rural nations of Southeast Asia have low travel propensities due to the level of economic development and the simple fact that the population is mainly dependent upon subsistence agriculture and has neither the time nor the income to devote to tourism. In contrast, densely populated urban areas normally indicate a developed economy with consumer purchasing power giving rise to high travel propensity and the urge to escape from the urban environment.

The distribution of population within a nation also affects patterns, rather than strictly levels, of tourist demand. Where population is concentrated into one part of the country tourism demand is distorted. This asymmetrical distribution of population is well illustrated by the United States where two-thirds of the population live in the eastern one-third of the country. The consequent east to west pattern of tourist flows (and permanent migrants) has placed pressure on the recreation and tourist resources of the western states.

At the regional level concentration of population into cities also has implications for demand patterns with a recreation and tourism hinterland often developing around the city.

(iii) *Political influences*

Politics affect travel propensities in both democratic and totalitarian nations. In democratic nations the degree of government involvement in promoting and providing facilities for tourism varies. Typically, Conservative administrations act to nurture an environment in which the tourism industries can flourish, rather than the administration being directly involved in tourism itself. Socialist administrations, on the other hand, encourage the involvement of the government in tourism and often provide opportunities for the 'disadvantaged' to participate in tourism. Democracies may also control levels of propensity for travel abroad by limiting the amount of foreign currency that can be taken out of a country. Commonly this occurs when a nation's own currency is weak or the economy faltering. A weak currency will also deter people from travelling abroad.

Currency controls are more common in Communist planned economies where levels of control of international tourism can be considerable. In Communist planned economies tourist organizations are centralized and act as an arm of the administration. Residents' travel is often curtailed and inbound tourism inhibited by the need to obtain visas. Despite this, Communist nations have strong constitutional protection of their citizens' right to free time and domestic holidays.

In a more general sense, unstable political regimes where civil disorder or war is prevalent may forbid non-essential travel, and inbound tourism will be adversely affected.

(iv)   *Patterns of tourist demand*

Generation of domestic tourist demand is an important consideration in world tourism because the great majority of tourist flows are domestic, although as many trips go unrecorded, domestic tourism volumes are notoriously difficult to obtain.

The volume of domestic tourism generated by a country is dependent upon geographical factors such as a country's size, proximity to other tourist destinations, and the richness of its tourist resources. In Europe, the Netherlands and Belgium have low domestic travel volumes due to the ease of reaching other countries, as well as the small size of their own countries. On the other hand, the USA offers a varied range of high quality tourist destinations resulting in a high volume of domestic tourism. Here, the cost and effort of leaving the country also act as a disincentive to international tourism (see Appendix 4).

International tourism in the world is expanding, though not as rapidly as domestic tourism. The majority of this growth has occurred since 1950 with international tourist arrivals almost trebling between 1950 and 1960. In 1960 arrivals stood at just over 70 million, a figure which had more than doubled by 1970 (to almost 160 million arrivals). This growth slowed during the 1970s due to the world recession, the energy crisis, and political uncertainties in many parts of the world, but the decade was characterized by the rise of oil-rich countries, and some Latin American countries, as major tourist generators.

As would be expected from the above sections the major holiday and business tourist-generating countries (Japan, and countries in Western Europe and North America) are all in the high mass consumption stage (Table 2.1). In the future it would be expected that countries in the drive to maturity stage of economic development will become important generators of tourism. Appendices 5, 6 and 7 provide a statistical summary of international tourism and related social and economic factors for selected countries in the world.

The personal view

Two sets of personal factors influence travel propensity. The first group of factors can be termed *life style* and include income, employment, holiday entitlement, educational attainment, and mobility. A second group come under the term *life cycle* where the age and domestic circumstances of an individual affect both the amount and type of tourism demanded. Naturally these factors are inter-related and complementary. A high status job is normally associated with an individual in middle age with a high income, above-average holiday entitlement, education, and mobility. The interweaving of these variables, coupled with their rapid growth throughout the twentieth century, have combined to make leisure, recreation, and tourism a major force in the developed world.

(i)   *Income*

Tourism is a luxury, an expensive activity that demands a certain threshold of income before an individual can choose to take part. Gross income is the total amount earned, but gives little indication of the money available to spend on tourism. Disposable income represents the money that actually reaches the public's hands to dispose of as they please, but demands on disposable income include essentials such as housing, food, and clothing. The most useful measure of the ability to participate in tourism is discretionary income, that is, the income left over when tax, housing, and the basics of life have been accounted for. Clearly, two households with the same gross incomes may have very different discretionary incomes.

A low discretionary income markedly depresses travel propensity. As discretionary income rises, the ability to partake of tourism is associated with the purchase of leisure-oriented goods, until, with a high discretionary income travel may reach a peak and then level off as the demands of a high-status job, and possibly frequent business trips, reduce the ability and desire to travel for pleasure.

(ii)   *Employment*
The nature of employment not only influences travel propensity by determining income and holiday entitlement, but it also has an effect upon the type of holiday demanded. A more fundamental distinction is between those in employment and those unemployed. The impact of unemployment on tourism demand is obvious, but the nature of demand is also changed with employment uncertainty encouraging later booking of trips, more domestic holidays, shorter lengths of stay, and lower spending levels.

(iii)   *Paid-holiday entitlement*
A variety of holiday arrangements now exist world-wide, with most nations having a number of one-day national holidays, as well as annual paid-holiday entitlement by law or collective agreements. Individual levels of paid-holiday entitlement would seem to be an obvious determinant of travel propensity, but in fact, the relationship is not straightforward. However, it is possible to make a number of generalizations.

Firstly, low levels of entitlement do act as a real constraint upon the ability to travel, whilst a high entitlement encourages travel. This is in part due to the inter-relationship between entitlement and factors such as job status, income, and mobility. Secondly, as levels of entitlement increase, the cost of tourism may mean that more of this entitlement will be spent at home. Thirdly, patterns of entitlement are changing. Entitlement is increasingly used as a wage bargaining tool and the introduction of flexi-time, work sharing, and long weekends will release blocks of time which may be used for short holiday breaks.

(iv)   *Other lifestyle factors*
Level of educational attainment is an important determinant of travel propensity as education broadens horizons and stimulates the desire to travel. Also, the better educated the individual, the higher his or her awareness and susceptibility to information, media, advertising, and sales promotion.

Personal mobility (generally the use of a motor car) is an important influence on travel propensity, especially with regard to domestic holidays. This variable will be discussed in Chapter 5.

(v)   *Life cycle*
The propensity to travel, and indeed the type of tourism experience demanded, is closely related to an individual's age. Whilst the conventional measurement is chronological age, domestic age better discriminates between types of tourist demand and levels of travel propensity. Domestic age refers to the stage in the life cycle reached by an individual and different stages are characterized by distinctive holiday demand and levels of travel propensity (Table 2.2).

(vi)   *Personality factors*
No two individuals are alike and differences in attitudes, perceptions, and motivation have an important influence on travel decisions. *Attitudes* depend on an individual's perception of the world. *Perceptions* are mental impressions of, say, a place or travel company and are determined by many factors which include childhood, family, and work experiences. As perceptions will be influential in making the decision to travel, it is important for planners and managers in tourist destinations to foster favourable 'images' of their locations in the public's mind.

Attitudes and perceptions in themselves do not explain why people want to travel. The inner urges which initiate travel demand are called *travel motivators*. Gray outlined a twofold classification of travel motivators.

Table 2.2 Domestic age and tourism demand

Adolescence/young adult

At this stage there is a need for independence and a search for identity. Typically, holidays independent of parents begin at around 15 years, constrained by lack of finance but compensated by having few other commitments, no shortage of free time, and a curiosity for new places and experiences. This group have a high propensity to travel, mainly on budget holidays using surface transport and self-catering accommodation.

Marriage

Before the arrival of children young couples often have a high income and few other ties giving them a high travel propensity, frequently overseas. The arrival of children coupled with the responsibility of a home mean that constraints of time and finance depress travel propensity. Holidays become more organizational than geographical with domestic tourism, self-catering accommodation, and visiting friends and relatives increasingly common. As children grow up and reach the adolescence stage, constraints of time and finance are lifted and parents' travel propensity increases.

Retirement

The emergence of early retirement at fifty or fifty-five years is creating an active and mobile group in the population who will demand both domestic and international travel. In later retirement lack of finance, infirmity, and often the loss of a partner act to offset the increase in free time experienced by this group. Holidays become more hotel-based and travel propensity decreases.

Firstly, wanderlust is simply curiosity to experience the strange and unfamiliar. It refers to the basic trait in human nature to see, at first hand, different places, cultures and peoples. Secondly, sunlust can literally be translated as the desire for sun and a better climate, but in fact it is broader than this and refers to the search for a better set of amenities than are available at home. It is unusual to travel for one motivator alone and instead some combination of the two is more common.

The interaction of personality attributes such as attitudes, perceptions, and motivation allow different types of tourist to be identified. One classification by Cohen (1972) is particularly useful. He uses a classification based on the theory that tourism combines the curiosity to seek out new experiences with the need for the security of familiar reminders of home. Cohen proposes a continuum of possible combinations of novelty and familiarity and, by breaking up the continuum into typical combinations of these two ingredients, a fourfold classification of tourists is produced (Table 2.3).

Suppressed demand

Throughout this chapter the concern has been to identify factors which influence effective tourist demand. Yet tourism is still an unobtainable luxury for the majority of the world's population, not just in undeveloped and developing countries, but also for many in the developed world. Lansing and Blood identified five major reasons why people do not travel: expense of travel, lack of time, physical limitations (such as ill health), family circumstances, and lack of interest. It is not uncommon for individuals to experience a combination of two or more of these barriers. For example, a one-parent family may find lack of income and time will combine with family circumstances to prevent tourism travel. Obviously it is just these groups who would most benefit from a holiday and tourism planners are increasingly concerned to identify these barriers and devise programmes to encourage non-participants to travel. Perhaps the best known example of this is the *social tourism movement* which is concerned with the participation in travel by people with some form of handicap or disadvantage, and the measures used to encourage this participation.

Table 2.3   Cohen's classification of tourists

The organized mass tourist
Low on adventurousness he/she is anxious to maintain his/her 'environmental bubble' on the trip. Typically purchasing a ready-made package tour off-the-shelf, he/she is guided through the destination having little contact with local culture or people.

Institutionalized tourism
Dealt with routinely by the tourism industry – tour operators, travel agents, hoteliers and transport operators.

Familiarity

The individual mass tourist
Similar to the above but more flexibility and scope for personal choice is built-in. However, the tour is still organized by the tourism industry and the environmental bubble shields him/her from the real experience of the destination.

The explorer
The trip is organized independently and is looking to get off the beaten track. However, comfortable accommodation and reliable transport are sought and whilst the environmental bubble is abandoned on occasion, it is there to step into if things get tough.

Non-institutionalized tourism
Individual travel, shunning contact with the tourism industry except where absolutely necessary.

The drifter
All connections with the tourism industry are spurned and the trip attempts to get as far from home and familiarity as possible. With no fixed itinerary, the drifter lives with the local people, paying his way and immersing himself in their culture.

Novelty

Adapted from: Cohen, E., 'Toward a Sociology of International Tourism', *Social Research*, Vol. 39, No. 1, pp. 164–82, 1972.

Summary

Tourism is a major contribution to the quality of life in the twentieth century and demand for tourism is made up not only of those who participate, but also those who do not travel for some reason. Travel propensity is a useful indicator of tourism participation as it gives the proportion of a population who actually engage in tourism. Travel frequency refers to the average number of trips taken by those participating in tourism, during a specified period.

Travel propensity is determined by a variety of factors which can be viewed at two scales. At the world scale, those countries with a high level of economic development and a stable, urbanized population are major generators of tourism demand. The political regime of a country is also relevant here. At the individual scale, a certain level of discretionary income is required to allow participation in tourism, and this income, and indeed, the type of participation, will be influenced by such factors as job type, life-cycle stage, mobility, level of educational attainment, and personality. Even within the developed world, many are unable to participate in tourism for some reason. Demand for tourism is therefore concentrated in the developed Western economies and predominates amongst those with high discretionary incomes.

THREE

The geography of resources for tourism

LEARNING OBJECTIVES

After reading this chapter, you should be able to:

1 *Appreciate the nature of resources for tourism.*
2 *Understand the significance of latitude in determining climate and describe the distribution of world climates and their significance for tourism.*
3 *Be aware of the major climatic elements and explain how each affects tourism.*
4 *Distinguish the methods used to classify and evaluate resources for tourism.*
5 *Outline the main factors favouring the development of tourist resources.*

Introduction

Technology now allows tourists to reach most parts of the world, yet only a small fraction of the world's potential tourist resource base is developed. One reason for this is because tourists demand attractions which are not possessed by their own place of residence. Clearly, tourism does not occur evenly or randomly in space, various types of tourism will have differing requirements for favourable growth, and certain sites, regions, or nations will be more favourable for development than others. This chapter examines tourist resources at three scales; the world, the national, and the local scale.

Resources for tourism

Tourist resources have three main characteristics. Firstly, the concept of tourist resources is normally taken to refer to tangible features which are considered of economic value to the tourism industry and indeed recognized as valuable assets by the tourists themselves.

Secondly, tourist resources themselves are often not used solely by tourists. Apart from resort areas where tourism is the dominant use of land, tourism shares space with agriculture, forestry, water management, or residents using local services. Tourism is a significant land use but rarely the dominant one and this can lead to conflict. Tourism is 'fitted in' with other uses of land. This is known as multiple use and the resolution of conflicting claims by recreationists and others must be achieved by skilful management.

Finally, tourist resources are perishable. Not only are they vulnerable to alteration and destruction by tourist pressure, but in common with many service industries, tourist resources are also perishable in another sense. Tourist services such as accommodation are impossible to stock and have to be consumed when and where they exist.

The world scale

Climate

Climate is one of the key factors influencing the development of tourist resources. Most outdoor recreation from sunbathing to skiing is dependent on favourable weather conditions. Air travellers need accurate information on climatic conditions – especially temperatures – as only a limited range of clothing can normally be taken (see Figure 3.1). Climate largely determines the length of the holiday season in a resort, although this is also influenced by external factors such as the timing of school holidays in the generating area. The oper-

ators of tourist facilities have to cope with seasonal variations in demand, and the problem of seasonality is a major one as regards employment and profitability.

The world climate scene

Climate is the long term weather conditions at a particular location. It is determined by three main factors: latitude; continental or marine influences; and relief.

Latitude or distance from the Equator is the primary factor, as this will indicate the angle of the sun's rays at any given time of the year. Due to the earth's rotation the Northern Hemisphere is tilted toward the sun in June, when it is shining directly overhead at noon on the Tropic of Cancer (latitude 23.5° North). North of the Arctic Circle there is

Figure 3.1 *Temperature and clothing – holiday travel in January. The upper row of numbers refers to the insulation value of clothing in clos (units of thermal resistance).*

continuous daylight at this time but the low angle of the sun's rays ensures that its heating power is limited even in mid-summer. The Southern Hemisphere, tilted away from the sun is experiencing winter, and Antarctica continuous darkness. By December on the other hand, the sun's overhead path has moved south from the Equator to the Tropic of Capricorn (latitude 23.5° South), and this marks the onset of winter in the Northern Hemisphere. Generally speaking the zone between the Tropics enjoys a warm climate all year round as the sun is always high in the sky at midday. The result of increasing distance from the Equator is a shorter summer and a greater difference in day length between summer and winter.

This simple model of temperature decrease from Equator to the Poles is complicated by the fact that most of the world's land area is located in the Northern Hemisphere. Land surfaces heat and cool more rapidly than large areas of water. The oceans therefore act as a heat source, so that coastal locations and islands enjoy a climate which is relatively equable compared to the extreme variations of temperature characteristic of continental heartlands such as Central Asia. In Western Europe winters are milder than would be expected for the latitude due to the influence of the warm ocean current known as the Gulf Stream and its continuation, the North Atlantic Drift.

Climatic elements and tourism

Relief has a major effect on weather patterns. Climbers are well aware that average temperatures fall considerably while ascending a mountain. The thinner atmosphere at high altitudes also means that more solar radiation reaches the ground by day, but that heat is lost more rapidly from the ground at night. Great climatic contrasts are found within mountain regions, providing varied habitats, or life-zones, for plants and animals. Mountain barriers profoundly modify the climate of adjacent lowlands, since moist air from the seas is forced to rise over them, becoming drier and warmer as it descends.

Temperature is the most important variable affecting tourism and outdoor recreation.

However, at high temperatures it is the *humidity factor*, relating to the amount of moisture in the air, which is equally significant. A dry heat is widely recognized as being more agreeable than sultry conditions, where it is difficult to keep cool through perspiration. Figure 3.2 shows the relationship between air temperature, relative humidity, and the comfort of the 'average' tourist. The concept of effective temperature is used to assess the effect of warm weather, especially under humid conditions on sedentary normally clothed individuals (see Appendix 8 for its derivation). Obviously people vary considerably in their response to heat or cold, according to their rate of metabolism, ethnic origin, body build, and age, while acclimatization is also important. Figure 3.2 can be used to investigate the suitability of an area's climate for tourism, once the average monthly daytime values of temperature and relative humidity have been obtained. They can then be plotted as co-ordinates on a transparent overlay. Five such climographs appear in Figure 3.3. It will be seen that the climate of Majorca most closely approaches the optimum.

The duration of bright *sunshine* and its intensity depend on latitude, altitude, aspect, and the degree of exposure to moisture-bearing air masses. The Equatorial belt is much less sunny than the Mediterranean, but in both regions the amount of ultra-violet radiation reaching the earth's surface is much greater than in northern Europe, producing the sought-after tan or sunburn. At high altitudes, sunlight reflected from snow or rock faces provides considerable warmth even though air temperatures may be scarcely above 0°C – this explains why it is possible to ski and sunbathe nearby, in mountain resorts.

The frequency of *precipitation* is another important consideration for holidaymakers and resort planners. For example, in the Tropics there is usually a well-defined division of the year into rainy and dry seasons, and rain often occurs in short heavy downpours. In contrast mid-latitude countries such as Britain and New Zealand receive less annual rainfall than many tropical countries but they experience many more rainy days and there is no dry season. The amount of snowfall and the

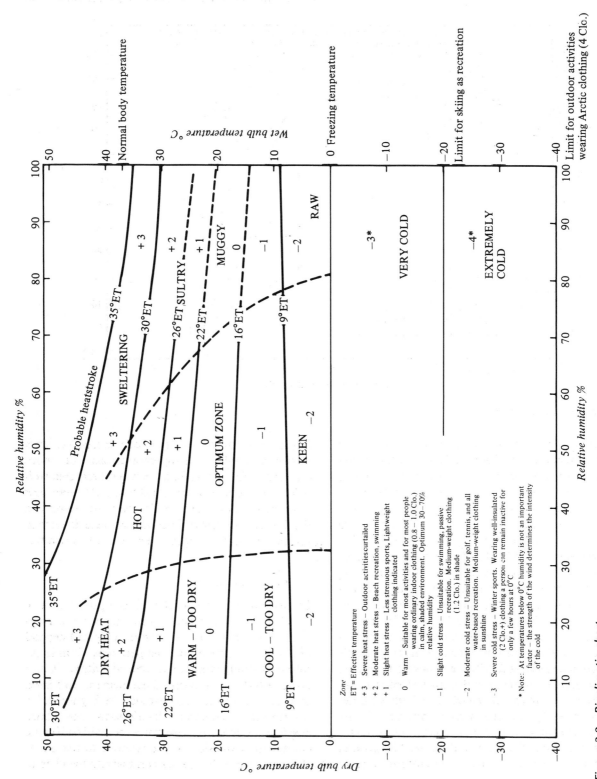

Figure 3.2 Bioclimatic chart
Adapted from Terjung, W. H., 'Physical Climates of the Coterminous United States', Annals of the Association of American Geographers, no. 56, 1966, pp. 141–79.

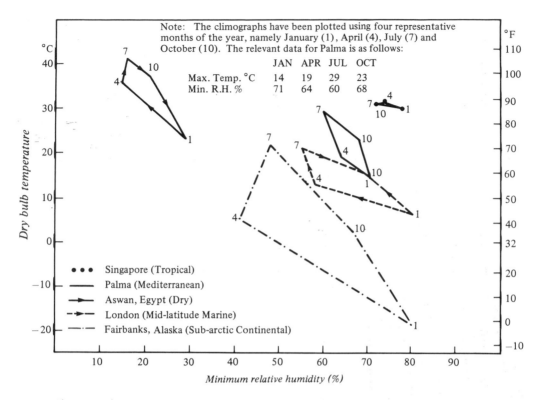

Figure 3.3 *Climographs*

duration of snow cover are of vital importance to ski resort operators. Suitable locations for winter sports are mainly found in mid-latitude mountain regions where temperatures consistently fall below 0°C for several months and the air is not too dry.

Winds are caused primarily by differences in barometric pressure and secondly by topography. A knowledge of the land and sea breezes characteristic of coastal areas is essential for the yachtsman, while the glider pilot is interested in the peculiarities of mountain winds, such as the Föhn of the Alps and the Chinook of the Rockies. In tropical islands sea breezes mitigate the high temperatures and humidity, so that the climate is more agreeable than some mid-latitude cities in summer where the air is calm and polluted with fumes from industry and motor vehicles. In middle and high latitudes winds intensify the sensation of winter cold by increasing evaporation from the skin; the resultant heat loss is called the wind chill factor. This is often converted to an 'equivalent temperature', and as

Figure 3.4 shows strong winds combined with relatively mild air temperatures can be more dangerous for hill-walkers than temperatures well below 0°C under calm conditions. At very low temperatures especially under blizzard conditions there is also the risk of frostbite or severe damage to the skin tissues of unprotected parts of the body.

World climatic regions

For each tourist activity there is an optimal climate which allows participation in comfort for a maximum number of days each year. This will depend on a combination of temperature, humidity, solar-radiation, windspeed, and visibility. It is a difficult task to synthesize these elements in a form that can be readily understood. In Figure 3.5 a conventional climatic classification has been employed rather than one based on the bioclimatic chart with a division of the world into ten major climatic groups. Table 3.1 summarizes the charac-

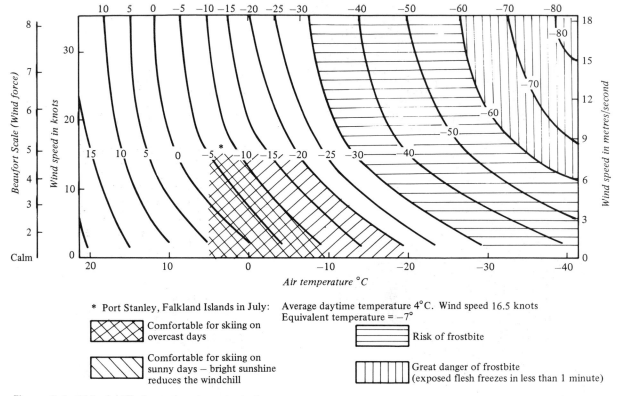

Figure 3.4   *Windchill chart showing equivalent temperatures*

teristics of these groups and their significance for tourism. The Mediterranean climate is probably the most agreeable for tourism. The tropical zone has great potential although health hazards pose a major constraint in many areas where living standards are low.

World physical features

The distribution of land and sea has a fundamental influence upon the world's climate and also the location of tourism. 71 per cent of the earth's surface is made up of the four oceans; Pacific, Atlantic, Indian, and Arctic, with the remaining 29 per cent of the earth's surface comprising the seven continents; Asia, Africa, North America, South America, Antarctica, Europe, and Australasia (in descending order of size). The distribution of land between the Northern and Southern Hemisphere is unequal as almost 40 per cent of the Northern

Hemisphere is made up of land whereas over 80 per cent of the Southern Hemisphere is ocean.

World landforms

The land surface of the earth is comprised of a variety of landforms which can be broadly classified into four types; mountains, plateaux, hill lands, and plains.

About 75 per cent of the earth's surface is *mountain or hill land*. These landforms are particularly attractive for tourist development, not only for their winter-sports opportunities but also because the more rarified air is clear, crisp, and ideal for walking, sightseeing, and photography. Many mountain resorts have developed to give relief from high temperatures in the lowlands. Mountainous areas are sparsely populated and some are designated national parks for their outstanding natural features and beauty. *Plateaux and*

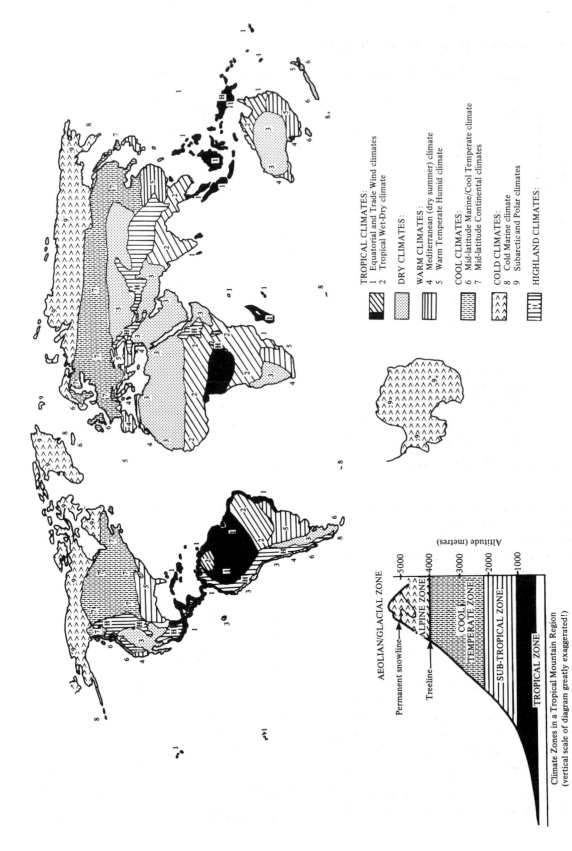

TROPICAL CLIMATES:
1 Equatorial and Trade Wind climates
2 Tropical Wet-Dry climate

DRY CLIMATES:

WARM CLIMATES:
4 Mediterranean (dry summer) climate
5 Warm Temperate Humid climate

COOL CLIMATES:
6 Mid-latitude Marine/Cool Temperate climate
7 Mid-latitude Continental climates

COLD CLIMATES:
8 Cold Marine climate
9 Subarctic and Polar climates

HIGHLAND CLIMATES:

AEOLIAN/GLACIAL ZONE

Altitude (metres)

Permanent snowline
Treeline

ALPINE ZONE

COOL
TEMPERATE ZONE

SUB-TROPICAL ZONE

TROPICAL ZONE

Climate Zones in a Tropical Mountain Region
(vertical scale of diagram greatly exaggerated!)

Figure 3.5 World climates

Table 3.1 World climatic regions and tourism

Climatic region	Physical characteristics	Significance for tourism	Examples of areas
1 Tropical trade wind and Equatorial climates	Moderately high temperatures and high humidity year-round. No real 'dry season'. On-shore winds have some cooling effect on island and windward coasts. Lush vegetation including rain forest.	High effective temperatures discourage strenuous activity. Warm water temperatures year-round encourage beach tourism.	Islands of the Caribbean, South Pacific and Indian Oceans, Amazon basin.
2 Tropical wet-dry climate	Much greater seasonal differences, especially in rainfall. A long dry season often divided into the 'cool dry' – (warm days and cool nights) and the 'hot dry', where the heat is usually associated with low humidity. The rainy season typically lasts from June to November in the Northern Hemisphere and from December to May in the Southern Hemisphere. Savanna grassland typical of many areas.	Dry season may be suitable for sightseeing, safaris, and beach tourism. High effective temperatures in rainy season deter tourists and storms may disrupt communications.	India, Gambia, Zambia, Centre-West of Brazil, Northern Australia.
3 Dry climates	Little or no rainfall. High daytime summer temperatures, but low humidity except in some coastal areas, (e.g. Persian Gulf). Intense solar radiation. Nights are much cooler and can be very cold in winter in mid-latitude interior locations (e.g. Soviet Central Asia).	Abundant sunshine favours outdoor recreation most of the year. Major problems include water supply, dust storms and extreme summer heat.	Egypt, South West USA, Central Australia, Namibia.
4 Mediterranean climate	Warm-hot dry summers, cool winters with moderate rainfall. Abundant sunshine.	Particularly favourable, permitting beach tourism for most of the year.	Majorca, Southern California, Cape Town, Central Chile.
5 Warm temperate humid climate	Warm-hot humid summers. Abundant rainfall, especially in summer. Cool winters, subject to occasional cold spells in some areas.	High effective temperatures in summer may deter active recreation. Suitable for watersports most of the year.	Georgia (USA), Georgia (USSR), South China, New South Wales, Uruguay.

Table 3.1 *continued*

Climatic region	Physical characteristics	Significance for tourism	Examples of areas
6 Cool temperate climate	Rather cool summers. Abundant rainfall year-round. Weather highly variable. Mild-raw winters, windy on exposed coasts and uplands.	Beach activities comfortable only during the summer months. Favours the more strenuous types of outdoor recreation. All-weather indoor facilities desirable.	British Isles, Vancouver Island, South Island of New Zealand, Southern Chile.
7 Mid-latitude continental climates	Pronounced seasonal changes. Warm humid summers with moderate rainfall. Cold winters with snow cover for several months, but weather is usually calm and settled. Large areas of coniferous forest in the north.	Summers suitable for outdoor recreation. Winters suitable for skiing and other snow-based activities.	Sweden, Ontario, Hokkaido.
8 Cold marine climate	Cold and damp, no real summer, raw winters. Overcast skies and strong winds prevalent year-round.	Generally unfavourable for recreation, but rich bird and marine animal life attracts naturalists.	Aleutian Islands, South Georgia.
9 Subarctic and polar climates	Cold and dry. Period of summer warmth brief or absent, despite long hours of daylight. Very cold winters with excessive windchill and long hours of darkness. Low precipitation. Tundra with much surface water in summer due to poor drainage. Mountainous areas, as in Greenland and Antarctica are permanently ice-covered.	'Permafrost' inhibits construction of tourist facilities, while frequent blizzards and 'white-outs' result in high transport costs. Scope for adventure holidays involving a high degree of preparation: dog sledging, skiing and hunting in late winter/spring. Canoeing and fishing possible in more favoured areas in summer.	Baffin Island, Spitzbergen, Northern Alaska.
10 Highland climates (mountains and plateaus above 1500 metres)	Altitude main factor, but great differences in temperature between sunlit and shaded locations. Intense ultra-violet radiation, low humidity and absence of dust and pollen at high altitudes. Interesting plant and animal life.	Attracts a wide spectrum of recreationists, including trekkers, climbers and naturalists. Above 4000 metres the thin air may restrict strenuous activities. In tropical countries mountains give relief from the heat of the lowlands (e.g. the health resorts of India and Malaya). In middle latitudes a reliable snow cover at altitudes of 1500–3000 metres encourages development of ski resorts.	Bolivia, Ethiopia, Tibet, Colorado, Alps.

plains are less scenic but are important because they house most of the world's population. Coastal plains are ideal for resort development providing flat areas of building land with ready access to the beach and sea.

Within each of these four landform categories there are a variety of minor features resulting from variations in the underlying rock. Volcanoes, hot springs and geysers are one group of attractions while areas of karst limestone give rise to caves, gorges and sinkholes.

The *coast* has long been used for holidays and recreation throughout the world. Sandy beaches, coves, safe bathing, and a protective backland of dunes and low cliffs will encourage tourist development and a wide range of recreational activities. Islands, or groups of islands, have a particular appeal for tourism. Other features attractive to tourism include barrier islands and spits resulting from longshore drifting, estuaries suitable for sailing and fishing, and the coral reefs and atolls found in many tropical areas which provide an ideal environment for diving. However, although the coast is widely used for tourism, tourism often has to share use of the coast with other, less attractive, uses (such as oil refining).

Inland waters lure many visitors and act as a focus for tourist and recreational activities. Water resources for tourism can be viewed as nodes (lakes, reservoirs), linear corridors (rivers, canals), or simply as landscape features (such as the Victoria Falls). Most activity takes place in the shallow waters near to the shore where bathing, fishing, and boating encourage the development of tourist resorts and second homes. Lakes are more commonly distributed in the higher latitudes, particularly recently glaciated areas such as northern Europe and North America. Pollution can be a problem as, unlike the tidal nature of the sea, lakes have no natural cleansing mechanism. The lakes of northern Europe are readily accessible to major population areas but those of North America, Asia and Africa are more distant from major population centres. Rivers are more widely distributed than lakes and cruising on major rivers and inland waterways plays a major role in tourism. However, like the coast, tourism has to share the

use of rivers with other uses which may not be compatible.

The national scale

At the national scale tourist development involves either finding regions to develop for tourism or, in areas already developed, alleviating problems of congestion or over-use. These activities demand accurate methods of classifying tourist resources and evaluating their potential.

Classification of resources for tourism

Tourist attractions

Tourist attractions give rise to excursion circuits and spawn an industry of their own. The simplest approach to identifying attractions in an area is to draw up an inventory, or checklist, by defining the range of attractions, counting them, and either listing or mapping the result. Peters (1969) has classified attractions into cultural (museums, historic buildings), traditions (music, folklore), scenic (wildlife, national parks) and other attractions (health resorts, etc.) Of course, different forms of tourism will require differing types of attraction. For example, business tourism gravitates towards major population and commercial centres which are highly accessible and ideally will have a range of other complementary attractions.

Increasingly, tourist attractions, and the tourist resource base in general, are suffering from increased use and need effective visitor management. This can only be achieved if tourist attractions are not considered simply as point attractions but as an integral part of the tourist resource base.

A broader view of the tourist resource base

One of the most useful classifications of the *total resource base* for tourism and recreation is that of Clawson (1966). Clawson's classification allows the inclusion of a continuum of resources from intensive resort development to wilderness and, therefore, incorporates both resource and user characteristics. Clawson's three basic categories are; user-

Table 3.2 Clawson's classification of recreation resources

User-oriented	Intermediate	Resource-based
Based on whatever resources are available. Often man-made/artificial developments (city parks, pools, zoos etc.). Highly intensive developments close to users in large population centres. Focus of user pressure. Activities include golf, tennis, picnicking, walking, riding etc. Often highly seasonal activities, closing in off-peak.	Best resources available within accessible distance to users. Access very important. More natural resources than user-oriented facilities but experience a high degree of pressure and wear. Activities include camping, hiking, picnicking, swimming, hunting, and fishing.	Outstanding resources. Primary focus is resource quality with low-intensity development and man-made facilities at a minimum. Often distant from users, the resource determines the activity (sightseeing, scientific and historic interest, hiking, mountain climbing, fishing, and hunting).

Activity paramount ⟷ Resource paramount

Artificiality ⟷ Naturalness

⟵ Intensity of development

Distance from user ⟶

Adapted from: Clawson, M. and Knetsch, J. The Economics of Outdoor Recreation, Johns Hopkins University Press, Baltimore, 1966.

oriented areas of highly intensive development close to population centres, resource-based areas where the type of resource determines the use of the area, and an intermediate category. As with most classifications the reality is a continuum rather than a series of discrete classes (Table 3.2).

A second broad classification is that proposed by the Outdoor Recreation Resources Review Commission (ORRRC) of the United States. The system classifies areas according to physical resource characteristics, level of development, management, and intensity of use. Six classes are produced ranging from high-density, intensively-used areas to sparsely-used primitive areas (Appendix 9).

Evaluation of resources for tourism

Measurement of the suitability of the resource base to support different forms of tourism is known as resource evaluation. The main problem here is to include the varied requirements of different users. For example, pony trekkers need rights of way, footpaths or bridleways, and attractive scenery. Combination of these various needs is the aim of a resource evaluation system (see Appendix 10).

The local scale

Conditions favouring tourist development

For the tourist resource base to be developed someone, or some organization, has to act. These agents of development can be either in the private or the public (government) sector.

The public sector is not only involved in tourist development at the local scale but at all levels including the international. Typically, at the national and international levels involvement is with planning and co-ordination of tourism development. At the local scale the public sector is likely to be involved in encouraging and providing tourist development. Normally, because of the scale and extent of development, the public sector takes on responsibility for providing the initial tourist infrastructure. Infrastructure includes all tourist development on and below ground such as roads, parking areas, railway lines, harbours, airports, and runways, as well as the provision of utilities.

Private sector developers typically take on the responsibility of providing the tourist superstructure, including accommodation, entertainment, shopping facilities, restaurants, and passenger transport terminals. Clearly, these development tasks reflect the motives of the two sectors; the private sector looking for profit and a return on investment, while the public sector is anxious to provide an environment conducive to tourist development.

At the local scale *accessibility* is a vital consideration for tourist development, especially for business travel. For successful tourist development, access from the major tourist-generating areas is vital and may be a deciding factor in the success of the development. Resorts in the Mediterranean owe their success to their proximity to the major tourist markets. Other factors favouring the development of tourist resources at the local scale include land availability, suitable physical site attributes (soil, topography, etc.), and a favourable planning environment with zoning for tourist development. Many governments may also actively encourage tourist development by providing finance at generous rates.

Tourist resorts

At the local scale development of tourist resources leaves a distinctive imprint upon the landscape. Nowhere is this clearer than in the *resort landscapes* of the developed world. Indeed, in Western Europe alone over four hundred resorts can be identified, and Lavery (1971) has classified them into eight basic types, based on their function and the extent of their hinterland (Appendix 11).

Resort townscapes have a distinctive morphology and blend of services catering for the visitor. Typically, a concentration of tourist-oriented land

and building uses is found adjacent to the main focus of visitor attraction (beach, lake, or falls). This area of tourist-related functions is termed the *recreational business district* (RBD) and its nature will vary with the type of resort and the predominant tourist use. The RBD develops under the twin influences of the major access route into the resort and the location of the central tourist feature. For example, in seaside resorts the RBD often develops parallel to the coast with a promenade (boardwalk in the USA) a road, and a first block of premier accommodation and shops. Beyond this the intensity of tourist functions and land values decreases in a series of zones around the RBD (Figure 3.6).

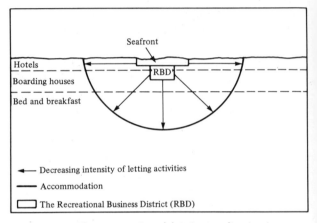

Figure 3.6 The recreational business district in an idealized coastal resort
Source: Wall, G., 'Car-owners and Holiday Activities' in Lavery, P., *Recreational Geography*, David & Charles, 1971, pp. 97–111.

A resort's success is subject to the whims of fashion and taste. As the resort develops and changes, so does the clientele with Cohen's (1972) explorers and drifters discovering the town in the early days, to be ousted by 'institutionalized' tourists as the resort matures (Table 2.3). Commercialization can lead to the resort's eventual decline and stagnation as increased visitor numbers exceed capacity limits and lead to the physical deterioration of the resort's fabric. Increasingly, visitors desert the resort for newer, often purpose-built, attractions elsewhere. At this stage rejuvenation of the resort is necessary if bedspaces are to be filled and the physical 'plant' of the resort efficiently utilized. Rejuvenation can take the form of man-made attractions such as casinos, indoor leisure centres, diversification into conference tourism, or upgrading accommodation.

The pleasure periphery

Different forms of tourism obviously demand different blends of resources but certain generalizations can be made. Christaller stated that tourism avoids central places and agglomerations of industry and is drawn instead to the coastal and mountain peripheries of settlement districts. For example, Western Europe is ringed by a 'pleasure periphery' of resorts, about two hours or less flying time from their main markets.

Winter sports tourism also fits Christaller's statement. It requires good snow cover and hilly terrain and thus most ski developments are located peripheral to major population centres in areas like northern Europe, the Alps, Pyrenees, Andes, and Colorado in the USA. Obviously not all tourism fits Christaller's generalization and exceptions include tourism in capital cities, historical and cultural centres, and some health and spa tourism. However the generalization is useful and goes some way towards explaining tourism's value as a regional development tool in the peripheral areas of many countries where tourism is and often can be, the only significant employer and user of local resources.

Summary

Certain factors favour the development of tourist resources and this explains why the world pattern of tourism supply is uneven. Developed tourist resources are cultural appraisals, considered by society to be of economic value. They are usually shared with other users and are both fragile and perishable. At the world scale climate and physical features are key factors influencing tourist development. World climates are determined by latitude, altitude, and factors such as the distribution of land, sea, and mountains. The optimal climate for tourism is the Mediterranean type. Of the range of physical features in the world, coasts, mountains, and inland water are the most popular locations for tourist development.

At the national scale, classifications of tourist attractions which include the whole tourist resource base are useful. Evaluations of the potential of the resource base to satisfy tourists' demands allow possible future areas for recreation and tourism to be identified. These evaluations can then be applied to the local scale where resultant resort developments have a distinctive morphology and mix of service functions. These factors have led to the development of tourism peripheral to large population centres and a concentration of tourism in mountain and coastal areas.

FOUR

The elements of transport for tourism

LEARNING OBJECTIVES

After reading this chapter, you should be able to:

1 *Appreciate the close relationship between tourism and transport.*
2 *Understand the principles of spatial interaction between places and understand their importance to tourism geography.*
3 *Describe the four main physical elements of a transport system – the way, terminal, carrying unit, and motive power.*
4 *Identify the costs involved in running a transport system.*
5 *Compare and contrast the distinguishing features of the main transport modes, and recognize their particular contributions to tourism.*
6 *Understand the components of transport networks.*

Introduction

In Chapter 1, three components of tourism were identified; the tourist-generating areas, tourist-destination areas, and the links between them. This chapter introduces some of the basic principles of

transport geography and illustrates their application to tourism, while the following chapter examines the geographical characteristics of the most important transport modes for tourism. Tourism and transport are inseparable. Tourism is about being elsewhere and transport bridges the gap between origin and destination. Consideration of transportation is important to those concerned with tourism for a number of reasons.

Firstly, in a historic sense, transportation has developed hand in hand with tourism. Improvements in transport have stimulated tourism and, in turn, tourism demand has prompted such transport developments as the growth of charter air services to serve the leisure market. Secondly, transportation renders tourist destinations accessible to their markets in the tourist-generating areas. All tourism depends on access, indeed, accessibility, or lack of it, can make or break a destination. Thirdly, transport for tourism involves considerable public and private investment and represents a major sector of the tourist industry in terms of employment and revenue generated. Tourism then, is transformed by, and has helped to transform, the world communications map.

Principles of interaction

In Chapter 1, the basic principle of *spatial interaction* between two places was outlined in terms of a supplying area containing a surplus of a commodity (such as sunshine) and the origin area having a demand for that commodity. In geography this is known as spatial differentiation with transport linking the two areas.

Ullman suggested that three main factors are responsible for spatial interaction and, therefore, transport development; complementarity, intervening opportunity, and transferability. *Complementarity* is a way of saying that places differ from each other and that in one place there is the desire to travel and in the other place the ability to satisfy that desire. This complementarity of demand and supply will produce interaction between areas and a transportation system will be required. One example of complementarity is the flow of tourists from north eastern states of the USA to resorts in the western states and Florida.

While Ullman's idea of complementarity makes interaction possible, there may be competing attractions. For example, for a resident of Munich wishing to take a summer holiday in a Spanish resort, mainland Spain is closer than one of the Canary Islands. Mainland Spain is, therefore, an *intervening opportunity*, even though perfect complementarity exists between Munich and the Canary Islands.

Ullman's third factor is *transferability*, or friction of distance. This refers to the cost (in time and money) of overcoming the distance between two places. If the time and money costs of reaching a destination are high, then even perfect complementarity and lack of intervening opportunities will not persuade movement to take place.

Ullman's three factors explain why interaction takes place between places and, if two places have no interaction, it can usually be explained by referring to complementarity, intervening opportunity, or transferability.

The elements of transport

If interaction does take place, a transport system will be needed. But what will this system consist of? Some distinguish between three elements only – the way, the terminal, and the vehicle. But it is probably more meaningful to follow Faulks (1982) who has identified four basic physical elements in any transport system; the way, the terminal, the carrying unit, and motive power. For each mode of transport, the characteristics of these elements vary and it is, therefore, useful to examine each element in turn.

The way

The way is the medium of travel used by the various transport modes. It may be purely artificial such as roads, railways, or tram-tracks; it may be a natural way such as air or water; or it can be a combination of the two (such as inland waterways). A variety of distinctions are important. Firstly, where the way has to be provided artificially a cost is incurred. The cost of the way is influenced by a second distinction; whether the user shares the way with others (for example, roads) or has sole use of a specialized way (for example, railways). A further distinction is that on roads and inland waterways, vehicles are controlled almost exclusively by their drivers or operators with a minimum of traffic control (such as traffic signals). In contrast, air traffic, railways, and to some extent shipping, are subject to traffic control, signals, or some other navigational aid. This adds to the cost of the way.

The nature of the way is an important consideration for the carrying units, terminals, and motive power. For example, the natural way of the aircraft – the sky – is freely available and is extensively used for tourist travel. But the way does influence the development of the transport mode as aircraft have to be robust to ensure safety and comfort, and the carrying unit is thus expensive. Also, specialized terminals are required which are both expensive and often located at some distance from the destination which they serve.

The terminal

A *terminal* gives access to the way for the users and is the furthest point to which the transport system extends – literally the end of the line. Terminals can also act as interchanges where travellers may transfer between modes (train to bus, aircraft to train). Terminals vary tremendously in their design and the amenities provided, since they are largely dependent on the type of journey involved.

The carrying unit

Each 'way' demands a distinctive form of *carrying unit*; aircraft for the sky, ships for the sea, vehicles for roads, and trains or trams for rails. Some carrying units such as aircraft, ships, and road vehicles are very flexible as their use of the 'way' rarely restricts other vehicles. However, trains and trams are confined to a track where overtaking is virtually impossible and break-downs can cause extensive delays. A second consideration is whether the carrying unit can be adapted to other purposes (for example, some cruise ships are converted passenger liners).

Motive power

The historical development of *motive power* technology reads almost like a history of tourism. It begins with the natural power of horse-drawn carriages and sailing vessels, continues with the artificial power of steam for railways and ships, the internal combustion engine for road transport vehicles, and the rapid advance of air transport, to jet propulsion. Now, tourism is reliant almost exclusively on artificial power, for reaching a destination, although activity holidays such as cycling, pony-trekking, and sailing are increasingly popular. Motive power combines with the 'way' and the carrying unit to determine the speed, range, and capacity of the transport mode in question.

Finally there is the question of size. Here the most important consideration is to find the combination of carrying unit and motive power that can hold the maximum number of passengers while still allowing efficient utilization of the transport system. Increasing size does bring its own problems; jumbo jets, for example, require longer runways.

Transport costs and pricing

Transport costs and pricing are fundamental to the geography of tourism. The distinctive cost structure of each mode influences consumer choice and thus determines the volume of traffic on a route. There are two basic types of transport cost. The first is *social costs*. These costs are not paid for by the user of the transport but are borne by the community: an example of this is the unquantifiable cost of aircraft noise to residents living near international airports. Secondly, *private costs* are paid for by those who use or operate the transport system, directly or indirectly.

When considering the private costs of operating transport, a basic distinction needs to be made between fixed and variable costs. *Fixed costs* (or overheads) are incurred before any passengers are carried or, indeed, before a carrying unit moves along the 'way'. These costs are 'inescapable' and include items such as interest on capital invested in, and depreciation of the 'way', the terminals, and the carrying units; maintenance; and administration. The most important feature of fixed costs is that they are not only inescapable, but they do not vary in proportion to the level of traffic on a route, the distance travelled, or the numbers carried. For example, the control tower of an airport has to be manned independent of the number of aircraft movements at the airport.

Variable costs (or running costs) do depend upon the level of service provided, distance travelled, and the volume of traffic carried. Here costs include fuel, crew wages, cleaning and the maintenance of carrying units. These costs are 'escapable' because they are only incurred when the transport is operating and can be avoided by cancelling services.

The distinction between fixed and variable costs is a very important one because the different modes of transport have differing ratios of fixed to variable costs. Railways, for example, have to provide and maintain a track. This means that the total costs of a railway system contain a high proportion of fixed costs whereas for road transport the fixed costs are low. This means that the cost per passenger kilometre decreases rapidly for rail, but more slowly for road transport. In other words, railways are uneconomic if they are only carrying a few passengers because each has to make an unacceptably large contribution to fixed costs. On the other hand road transport is much more competitive as the greater part of the costs are variable.

The distinction between fixed and variable costs is not a sharp one and in fact the two types of cost do blur. For example, costs of staffing and equipping a terminal may increase with the volume of traffic. These costs are known as *semi-fixed*. Clearly, the time period has to be defined in distinguishing between fixed and variable costs. While it can be said that crew wages are a variable cost, in fact crew are retained and have to be paid irrespective of the utilization of the transport system in the short term. Their wages are therefore a short-term fixed cost but not long term, as longer-term staffing can normally be adjusted to the volume of business.

The ratio of fixed to variable costs is an important consideration for transport operators in the tourism business. Compared to many activities transport has a high proportion of fixed costs. Its product is also perishable because, if a seat is not sold on a flight, it cannot be stored and sold at a later date. These two factors mean that operators must achieve a high utilization of their systems. This means not allowing carrying units to be idle for long periods of time without making a contribution to fixed costs and achieving a high load factor (i.e. the number of seats sold compared to the number available).

The *marginal cost principle* is of particular interest to the transport operator. Simply, marginal cost is the additional cost incurred in order to carry one extra unit of output (say a passenger). The operator determines a load factor which covers the fixed costs of the journey and the variable cost of each passenger carried. If the journey is budgeted to break even at, say, a load factor of 80 per cent, then every extra passenger carried over this level will incur a small marginal cost (because variable costs are low) and therefore represents a substantial profit for the operator. Unfortunately the opposite also applies. For every passenger below the 80 per cent level a loss will be incurred.

A related problem is the fact that much tourist demand tends to be highly peaked both on a weekly and annual basis. This means that air transport fleets may only be fully utilized at certain times of the year. Both in Europe and North America one solution to this was the creation of the winter holiday market in the late 1960s to utilize idle aircraft and make a contribution to fixed costs. Another solution is to use differential pricing. Here operators offer low fares for travel in the off-peak period (on particular days of the week, or in particular months) to increase the traffic at these times.

Transport modes

In transport the term *mode* is used to denote the manner in which transport takes place. As has been seen, all forms of transport comprise a 'way', terminal, carrying unit, and motive power, and it is the distinctive technologies of these basic components which are applied by differing modes to give each mode its own characteristics.

Technology determines the appropriateness of each mode for a particular type of journey. It also ensures that some modes overlap in their suitability for journeys and may lead to competition on certain routes. In other cases transport modes are complementary as in the case of rail or road links from airports into cities, or fly-drive holidays where the advantages of air transport are used to reach the destination and the flexibility of motor transport for touring the destination (see Table 4.1). So which transport modes are most suitable for what purposes?

The main advantage of *road transport* is the door-to-door flexibility it allows. This means that journeys by other transport modes often begin or end with a road journey. This combined with the fact that road vehicles can carry only a small number of passengers and have a relatively slow average speed, makes them particularly suitable for short to medium distance journeys. The main disadvantage of road transport is that it is shared by many users and this can lead to congestion at times of peak demand; with an industry subject to annual and weekly peaks like tourism this can be a major handicap. Since the Second World War the private car has become the dominant transport mode for

Table 4.1 Characteristics of transport modes

Mode	Way	Carrying unit	Motive power	Advantages	Disadvantages	Significance for tourism
Road	Normally a surfaced road, although 'Off Road Recreational Vehicles' are not restricted.	Car, bus, or coach. Low capacity for passengers.	Petrol or diesel engine. Some use of electric vehicles.	Door to door flexibility. Driver in total control of vehicle. Suited to short journeys.	Way shared by other users leading to possible congestion.	Door-to-door flexibility allows tourist to plan routes. Allows carriage of holiday equipment. Acts as a link between terminal and destination. Acts as mass transport for excursions in holiday areas.
Rail	Permanent way, with rails.	Passenger carriages.	Diesel engines (diesel/ electric or diesel/ hydraulic). Also electric or steam locomotives.	Sole user of the way allows flexible use of carrying units. Suited to medium or long journeys, and to densely populated urban areas. Non-polluting.	High fixed costs.	In mid-nineteenth century opened up areas previously inaccessible for tourism. Special carriages can be added for scenic viewing etc. Trans-continental routes and scenic lines carry significant volume of tourist traffic.
Air	Natural.	Aircraft. High passenger capacity.	Turbo-fan engines; turbo-prop or piston engine.	Speed and range. Low fixed costs. Suited to long journeys.	High fuel consumption and stringent safety regulations make air an expensive mode. High terminal costs.	Speed and range opened up most parts of the world for tourism. Provided impetus for growth of mass international tourism.
Sea	Natural.	Ships. Can have a high degree of comfort. High passenger capacity.	Diesel engine or steam turbine.	Low initial investment. Suited to either long distance or short ferry operations.	Slow. High labour costs.	Confined to cruising (where luxury and comfort can be provided) and ferry traffic.

most types of tourism, accounting for up to 75 per cent of international tourism journeys in 1980.

In contrast to the road, *the railway* track is not shared and extra carrying units (carriages) can be added or removed to cope with demand. This is particularly important in holiday areas where special trains may be run. Also, special facilities can be provided on rolling stock – such as dining-cars, or special viewing cars for scenic routes. The railway's main disadvantage however, is that the track, signalling and other equipment has to be paid for and maintained by the single user of the 'way'. Providing railway track is particularly expensive as the motive power can only negotiate gentle gradients. This means that moving earth, blasting rock cuttings, and constructing tunnels, is a major cost consideration, especially on long routes, and in mountain regions. Railways are, therefore, characterized by high fixed costs and a need to utilize the track and rolling stock very efficiently to meet these high costs. The railway's speed and ability to carry large numbers of passengers make it suitable for journeys of say 200 to 500 kilometres between major cities.

The most influential developments for international tourism since the Second World War have occurred in the *air transport mode*, where technological advances have opened up many parts of the world to tourism. Indeed, no part of the world is now more than twenty-four hours flying time from any other part. The main advantages of the air transport mode are twofold. Firstly, the 'way' allows the aircraft a direct line of flight unimpeded by barriers such as mountain ranges, oceans, or jungles; and secondly, the superior speeds which can be reached in everyday service. The air transport mode has a high capacity to carry passengers and is ideally suited to movements of over 500 kilometres, for journeys over difficult terrain, and also short journeys where a change of transport mode would otherwise be necessary. (For example a journey from North Island to South Island, New Zealand, where the Cook Strait has to be crossed.) Air transport does have the disadvantage of needing a large terminal area which may be some distance from the destination which it serves. The mode is also expensive due to the large

amounts of power expended and the high safety standards demanded. Overall, it is estimated that around 15 per cent of international tourism uses air transport.

Sea transport lacks the speed of air travel – an aircraft can cross the Atlantic twenty or more times while a ship makes a single return journey. Most of the long-haul passenger traffic has, therefore, been lost to air simply because the ship is so slow. However, ships expend relatively little power, they are large, and can provide a high degree of comfort. This has led to the development of the cruise market which is travel for travel's sake. Sea transport is ideally suited to short sea crossings, providing a roll-on roll-off facility for motor vehicles. A terminal facility is needed and this can be either artificial (such as Takoradi, Ghana), or natural (such as San Francisco Bay). One innovation is the development of hydrofoils and hovercraft which are, in a sense, an attempt to combine the advantages of the air and surface transport modes.

Transport routes and networks

Transport routes do not occur in isolation from the physical and economic landscape of the world. Mountain ranges, extensive hilly terrain, river valleys, waterlogged ground, or even climatic factors influence the location of transport routes, as do the location of major cities, political boundaries, and the tourist-generating and destination areas. However, not all modes of transport are equally affected by these factors. For example, mountains do not affect air transport routes although they will influence the location of air terminals. In contrast, railways are very much influenced by topographical features. These factors, combined with considerations of technology and investment, ensure that transport routes remain relatively stable channels of movement.

The fact that some modes of transport have a restricted 'way' – road, railway tracks, or canal – will automatically confine movement into a series of channels. For navigational purposes those modes of transport which use natural ways – the sea or the air – are also channelled and movement does not take place across the whole available surface of the earth. Looked at on a world, regional, or even local scale these channels of movement link together to form networks of transport routes such as world cruising networks, regional coach or rail networks, or the local networks of tourist excursion circuits.

Each *transport network* is made up of a series of links (along which flows take place) and nodes (terminals or interchanges). Geographers now analyse and describe these route networks in a variety of ways. The most straightforward technique is a flow map which shows the volume of traffic on each route. Simple 'eyeballing' of the map gives a rough indication of major nodes and links.

A more accurate approach is to analyse and summarize the network using graph theory with a series of descriptive measures. However, before this can be done the transport network must be reduced to its essential elements of nodes and links. A good example of this is the map of the London Underground system which reduces the network to its essential structure.

In theory, the more links there are in a network, the greater the connectivity of that network. But in fact, even very dense transport networks can be ill connected. By calculating the ratio between the number of links and the number of nodes, a simple measure of connectivity is produced. This is known as the beta index and ranges from 0 for a network with just nodes and no links to 1.0 or more for complex networks.

The accessibility of places on a network is of particular interest to tourist geographers as, once a node is linked to another, it becomes accessible. It must be noted though that scale is important here.

For example, at the local scale many places may be highly accessible, but when viewed at the world scale they become relatively inaccessible. One useful measure of network accessibility is network density – simply by dividing the total area of the network by the total unit length of the network.

Summary

Transport is created or improved because it satisfies a need for spatial interaction between two places. This interaction may be explained by three basic principles; complementarity, transferability, and intervening opportunity.

Once spatial interaction exists, a transport system will be required, and in general terms the main physical elements of the system will comprise: a 'way' (road, rail, sea, air); a terminal; a carrying unit (ships, trains, aircraft); and motive power (such as a diesel engine).

The costs of the transport system can be divided into social costs, which are the costs to the community, and private costs, which are borne by the user or operator of the system, and which comprise fixed costs (or overheads) and variable costs (running costs). The combination of the physical elements and cost structure of a system result in the suitability of different transport modes (road, rail, sea, or air) for different types of journey.

Each transport mode operates along a channel of movement, determined by the nature of the 'way' (road or rail), or navigational convenience (sea or air). Transport networks are therefore made up of stable links along which movement takes place, and nodes, or terminals.

FIVE

The geography of transport for tourism

LEARNING OBJECTIVES

After reading this chapter, you should be able to:

1 *Identify the Greenwich Meridian, the various time zones and the International Date Line, and illustrate their importance to the traveller.*
2 *Outline the advantages of each mode of transport for the different types of traveller.*
3 *Plot the major routes, by air, by sea, and overland, between the tourist-generating areas and the destination areas.*
4 *Explain the role of London and other major world cities as transport interchanges.*
5 *Appreciate the environmental problems arising from the growth in demand for transport.*

Air transport

Of the many forms of transport used by tourists, it is the *jet aircraft* which has captured the imagination, since it has opened up many formerly remote areas as holiday destinations. It must be emphasized that only a small percentage of the world's population has ever used airlines, and even in developed countries surface modes of transport carry many more times their volume of passengers. However, air transport has done most to bring about far reaching changes in the nature of international tourism and the structure of the travel industry since the 1950s.

Air travel is dependent on *petroleum* which, like most natural resources, is far from evenly distributed among the nations of the world. There is the ever present possibility of another energy crisis, perhaps more severe than those which took place in 1973 and 1979. Oil reserves are being depleted, not only by demand from civil aviation but from other sectors of the transport industry, from manufacturing industry, and from the private motorist and consumer. The USA, which has half the world's motor vehicles and an even higher proportion of its civil aircraft, has the highest per capita energy consumption. Since the 1960s the USA, Western Europe, and Japan have become increasingly dependent on imports of petroleum from the politically sensitive countries of the Middle East.

Time zones and air travel

Much international travel necessitates a time change if the journey is in any direction other than due north or south. These differences in time result from the earth's rotation relative to the sun; at any given moment at one locality it is noon, while half the world away to the east or west, it is midnight. The sun appears to us to be travelling from east to west and making one complete circuit of the earth every twenty-four hours. Looked at from a vantage point in space, the earth is in fact making a complete turn on its axis through 360° of longitude, this means that for every 15° of longitude the time is advanced or put back by one hour; places that lie east of the Greenwich Meridian have a later hour, those to the west an earlier hour due to this apparent motion of the sun.

Theoretically every community could choose its own local time. It was primarily the development of the railways which made it necessary to standardize timetables, using an *international system of time zones* based on the Greenwich Meridian. Since 1884 the world has been divided into twenty-four time zones in which standard time is arbitrarily applied to wide belts on either side of a particular meridian which is usually a multiple of 15° (see Appendix 12). Travellers passing from one time zone to another will therefore adjust their watches by exactly one hour (with the exception of a few parts of the world where the standard time differs by thirty minutes or so from neighbouring areas). Countries in the Western Hemisphere have time zones which are designated with a minus number as so many hours 'slow' behind Greenwich Mean Time (GMT). GMT is the standard time on the Greenwich Meridian passing through London. Countries in the Eastern Hemisphere have time zones designated with a plus number as so many hours 'fast' on GMT. Only when it is noon on the Greenwich Meridian is it the same day worldwide; at all other times there is a twenty-four hour difference between each side of the 180° meridian.

In 1884 the International Date Line was established as the boundary where each day actually begins at midnight and immediately spreads westwards. It corresponds to the 180° meridian (except where deviations are necessary to allow certain territories and Pacific Islands to have the same calendar day). The calendar on the western (Asian) side of the International Date Line is always one day ahead of the eastern (American) side.

Fast jet travel across a large number of time zones causes disruption to the natural rhythms of the human body which responds to a twenty-four hour cycle of daylight and darkness. This effect of jet lag differs considerably between individual travellers, and seems to be more disruptive on long west to east flights than on westbound journeys.

The world pattern of air routes

The shortest distance between two places lies on a great circle which, drawn on the surface of the globe, divides it into equal halves, or hemispheres. Aircraft can utilize *great circle routes* fully because they can ignore physical barriers. For example, the great circle route between Western Europe and the Far East is over Greenland and the Arctic Ocean. Aircraft can use great circle routes due to improved technical performance, pressurized cabins and greatly increased range (up to 10,000 kilometres for a Boeing 747). Aircraft can now fly 'above the weather' in the extremely thin air, uniformly cold temperatures, and cloudless conditions of the stratosphere at altitudes of between 10,000 and 17,000 metres. In middle latitudes pilots take advantage of upper air westerly winds which attain speeds as high as 350 to 450 kilometres per hour. These jet streams reduce the travel time from California to Europe by over an hour, compared to the time taken on the outward journey.

Even so, the 'freedom of the air' is to some extent an illusion. The movement of aircraft, particularly over densely populated countries, is channelled along designated airways or corridors. The development of air routes is determined firstly by the extent of the demand for air travel, secondly by the existence of adequate ground facilities for the handling of passengers and cargo, and thirdly by international agreement. The Chicago Convention in 1944 defined five *'freedoms of the air'* which are put into practice by bilateral agreements between pairs of countries. These freedoms are: the privilege of using another country's airspace; to land in another country for 'technical' reasons; the third and fourth freedoms relate to commercial point-to-point traffic between two countries by their respective airlines; and the fifth freedom allows an airline to pick up and set down passengers in the territory of a country other than its destination. In many parts of the world these freedoms are greatly affected by international politics. The Soviet Union for example prohibits overflying of vast areas of Siberia.

The routes and tariffs of the world's scheduled international airlines are to an extent controlled by the *International Air Transport Association* (IATA) to which most belong. IATA has divided the world into three Traffic Conference Areas for this purpose. Area 1 includes all of the North and South American continents together with Greenland, Bermuda, the islands of the Caribbean, and the Hawaiian islands; Area 2 includes Europe, Africa and adjacent islands, as well as the countries of South West Asia; Area 3 includes the remainder of Asia and the adjacent islands, together with Australia, New Zealand, and most of the Pacific Islands (Appendix 13).

Most of the world's air traffic is concentrated in three major regions – the eastern part of the United States, Western Europe, and East Asia. This is due partly to market forces originating from their vast populations, and partly because of the strategic location of these areas. The situation of London is especially advantageous, almost at the centre of the Earth's 'land hemisphere' in which over 90 per cent of the world's population – and an even higher proportion of the world's industrial wealth – are concentrated.

The 'air bridge' between Europe and North America across the North Atlantic is the busiest intercontinental route, linking the two greatest concentrations of wealth and industry in the world. The capacity provided by wide-bodied jets and vigorous competition between the airlines has brought fares within reach of the majority of the population, while the Atlantic has shrunk metaphorically speaking to a 'ditch' which can be crossed in a few hours.

The location of international airports

The growth of civil aviation has placed demands on the world's major airports that were not anticipated at the time they were built. A major international airport now needs several passenger terminals, adequate car parking, hotels with conference facili-ties, a cargo terminal, warehousing, and servicing facilities, and has all the problems associated with large urban areas such as traffic congestion on the access roads, crime, and pollution.

The largest jet aircraft in operation need runways of at least 3000 metres in length. In tropical countries, and especially at high altitudes, runways have to be even longer, as the lower density of the air means that jets have to make longer runs to obtain the lift to get airborne. A major international airport, therefore, requires a good deal of land. The physical nature of the airport site is important. It should be as flat as possible with clear unobstructed approaches. Such land is not abundant in the small islands which are popular with holidaymakers, or for that matter near many of the world's cities. In both Rio de Janeiro and Hong Kong airports had to be built on land reclaimed from the sea. Runways are aligned so that aircraft can take off against the prevailing wind and airports should be located up-wind of large concentrations of industry, which cause 'smog' and poor visibility. The local weather record is therefore important.

At the same time the airport must be in a location which is readily accessible from the large centres of population it is primarily meant to serve. However most are between twenty to thirty kilometres distant, and sometimes as much as fifty kilometres away (e.g. Narita serving Tokyo). Investment is needed to construct or improve a rapid surface transport link between the city centre and the airport to minimize total travel time. This is particularly important for business travellers on short haul flights. Generally there is a motorway link, or in densely populated areas a high speed railway – separated from the main network, or a helicopter link for business travel.

Despite their value for tourism and the national economy, proposals for airport expansion are fiercely opposed in developed countries. This is mainly due to the problem of noise pollution, and because land is scarce, especially in Western Europe. Consequently on short and medium haul routes there is a definite role for STOL (short take off and landing) aircraft and possibly for seaplanes and airships, none of which require extensive ground facilities. Helicopters are manoeuvrable, but noisy and expensive to operate, and have only a limited capacity. Except in North America the helicopter is not widely used for sightseeing excursions or as a service for business travellers.

Surface transport

Water transport

Unlike aviation, transport over land or water has developed since the dawn of civilization. Until the nineteenth century animal or even human muscle was the motive power for vehicles, and this, together with the primitive state of the roads explains why water transport was used wherever possible. Even today the 'freedom of the high seas' is internationally respected.

A distinction must be made between the long haul or line routes plied by shipping, and the short sea routes, especially those of Europe and the Mediterranean, where ferries provide vital links in the international movement of travellers by road and rail. Cruising needs a separate category here since it is essentially water-borne tourism rather than a point-to-point voyage.

Chapter 4 identified speed as the biggest limitation of water transport. A conventional vessel has to 'push' out of the way a volume of water equal to its own weight. This can be partly overcome by vessels using the hydrofoil principle (where the hull is lifted clear of the sea by submerged foils acting like aircraft wings) or hovercraft (where the entire vessel uses a cushion of air to keep it clear of the water). So far, neither hydrofoils or hovercraft are used on long ocean voyages due to their vulnerability in rough seas and strong winds, as well as their limited capacity and range of operation. Nevertheless they are successful on short sea crossings where their speed (up to three times that of a conventional ship), manoeuvrability, and fast turn-round in port give them the advantage.

The world pattern of shipping routes

Ships rarely keep to great circle routes, instead they ply 'sea lanes' determined by the availability of good harbours en route, and physical conditions –

sea areas characterized by persistently bad weather, floating ice, reefs, and sandbars are avoided. Economic considerations are foremost, the most important routes are those linking Europe with its main trading partners overseas. Tourists and emigrants now account for only a small fraction of the business due to competition from the airlines and the high labour and fuel costs involved in operating a passenger liner.

The North Atlantic routes also suffer from adverse weather conditions and sea states for much of the year; there are few sailings between September and May. Ships have to sail well south of Newfoundland from March to June to avoid the icebergs brought down by the Labrador Current. Off the Grand Banks of Newfoundland fogs are also frequent due to the mixing of the cold water of the south-flowing Labrador Current with the much warmer North Atlantic Drift.

Other important routes include those connecting Europe with the Middle East, India, the Far East – either via Cape Town or through the Mediterranean and the Red Sea, using the Suez Canal. The opening of the Suez Canal in 1869 shortened the sea route to India (formerly via the Cape of Good Hope) by 6000 kilometres and the distance to Australia by almost 2000 kilometres. It brought about a great revival in the prosperity of Mediterranean ports such as Genoa and Marseilles, and the development of supply centres and entrepôts.

The Panama Canal, cut in 1914 through the rugged isthmus linking the two Americas, has never handled a comparable amount of traffic to Suez (which is a sea level canal), as its capacity is limited by a number of locks. However, Panama is now the focus of many of the shipping routes of the Caribbean. Construction of the canal shortened the distance between Liverpool and San Francisco by 8000 kilometres, and greatly aided the development of the Pacific coast of South America. Formerly the Pacific could only be reached from Europe by a dangerous voyage round Cape Horn or through the Straits of Magellan.

Regions with a cold winter climate present severe obstacles to shipping. Whereas the harbours of the British Isles and Norway are kept ice free by the influence of the North Atlantic Drift, in Canada the mouth of the St Lawrence at a much more southerly latitude is closed from December to April. In Finland and Russia the Baltic seaports are kept open during most winters at considerable cost by fleets of icebreakers. The Soviet Union is at a disadvantage in having few ice-free ports and even these, such as Murmansk, are located far from the main centres of population. However, in summer seagoing vessels can penetrate great distances inland by using the very extensive system of rivers and canals.

Passenger traffic on the short sea routes is increasing rapidly throughout Western Europe largely as the result of the popularity of motoring holidays and the growth of trade between the countries of the EEC. The introduction of roll-on roll-off facilities has enabled the ports to handle a much greater volume of cars, coaches, and trucks and most ferries now operate throughout the year with greatly improved standards of comfort and service.

The great decline in the scheduled services offered by the passenger liner has been offset to some extent by the popularity of *cruising*. The chartering and operation of ships for inclusive tours began in the 1860s and reached its heyday in the 1920s. Typically such cruises lasted for several months and catered exclusively for upper income groups with both abundant leisure and wealth. The sea voyage, often undertaken for health reasons, was more important than the places visited. Since the 1950s fly-cruising has become important; here, clients are flown out to their destinations in the warm waters of the Caribbean, West Africa, and the Pacific, and once there, use the ship as a floating hotel. Cruise ships have become smaller, as few ports of call can accommodate 30,000 ton passenger liners and they are increasingly designed with a great deal of open-deck space for warm-water voyages.

The Caribbean is the most popular cruising destination. Its popularity is based on its position close to the American cruise market – the largest in the world; its ideal climate and island scenery; and the short sea distances between ports, with a wide choice of shore excursions. Winter is the main cruise season, but early summer is also popular.

Cruising in the Mediterranean is dominated by the North European market. There are a great many ports, usually of great cultural or historic interest, which can be visited. Areas for summer cruises include the Baltic and the Norwegian coast in northern Europe, and the equally spectacular Pacific coast of British Columbia and Alaska in North America. Cruises off the east coast of Asia and in the western Pacific are also becoming popular especially with Australians and the Japanese.

The location of seaports

The ideal seaport should have: a harbour with a good depth of water close inshore and free from obstructions such as reefs, sandbanks, or dangerous currents; a climate free from severe winter freezes, fogs and strong winds; land available for development; and a productive hinterland with easy surface access to the main population centres.

In fact few ports satisfy all these requirements. In many parts of the world – the Mediterranean and West Africa are important examples – good harbours are few and far between, and it has been necessary to construct artificial ones at great expense. As ships have grown larger, ports have shifted down-stream to estuaries or tidal sections of large rivers. Thus, Paris was replaced as a port by Le Havre while Southampton and Tilbury grew as passenger outports for London. Unfortunately, ports located on estuaries require constant dredging because of silt brought down by the rivers. The finest harbours are often located in mountainous regions, and suffer from the handicaps of poor hinterlands, difficult communications, and little room for expansion (the Norwegian fjords are a good example here).

Rail transport

In the nineteenth century the introduction of railways revolutionized transport and enabled large numbers of people to travel long distances relatively cheaply. The great *transcontinental railways* were built in the period before 1914 when there was no serious competition from other modes of transport. The first was the Union Pacific between Chicago and San Francisco completed in 1869 and which helped to open up California and the American West. The Canadian Pacific railroad between Montreal and Vancouver was built for political as well as economic reasons, because otherwise British Columbia would not have joined the Canadian Confederation; similar motivations were behind the Australian Transcontinental from Sydney to Perth which links Western Australia to the rest of the country. The longest railway of them all – the Trans-Siberian took fifteen years to complete (1891–1905) and still remains the vital life-line of Siberia. The journey from Moscow to Nakhodka – almost 10,000 kilometres – takes over a week.

Railway construction has virtually ceased in most countries, with the significant exceptions of the Soviet Union, Yugoslavia, China, and some African States – notably Zambia and Tanzania.

Since the 1950s the railways have come under increasing competition from the airlines for long-distance traffic and the private car for short journeys. The decline has been greatest in the United States where many major cities are now without any passenger train service. In France and Japan on the other hand, there has been considerable government investment in applying new technology to developing high-speed trains and upgrading the trunk lines between major cities. The growth of environmentalist feeling and concern at another future energy crisis may lead to a rail revival in other developed countries. It is significant that major cities throughout the world from Miami to Hong Kong are investing in 'rapid transit' – automated railway networks rather than urban motorways to handle the immense numbers of commuters and tourists. In mountain regions specially designed railways are used, as in Switzerland, to overcome the problem of steep gradients and these are tourist attractions in themselves.

Road transport

The main impetus towards an international system of highways has come about through the demands of an increasingly motorized population and the development of a long-distance coach services and road haulage. The popularity of the motor car is due to the fact that it provides comfort, privacy, flexibility in timing, and the choice of routes and destinations – and theoretically door-to-door service – except in cities where parking is a growing problem. The private car, especially in North America, has resulted in a completely new landscape of motels and drive-in facilities dedicated to the needs of the mobile traveller.

In developing countries, where car ownership is confined to a small minority, bus and lorry services are the recognized means of conveying passengers, mail, and freight. Vehicles are specifically adapted for the local terrain and climatic conditions, so that scheduled bus services can operate in desert and dry grassland areas, where there are no conventional roads. In tropical humid regions there is a fairly extensive network of dirt roads which are viable during the dry season but impassable after the rains. Many countries, notably Brazil, have largely by-passed 'the age of the locomotive' and are very conscious of the value of airports and highways as a means of achieving national unity and economic progress. International road projects in developing countries include the Pan American Highway system in Latin America and transcontinental systems in Africa and Asia which can be used, politics permitting, by overland expeditions and the more adventurous type of traveller.

In Western Europe and North America a growing network of motorways connects most major cities and industrial areas, though holiday resorts are generally less well served. Motorways have shortened journey times and appreciably reduced accident rates. Roads designed specially for sightseeing have been built in scenically attractive coastal and mountain areas. However, too much road building and the development that invariably goes with it can destroy the very beauty which the tourist has come to see.

Summary

The development of rapid means of communication, especially in the field of civil aviation, has done much to revolutionize the scale and structure of the travel industry. It has also meant that almost all countries of the world have adopted a system of time measurement based on the Greenwich Meridian. Air transport and shipping services form a worldwide network which is based largely on market forces, and needs to be examined on an international scale. This is less true of road and rail communications which are subject to more detailed control by national governments and are therefore best dealt with on a country by country basis.

Airports are closely integrated with surface forms of transport. The expansion of major international airports leads to demands on scarce land, energy, and human resources which are increasingly difficult to resolve. The jet aircraft is but one of many modes of transport, some of which have highly specialized roles (such as the hydrofoil and hovercraft) while others such as the private car, bus, and train are competing for a wider market.

SIX

The demand for tourism in the British Isles

LEARNING OBJECTIVES

After reading this chapter, you should be able to:

1 *Appreciate that socio-economic, technological, and institutional factors present a powerful force in British society enabling the demand for tourism to be realized.*
2 *Be aware of changes in the volume of domestic tourism in the countries of the British Isles, and the factors that have brought about these changes.*
3 *Distinguish between the major sectors of domestic tourism – holiday, business, and visiting friends and relatives.*
4 *Appreciate the volume and scope of British residents' tourism overseas and the factors that have brought this about.*
5 *Understand the recent influences upon the volume of inbound tourism to the British Isles and the nature of the overseas market for British tourism.*

Introduction

It can almost be said that holidays in the modern sense were invented in the British Isles, with their tradition of travel and exploration. The importance of tourism in the British Isles is clearly illustrated by the statistics. By 1984, overseas arrivals in Britain stood at almost fourteen million, trips by British residents overseas at well over twenty million, and domestic tourism in the region of 140 million trips (for all purposes). Tourist spending by the British was over eight billion pounds, and by inbound tourists, over four billion pounds.

Demand for tourism and recreation in the British Isles has grown at a phenomenal rate since the Second World War, not only in terms of volume, but also variety. The cause of this growth is rooted in the social and economic development of the British Isles since the Second World War; specifically, three major influences can be identified: social and economic; technological; and institutional.

Changes in post-war British society

Social and economic changes in the British Isles have combined to boost demand for both domestic and international tourism. Since 1945, rising per capita incomes have brought higher purchasing power. The 1960s were a particularly prosperous period of high employment in which the first real stirrings of mass demand for outbound tourism were experienced. The 1970s and 1980s have suffered the setbacks of energy crises, recession, and unemployment, but even so, real household disposable incomes per head rose by almost 10 per cent over the decade 1970 to 1980 (Figure 6.1).

The startling increase in car ownership has played its part in revolutionizing holidaying habits.

Car ownership more than doubled in the decade 1950 to 1960, and then doubled again in 1970. In Great Britain in 1980 car ownership stood at around fifteen and a half million vehicles (Figure

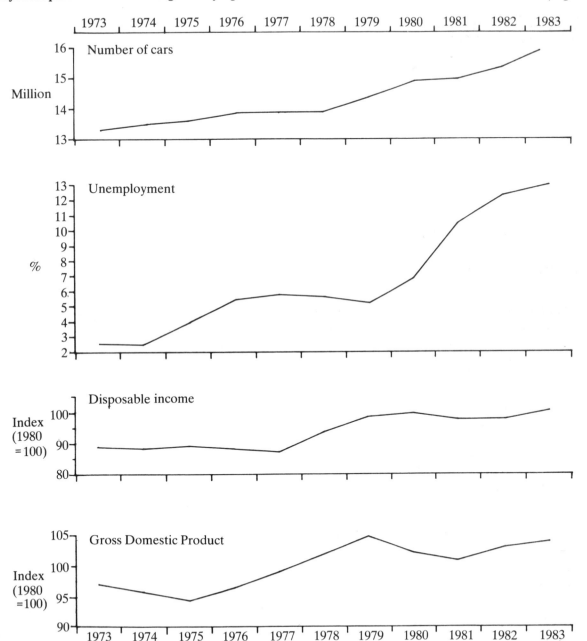

Figure 6.1   *British social and economic indicators*
Source: CSO, *Annual Abstract of Statistics*, HMSO, 1985; CSO, *Economic Trends. Annual Supplement*, 1985 edition, HMSO, 1985.

6.1), and facilities for motorists have grown accordingly. For example, by 1980 the length of British motorways reached over 2500 kilometres bringing many holiday destinations within reach of urban conurbations.

Increased affluence and personal mobility have been paralleled by an increase in educational levels and in consequence, a heightened awareness of opportunities for tourism. By 1980, almost half a million students were in full-time higher education.

The time available for holidays has also grown with increased holiday entitlement, three-day weekends, and various flexible working arrangements providing blocks of time for trips away from home. Through the 1960s for example, industry and services (e.g. retailing and banking) moved towards a five-day working week. This in itself is significant for the shorter-holiday market, but for the traditional long holiday, it is the annual entitlement which matters, and this has greatly increased since the Second World War. By 1980, nearly three quarters of manual workers were entitled to four weeks or more paid holiday.

Perhaps surprisingly, the increase in demand for tourism and recreation has come more from changes in society brought about by the above factors, than by any large increase in the population itself. Indeed, between 1961 and 1981 the population in Great Britain grew by only 4.5 per cent to approach 56 million by the mid-1980s. More important to tourism is the changing composition of the population. For example, the post-war baby boom produced a generation who began to demand tourism and recreation from the late 1970s. Similarly, the population is healthier and living longer and the retired population rose from almost 8 million in 1971 to over 9 million by 1981. Again this change in the population has implications for the nature of tourism demand and provision of facilities to the end of the century and beyond.

These changes in society have gone hand in hand with technological innovations (aside from transportation which was dealt with in Chapter 5). Breakthroughs in product design have brought a range of leisure goods within reach of the population (such as fibreglass boats, mountaineering equipment, etc.). Technology too, through the media, has brought awareness of holiday and recreational opportunities to all, specifically through television and radio programmes featuring holiday opportunities, or the guide books produced by tourist boards and motoring organizations. Finally, technology has not only begun to release the workforce from mundane tasks as microprocessors and robot engineering are introduced, but labour-saving devices have also helped to reduce the time spent on household chores.

The third factor which has boosted demand since 1945 has been the response of institutions such as government and the tourism industry. These include the proliferation of government agencies, such as tourist boards, and private sector initiatives, such as tour operators and travel agencies.

These three individual factors – social and economic, technological, and institutional – are each important in their own right, but when combined together, they present a powerful force in British society, enabling the demand for tourism to be realized.

British residents' demand for tourism

Britain's tradition of tourism has led to a high level of travel propensity in the population. Around 60 per cent of the British take a holiday in any one year, but over a period of three years, this figure rises to 75 per cent as some enter, and others leave the market in a particular year. Even so, there is a hard core of those who do not travel, especially the poor and the elderly. Not only is travel propensity high, but travel frequency averaged 1.5 trips per participant in 1980.

Domestic tourism in the British Isles

Taking the British Isles as a whole, domestic tourism for all purposes amounted to over one hundred and forty million trips in 1984, with the mainland UK accounting for over 95 per cent of these trips. In Eire, domestic tourism volume was around three million trips, and Britain's offshore holiday islands (the Channel Islands, the Isle of

Man, and the Scillies) accounted for one and a half million trips.

These aggregate figures do disguise differences between the various sectors in Great Britain (the British Home Tourism Survey shows that the holiday sector accounts for around 60 per cent of domestic tourism trips, business 15 per cent, and visiting friends and relatives 23 per cent). Each of these sectors have distinctive geographical patterns and show contrasting trends over time.

Holidays in Britain are inextricably linked to disposable income and general economic health. The 1970s began with strong demand for domestic holidays in Great Britain. However, over the decade demand fluctuated and, in the face of changing economic factors, the share of domestic tourism experienced an absolute decline as the share of overseas tourism by British residents increased.

Here, the recession of 1980–81 adversely affected demand for domestic tourism and a number of influences can be identified. Firstly, domestic tourism is dominated by those in the lower social grades who are more sensitive to price and changes in income or economic circumstances. Secondly, the industrial heartlands of the North, the Midlands, Scotland, and South Wales which traditionally generated high levels of demand for holidays at home have been particularly badly hit by the recession. In consequence, demand for holidays in Welsh and northern resorts has fallen. Finally, not only did inflation in the mid to late 1970s push up the cost of a holiday at home, but at the same time, recession bred uncertainty about employment and holiday decisions were delayed. However by the mid 1980s the increased cost of travel overseas, a weak pound and vigorous promotion of holidays in Britain saw a significant upturn in demand for domestic tourism and this looks set to continue through to the 1990s as disposable incomes rise.

An important distinction in the domestic market is between a long holiday (four nights or more) and a short holiday (one to three nights). For some times, the general trend has been a gradual decline in domestic long holidays and an increase in short, additional holidays. Clearly, many short holidays are taken as 'additional' holidays to complement the 'main' holiday (which may be taken in Britain or overseas). Indeed, the numbers of people taking more than one holiday are increasing, and by the early 1980s, 20 per cent of the British population took at least one additional holiday.

The generation of domestic holiday trips is broadly proportional to the distribution of population across the British Isles. However some areas have a relatively high holiday-taking propensity (the South East of England) while others are low (Scotland, the North West of England). England is the dominant domestic holiday destination in Great Britain with over 70 per cent of mainland trips in the early 1980s. Scotland and Wales each account for around 9 per cent of trips. Within the UK the West Country is by far the most popular destination, with one-fifth of total trips.

Of course, holiday choices are difficult to explain and are subject to the vagaries of changing tastes and fashion. However, the basic principle of spatial interaction is in operation in the domestic market, with a supplying area containing a surplus of a commodity, and the tourist-generating area possessing a demand for that commodity. For example, the South of England and the West Country are perceived to be sunny and warm, with the added advantages of an attractive coast, fine established resorts, and opportunities for touring. But set against these attractions is the problem of overcoming the distance to reach the holiday destination from home.

Domestic tourism demonstrates a clear pattern in time as well as space. The trend towards short, additional holidays has gone some way to reduce the acute seasonal peaking of domestic holidays, rooted in the timing of school and industrial holidays. Around 60 per cent of long holidays begin in July or August, but for short holidays, this figure falls to 25 per cent.

The business and conference sector of the domestic market has grown steadily and by 1980 represented 15 per cent of total trips, but 25 per cent of total expenditure due to the high spending nature of business and conference tourists (British Home Tourism Survey). Indeed, the UK is now estimated to account for 10 per cent of the international conference market. This lucrative sector is hotly competed for by resorts, towns, and cities across the British Isles, because it is not concentrated in the summer peak, tends to use serviced accommodation, and brings a high-spending clientele to the destination.

The visiting friends and relatives sector is a particularly important one for Ireland and Northern Ireland, where it has implications for accommodation planning as these tourists, by definition, do not stay in commercial accommodation.

Demand for overseas travel

Great Britain is a major generator of international tourism, ranking fourth in the world, and beaten only by the United States, West Germany, and France. By 1984, British residents made well over twenty million trips abroad and spent over four billion pounds in the countries visited. Of course, these overall totals again disguise the fact that a variety of sectors of tourism are involved. The International Passenger Survey identifies the major sectors of holiday tourism (about two-thirds of the total), business travel (around 15 per cent), and 'visiting friends and relatives' (around 13 per cent).

In the holiday sector, around 20 per cent of Britons took a holiday abroad in the early 1980s, representing almost twelve million trips, compared to five million in 1970, and only three and a half million in 1960. In part, this rapid growth stems from economic circumstances, but the activities of the travel trade over the last thirty years have now brought a holiday overseas within reach of a large percentage of the population. What has happened is that the increased organization of the travel industry, coupled with the growth of travel intermediaries, such as travel agents and tour operators, has taken much of the responsibility for organizing a holiday away from the tourist. Add to this sophisticated marketing and pricing techniques, and it is clear that the travel industry has done much to convert suppressed demand into effective demand for holidays overseas.

The fact that the real price (after adjusting for inflation) of overseas inclusive tours fell by 25 per cent between 1965 and 1972 fuelled demand. This price reduction was due, in part, to the use of more

economic jet aircraft and also the availability of winter holidays, but mostly it was due to fierce competition between tour operating companies. However, the recession of 1974, coupled to the sharp increase in oil prices, reduced demand for inclusive tours. This decline put a major tour operating group (Clarksons) into liquidation. By 1975 demand for inclusive tours had stabilized to around 4.3 million.

The mid 1970s saw fluctuations in the numbers of holidays taken abroad as the oil crisis, weak sterling, economic recession, and higher holiday prices took their toll. By 1978 however, a stronger pound, cheaper air fares and inclusive tours, and vigorous marketing, contributed to a growth in overseas holiday-taking of 20 per cent per annum. At the same time, high inflation pushed up the price of domestic holidays and with the British beginning to view the annual holiday as a priority, overseas holidays grew in popularity.

By 1980, 6.3 million inclusive tours were taken, representing 54 per cent of all overseas holidays. Spain was the most important destination for air inclusive tours (Figure 6.2), but its share has progressively been diluted as the range of destinations on offer has diversified.

But in the rapidly changing tourism scene, the picture of strong demand for overseas travel began to change by the mid 1980s. A weaker pound, increased prices of Spanish hoteliers, the reintroduction of surcharges on inclusive tours, and adverse publicity in major overseas resorts reduced demand for overseas travel and in turn, lower inflation at home boosted demand for 'value for money' holidays in Britain. This led to a further price war between tour operators in 1985.

The fact that by 1980, a staggering 50 per cent of the British population had experienced a holiday abroad has led to an increased number who feel confident to travel independently. For these travellers, France is still the most important destination with its convenient surface links to the British Isles. The USA is the only non-European country with considerable drawing power for British tourists and over the decade 1970 to 1980 it steadily increased its share of the British overseas holiday market. However, the major influence on visits to the USA (and the reverse flow) is the dollar-sterling exchange rate.

Throughout the 1970s business travel has kept a relatively constant share of travel out of Great Britain at around 15 per cent. Visits to the EEC and North America account for around three-quarters

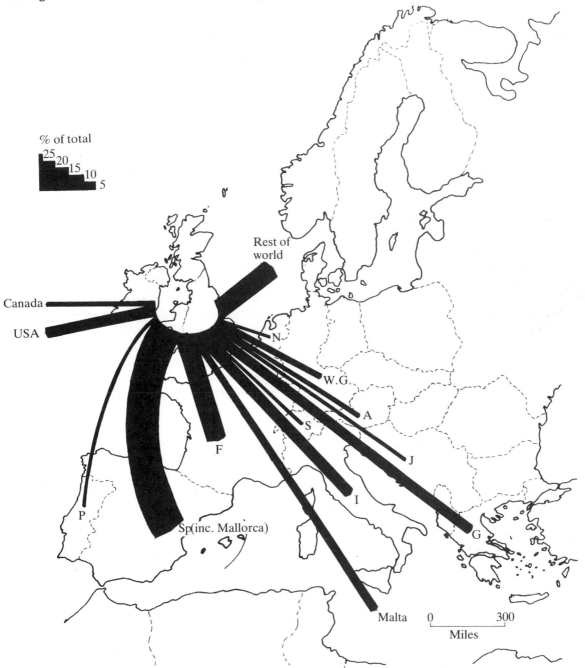

Figure 6.2 *Overseas destinations of British holidays*
Source: British Tourist Authority, *British National Travel Survey*, BTA, 1981.

of all outbound trips. Growth of trade with EEC countries has led to an increase in sea travel (almost a quarter of all outbound business travel).

Demand for tourism in the British Isles from overseas

Britain is a major recipient of overseas tourists in the global scene, and nationally, tourism is an important invisible currency earner. The ebb and flow of tourist movements in and out of the British Isles is due to the relative strength of sterling against other currencies, the health of the economy, and the marketing activities of both public and private tourist organizations.

The early 1960s saw between three and four million overseas visitors come to Britain, but with the devaluation of sterling in 1967, Britain became a very attractive destination and numbers increased to almost seven million visits by 1970. By the mid 1970s, the weakness of the pound against other currencies, made Britain the 'bargain basement' of the Western World, and arrivals leapt to eleven million in 1976. The weakness of the pound, coupled to the depressed demand for overseas travel by the British in the mid-1970s, meant that spending by British residents overseas was easily outpaced by this boom in inbound travel, and Britain enjoyed a surplus on its balance of payments travel account. In other words, spending by overseas visitors to Britain was greater than spending by British residents overseas.

By 1978 sterling was a stronger currency, and Britain was experiencing high inflation. These two factors had the effect of increasing the real price of tourism services and goods in Britain, and increased taxation on goods in the early 1980s led to a 'price shock' for overseas visitors. Britain was no longer a cheap destination and both visitor numbers and spending in real terms declined accordingly. This led to a deficit on the balance of payments travel account, the first for many years. Nevertheless, taking the decade as a whole, Britain's performance as a tourist destination is impressive. Flows of overseas tourists increased by 86 per cent and even at the latter part of the decade,

Britain maintained its share of world tourism. The weakening of the pound in the mid 1980s suggests a return to the boom of the mid 1970s as Great Britain once again becomes a very attractive destination for overseas visitors. By the late 1980s visitor numbers are expected to accelerate to around twenty million.

In contrast to the UK Ireland achieved only very slow growth in overseas arrivals over the decade (around 1 per cent per annum), and high inflation and unfavourable exchange rates have led to slight reductions in arrivals in the early 1980s.

Again, these overall figures conceal variations in the different segments of the flow of overseas visitors to the British Isles. Holiday visits grew rapidly until 1977 (to almost half of total arrivals), but have declined slowly since that date. Visiting friends and relatives was a growing sector throughout the 1970s, and reached 20 per cent of total arrivals by 1980. This is a particularly important sector of the Irish market, where over 50 per cent of UK visitors are ethnic Irish visiting the 'old country', and many North American visitors also have Irish connections. Business travel has also grown continually since 1970, and by 1980 it too accounts for 20 per cent of total arrivals, though high spending in this sector makes it worth 25 per cent of total overseas visitor spending. North America and the EEC account for almost 70 per cent of inbound business travel.

The origin of overseas visits to the British Isles has changed over the decade 1970 to 1980. Not only have the sources of travel to the British Isles become more diverse, but visits from all major source areas have more than doubled (with the exception of North America). Visits from North America remained static over the decade at about two million per annum, though of course, in a period of growth this means that the share of North American visits has fallen (30 per cent in 1970; 17 per cent by 1980). As the pound weakened against the dollar in the mid 1980s this picture reversed and by 1984 North American visits passed three million. Western Europe accounts for over 60 per cent of all visits, and the rest of the world for the remaining 20 per cent.

The majority of overseas visitors to Ireland

originate from the UK (70 per cent) and again the strength of sterling against the Irish punt looks set to maintain this high share. However, dependence on one market leaves Eire vulnerable to changes in the UK economy.

Within Britain both the geographical and seasonal distribution of overseas visitors is very concentrated. Geographically, almost 90 per cent of visitors are to England, with Scotland (9 per cent) and Wales (3 per cent) taking much smaller shares. Even within England, the pattern is concentrated upon London, which takes 60 per cent of the spending by overseas visitors to England. Obviously, London is the capital city, a major gateway, and business centre, and would be expected to receive the lion's share of overseas visits. However, tourist authorities are anxious to spread the benefits of this spending to other areas. This can be achieved by promoting the regions of Britain and encouraging motoring and touring holidays (especially from Western Europe). Equally, encouraging traffic through regional ports and airports may reduce the concentration upon London and indeed, these measures are meeting with some success. Seasonally, the third quarter of the year accounts for almost 40 per cent of overseas visits to Britain and over 50 per cent of those to Eire.

Around 60 per cent of visitors to Britain arrive by air and 40 per cent by sea, although those from Western Europe are more likely to come by sea (over 50 per cent) and from North America by air (over 90 per cent). Sea transport had become increasingly popular with visitors to Eire (50 per cent of the total in 1982). Britain attracts slightly less than half a million day excursionists, with the cross Channel ports and ferries accounting for a large percentage of this traffic.

Summary

The British Isles are a major generator of both domestic and international tourism. Demand for tourism has grown rapidly since the Second World War for reasons which are rooted in the social and economic development of the countries concerned.

Around 60 per cent of the British population now take a holiday in any one year, but even so there is a hard core of those who do not travel. The majority of domestic tourism trips are to the UK mainland. Business tourism is a growing sector of the domestic market.

British residents' demand for holidays abroad has increased steadily since the Second World War and Britain now ranks fourth in the league table of world tourism generators. A combination of economic circumstances and the response of the travel industry has converted suppressed demand into effective demand for holidays abroad. Spain is still the most important destination for British holidays abroad.

Britain is a major recipient of overseas tourists and this demand is influenced by the relative strength of sterling, the health of the economy, and the marketing activities of tourist organizations. Within the British Isles the distribution of overseas tourists is concentrated in England, and especially London, and into the third quarter of the year.

SEVEN

The supply of tourism in the British Isles

LEARNING OBJECTIVES

After reading this chapter, you should be able to:

1 *Distinguish between the major physical regions of the British Isles.*
2 *Understand the major weather patterns of the British Isles.*
3 *Identify the major public agencies responsible for administering tourism in the British Isles.*
4 *Explain the main influences on the distribution of accommodation in the British Isles.*
5 *Understand the geographical patterns of transportation in the British Isles and recognize their significance for tourism.*
6 *Demonstrate a knowledge of the tourist regions, resorts, business centres, and tourist attractions of the British Isles.*

The physical setting for tourism

Physically, the British Isles are an offshore group of islands only 300,000 square kilometres in area, but they comprise a rich variety of landscapes and weather conditions. These islands have a distinctive overall identity and an intrinsic appeal, defined by their coastlines and separated from mainland Europe by the 'Narrow Seas' which act as an effective frontier.

Three physical regions provide the setting for

tourism in the British Isles. The *highland zone* includes Central and North Wales, the Southern Uplands, and the Highlands and Islands of Scotland. Here rocks are older, often impermeable, and high rainfall gives leached, infertile soils. Population is thinly scattered and land use dominated by livestock rearing. The *upland zone* includes Exmoor, Dartmoor, the Brecon Beacons and Black Mountains, and the Pennines; and in Scotland, Caithness, The Lothians, and Orkneys. Here the rocks are younger, land-forms more rounded, and distinctive regional differences are apparent (contrast the Yorkshire Dales with Dartmoor). British national parks and national park direction areas are mainly in the highland and upland zones where they have been designated for their natural beauty and characteristic landscapes. The *lowlands* nowhere exceed 300 metres in altitude and encompass much of southern and eastern England and also Ireland (where much of the land is low-lying, below ninety metres). In England the lowlands are warmer and drier and land use is dominated by intensive agriculture and sprawling conurbations. The *coasts* are equally important for tourism. The western coasts are irregular with estuaries, cliffs, sandy coves, and islands contrasting with the east where smooth, low coasts are typical, with long beaches and spits, and low cliffs, or dunes.

The latitudinal extent of the British Isles (from 50° North to 60° North) gives a diversity of *climatic influences* and conditions. The location of the British Isles off the coast of mainland Europe does mean that the climate is tempered by maritime influences, especially in Ireland where moist, mild conditions predominate. The British Isles are a battleground of different air masses and conditions are dependent on either the nature of the dominant air mass at the time, or the wet stormy weather which results from the 'fronts' where the air masses meet. Low pressure systems are constantly coming in from the Atlantic and the Western Highlands and Uplands bear the brunt of these systems, sheltering the lowland zone.

In winter, temperatures are lowest in the north east of the British Isles and mildest in the south west, but in summer, the gradient changes to west-east, with cooler temperatures in the west. In the summer too, sunshine figures are a source of keen competition between resorts. The south coast has the highest average number of bright sunshine hours per day, with sunshine hours decreasing inland, to the north, and with altitude.

If sunshine is the goal of many holidays, precipitation is to be avoided (aside from snow in winter sports resorts). Highest precipitation is found in the higher ground of the west (Ireland, the Lake District, Wales, Scottish Highlands) which at 2500 millimetres per year, is about four times as much as parts of eastern England. Precipitation falling as snow is more common in the highland and upland zones, and the colder east. In the Cairngorms in Scotland snow can lie for more than one hundred days of the year and has led to a major development of winter sports in the Aviemore area. Any average figures are deceptive and the variety of influences upon weather in the British Isles means that there are considerable differences from the average experience.

The components of tourism

This section examines the various components of tourism in the British Isles from a geographical viewpoint. Tourism supports 1.5 million jobs in the British Isles indirectly or directly – jobs which are distributed throughout the tourism industry.

Amenities

The tourist resource base of the British Isles is remarkably diverse for a group of small islands. *Regional resources* embrace the ten national parks which have been designated in England and Wales, five national park direction areas in Scotland, and three national parks in Eire. In England and Wales, national parks comprise 9 per cent of the land area and are required to both preserve their natural beauty and enhance their enjoyment by the public. The forests in Britain and forest parks in Eire and Northern Ireland are also important features. The British Forestry Commission is charged with opening up the forests for recreation and tourism and are developing self-catering cabins in holiday areas.

The British Isles also contain major *inland water bodies*, but demand for their recreational use on the mainland outstrips supply. This has led to intensive management of lakes such as Windermere and Lake Bala, and the Norfolk Broads. In Northern Ireland and in Eire population pressures are much less extreme and the country's water bodies provide an important resource for fishing and cruising holidays. Linear features include canals and rivers, both of which are intensively used for tourism and recreation, as are heritage coasts and long-distance coastal footpaths. Government provision for tourism and recreation is complemented by conservation trusts and charities, such as the National Trust (with 200,000 hectares of amenity land).

It is in areas such as national parks and the hinterlands of major resorts that the most successful *tourist attractions* lie. Their very diversity of size, type, and ownership, make classification difficult but Patmore (1983) has identified three basic types of attractions.

Firstly, many attractions simply result from the opening of an existing resource – say an ancient monument or stately home. In England alone in 1980 over 1300 historic buildings and monuments attracted over 150 million visits. Secondly, some attractions have begun to add developments (such as the motor museum and monorail at Beaulieu Palace) to augment the attraction and broaden their appeal. The varying extent of provision in the 167 English and Welsh country parks means that they should also be included in this second category. The third type of attraction is one artificially created for the visitor, such as Alton Towers or even London Zoo. The government and the tourist boards are anxious to improve the professionalism of tourist attractions and to diversify the range of attractions on offer – which now include coal-mining museums, and theme parks.

Accommodation

Accommodation is concentrated into centres of demand such as the seaside and major cities. In the British Isles, around 50 per cent of beds in serviced accommodation are located at the seaside, especially in the south and south western coasts of England, and in North Wales. However, much of this accommodation is in outmoded Victorian and Edwardian buildings – establishments which do not meet the aspirations of twentieth century holidaymakers. Both the public and private sectors are trying to remedy this problem and ensure that accommodation supply matches demand. The real change in holiday tastes has been for self-catering accommodation. In 1951, 12 per cent of main holidays in England used self-catering accommodation, but by 1981, the figure was over 30 per cent. Self-catering developments were initially in holiday camps (still offering three million bedspaces), later in caravans (over four million spaces), and more recently in holiday flats. In major towns and cities, demand from business and overseas travellers keeps bed occupancy rates high. Here provision tends to be in the larger, expensive hotels (often of more then one hundred bedrooms).

Accommodation is also dispersed along routeways and in rural areas. Initially accommodation was found on coaching routes and later at railway termini and major ports. More recently, airports and air terminals have attracted the development of large, quality hotels (as at Heathrow and in West London). In rural areas accommodation is concentrated in South West England, Scotland, Wales, and the Irish rural areas of Cork, Kerry, Donegal, and Galway. There is a growing demand for farm holidays and self-catering cottages, as well as new 'time-sharing' developments. It is also the rural areas that bear the brunt of second-home ownership (estimated to stand at 500,000 in the British Isles).

It must be remembered that up to 50 per cent of tourists stay with friends and relatives and do not use commercial accommodation. This VFR sector is particularly important in Eire and Northern Ireland.

Transportation

Travellers entering the British Isles can do so through a variety of gateways, but in fact both air and surface transport networks focus on the south east of England. Over 80 per cent of international passengers travelling by *air* are channelled through the London airports and airlines are reluctant to move out from these gateways. Manchester has been identified as the UK's second major airport. Belfast, and airports on the offshore holiday islands, complete the network, and although holiday traffic to these islands is not inconsiderable, it has a highly seasonal pattern. Overall, Britain's major airports handle around forty million passengers annually in the early 1980s, with the three major Irish airports (Dublin, Shannon, and Cork) adding a further three million.

For *sea traffic*, there is again a concentration of passengers into southern England due to the dominance of cross Channel ferry routes. Elsewhere there is a diversification of routes such as those from Hull and Harwich on the east coast. A second concentration of routes is from the west coasts of mainland Britain to Eire and Northern Ireland.

In the domestic market, and for overseas travellers touring the British Isles, *surface transport* dominates. The British Rail intercity service carries around eighty million passengers annually. However, the coastal and inland holiday areas are served by the 'other provincial services' – branch lines that have had little investment since the war. British Rail also operates rail-based domestic holiday packages (Golden Rail). In the British Isles there are over forty private railways trading on nostalgia for the steam era. In Eire railways and coach/bus services are operated by CIE (Coras Iompair Eirann) allowing integrated travel across the country.

Since the Second World War, the use of the car has become more important than either rail or coach services, as road improvements have been completed and the real cost of motoring has fallen. In the decades 1955 to 1975 the use of the car for domestic holidays more than doubled, and the share of rail and coach travel fell accordingly. The 1980 Transport Act has revolutionized the coaching business in the UK by deregulating services. Coaches pose a very real alternative to rail travel on journeys of up to four hundred kilometres and the new generation of luxury coaches (such as the National Express Rapide services) have boosted passenger figures on coach services.

Administration

Public agencies with responsibility for tourism in the British Isles play a vital role in shaping the tourist 'product', both through their promotional activities and also by providing financial aid to tourist enterprises.

In Great Britain the 1969 Development of Tourism Act formed three statutory *national tourist boards*, (English, Scottish, and Wales Tourist Boards) and the British Tourist Authority (BTA) which was given sole responsibility for overseas promotion and any matters of common interest between the national tourist boards. The English Tourist Board (ETB) and the BTA both reported to the Department of Trade and Industry, (changed to the Department of Employment in 1985) while the Scottish and Wales Tourist Boards (STB and WTB) report to the Scottish Office and the Welsh Office respectively. In Eire the national tourist board is Bord Failte Eireann, established in 1955 with promotion (including overseas promotion) and development functions. The Northern Ireland tourist board (NITB) was one of the first statutory boards to be set up (in 1948). Britain's offshore holiday islands each have small, relatively independent boards reporting directly to their island governments.

The twin roles of promotion and development are effective tools with which to shape the supply of tourism in the British Isles. On the promotion side, the national boards in Great Britain are charged to promote their own countries within the UK and have back-up research and advisory powers. For development the boards were given the responsibility of providing and encouraging the provision and improvement of tourist facilities and amenities. In Eire, Bord Failte administers financial incentives for the improvement and addition of accommodation and tourist attractions.

The national tourist boards are supported by a *regional tourist board* (RTB) structure. There are twelve RTBs in England, three in Wales, and eight in Eire. In Scotland, all but four districts participate in the new structure consisting of thirty-two Area Tourist Boards (ATBS). At the *local level*, local authorities (county and district councils) have

National parks

1 Northumberland
2 Lake District
3 Yorkshire Dales
4 North York Moors
5 Peak District
6 Snowdonia
7 Pembrokeshire Coast
8 Brecon Beacons
9 Exmoor
10 Dartmoor

Figure 7.1 *Major tourist resources in the British Isles*

Key to regional maps
The maps show selected features considered to be of major significance for tourism.
Tourist centres and resorts have been categorized according to a particular
function, bearing in mind that most cities are in fact multi-functional

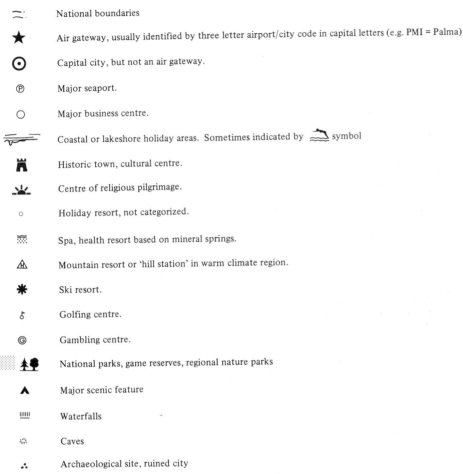

⌒	National boundaries
★	Air gateway, usually identified by three letter airport/city code in capital letters (e.g. PMI = Palma)
⊙	Capital city, but not an air gateway.
Ⓟ	Major seaport.
○	Major business centre.
~	Coastal or lakeshore holiday areas. Sometimes indicated by ⌇ symbol
♜	Historic town, cultural centre.
⛎	Centre of religious pilgrimage.
○	Holiday resort, not categorized.
▦	Spa, health resort based on mineral springs.
⚠	Mountain resort or 'hill station' in warm climate region.
✳	Ski resort.
♨	Golfing centre.
Ⓖ	Gambling centre.
▒ ♣♠	National parks, game reserves, regional nature parks
▲	Major scenic feature
⏜	Waterfalls
⁙	Caves
∴	Archaeological site, ruined city
⌇⏛	Inland waterway

The regional setting for tourism

The South

Tourism in the British Isles is heavily concentrated in southern England and London dominates the pattern as a business and tourism centre of world significance. London is the focus of national communications and its airports are important in considerable tourism powers available for promotion and development.

the international network of air services. It is particularly popular with overseas visitors who flock to its museums, historic buildings, and many other attractions. Tourism does add to the capital's congestion and efforts are being made to 'spread the load' to lesser-known attractions outside Central London, such as the former Docklands. Tourism helps to support the West End theatres and other amenities which Londoners take for granted.

Outside the capital, which has its own Visitor and Convention Bureau, the South is covered by four regional tourist boards, but the dividing lines between their areas do not provide sharp natural boundaries. Throughout the South the countryside is an important tourist resource. Inland, areas of outstanding natural beauty (AsONB) include the Chilterns and the North Downs, and the Cotswolds to the west boast mellow limestone buildings in tourist centres such as Broadway or Chipping Campden. The Thames Valley contains Oxford, Henley, and Windsor. Kent is studded with hop gardens, oast houses, and windmills, while to the west, in Hampshire and Dorset, the landscape changes to the woods and heath of the New Forest and the Purbecks.

The region's coast is one of contrasts. In the east the coasts of Kent and Sussex are occupied by important resorts, including Brighton with its good communications to London, and most of the Channel ports which are gateways to Britain. The industrialization of the Thames estuary, and parts of Kent do conflict with tourism, as do the naval dockyards and oil refineries in Hampshire, although the naval heritage of Southampton and Portsmouth is now exploited as a tourist resource. The Dorset coast takes in the fashionable resort of Bournemouth and smaller family resorts such as Swanage. To the south, the Isle of Wight is an important holiday destination with several family resorts.

The South West Peninsula has the valuable tourist resources of attractive coastline, fine scenery, and a mild, sunny climate (which has given rise to such slogans as 'The Cornish Riviera', and more recently 'The English Riviera'). Formerly the region suffered from remoteness, but the M5 motorway and increased car ownership means it continues to be the most popular tourist region for the British. Tourism is important for employment and income generation, although the seasonal nature of tourism is a problem.

The countryside of the South West contains two national parks – Dartmoor and Exmoor – with their associated facilities for visitors, and several AsONB including the Mendips and Quantocks. Exeter is an important regional and tourist centre, while Bristol is now developing a tourism industry based on business travel and its maritime history.

The coast of the South West is perhaps the best known feature. Major resorts include Torquay, Paignton, Weston-super-Mare, and Weymouth. The area has many smaller resorts (e.g. Lyme Regis), sailing and water-sports centres (e.g. Salcombe and Bude), and retirement havens (such as Budleigh Salterton). Much of the region's varied coastline is protected by heritage coast policies, or National Trust ownership, and provides other recreational opportunities such as long-distance coastal paths.

East Anglia and the Midlands

The middle part of England which extends from the eastern coast to the Welsh border covers three main regional tourist board areas. The lowland East Anglia region has many small market towns, such as Ipswich and Lavenham, which are well endowed with historic buildings. Major tourist attractions include Great Yarmouth and several smaller resorts, the university town of Cambridge, as well as historic Norwich, and the Lincolnshire bulb fields around Spalding. To the east the Essex marshes have yachting centres (Burham-on-Crouch) and major resorts at Clacton and Southend. East Anglia largely escaped the developments of the industrial revolution and has preserved much of its rural traditions.

The Norfolk Broads to the west of Great Yarmouth are perhaps Britain's best known area for water-based recreation and holidays. There are over 200 kilometres of navigable waterways and over 2000 powered craft for hire. There is no doubt of the commercial success of tourism in the area, but this has had costs. Detergents, human sewage, discarded fuel, and a lowered water table upset the ecological balance; banks are eroded and wildlife disturbed by the passage of boats; and the sprawl of boatyards and development despoil the landscape.

The Midlands are attracting tourists and day visitors to its countryside, historic towns, and industrial heritage. Cannock Chase is an important regional recreational resource located near the conurbation, and is developing facilities for visitors. Other countryside areas include the Malverns, Charnwood and Sherwood forests, and the Wye

Valley to the west, which attracts canoeing and activity holidays. The historic towns are dominated by Stratford-upon-Avon, popular with overseas visitors for its literary associations and Royal Shakespeare Theatre. Other important towns near the Welsh border are Ludlow, Shrewsbury, and Hereford. The National Exhibition Centre at the heart of the motorway system and with good rail and air connections enhances Birmingham as an important centre for business tourism. The industrial heritage is now undergoing a tourism revolution with restored railways, canals, and a new breed of museums such as the Ironbridge Gorge Complex, and the Potteries museum at Stoke-on-Trent.

The North

The northern part of England, which includes four regional tourist boards, is one of contrasts, from industrial heartlands, through the spectacular scenery of national parks, to its bustling resorts. The scenery of the area is evidenced by the fact that it contains five national parks. The Lake District Park is a major tourist area with its human-scale landscape, attractive towns and villages, and lakes – each with its own character. The Yorkshire Dales Park is characterized by a gentle landscape, criss-crossed by limestone walls, and dotted with field barns (some converted to shelters for walkers). The area is popular for educational visits (to areas such as Malham) and with cavers (around Ingleton). The Peak District Park is an area of moorland, notched by deep valleys as at Dovedale. Here too, educational visits and outdoor pursuits are important. The North York Moors Park contains heather-covered, rolling countryside with picturesque villages. The Northumberland National Park on the Scottish border contains Kielder Forest and Kielder Water – both recent additions to the landscape, while Hadrian's Wall to the south is of unique historic interest.

In these rural uplands, tourism brings income and jobs, supports rural services, and stems depopulation. But herein also lie seeds of conflict, as others argue that tourism interferes with farming operations and destroys the very communities that tourists visit.

The coasts of the North embrace major resorts. Blackpool's famous tower is jostled by a townscape of tourist facilities and small guesthouses; Scarborough is one of Britain's oldest resorts, an elegant town between two bays and its redeveloped Spa conference centre now adds a business dimension to its market. The region has a range of smaller resorts (such as Bridlington and Morecambe) and day-trip centres close to conurbations (such as Southport serving Merseyside). The undeveloped coast is also an important attraction. Much of the North Yorkshire coast is within the North York Moors National Park; Flamborough Head is a designated heritage coast.

The major conurbations are significant business travel centres; historic towns such as York and Chester attract overseas and day visitors alike, whilst the industrial heritage is also exploited for tourism. Bradford's tourism industry, based on the woollen textile heritage (with a little help from the Brontes), has been a notable recent example of an imaginative approach to developing tourism.

Wales

North Wales is an important tourist region with coastal resorts and the Snowdonia National Park. Here the traditional culture and Welsh language has persisted and is a tourist attraction in itself, along with castles such as Conwy and Caernarfon. The mountains and lakes of Snowdonia attract sightseers and outdoor enthusiasts to centres at Beddgelert and Betws-y-Coed and tourism now plays an important role in the rural economy. The coast is easily accessible from Merseyside and Manchester and includes such popular resorts as Rhyl and Llandudno, and major caravan developments in the east. Second-home development is significant in the area and is a source of controversy. The North Wales slate industry is now exploited as a tourist attraction, along with the narrow gauge railways built to serve the quarries.

Mid-Wales is also mountainous, thinly populated, and north-south communications are difficult. There are small seaside resorts (such as Aberystwyth and Aberdovey) popular with visitors from the Midlands; market towns (e.g. Newtown);

and former spas (such as Builth Wells) act as touring centres.

South Wales contains the majority of the population, towns, and industry of the country. It is now easily accessible from southern England via the Severn Bridge. The region contains attractive scenery in the Brecon Beacons National Park with its touring centres (e.g. Crickhowell) and the gentler countryside of Pembrokeshire (with the resort of Tenby and a coastal national park). The coast is an important recreational resource for the conurbations. The Gower peninsula and resorts of Barry and Porthcawl are particularly popular.

Scotland

Scotland occupies the scenic northern third of Britain, a predominantly unspoilt mountainous country, thinly populated outside the conurbations of Glasgow and Edinburgh. Its folklore and history are an important part of its tourist appeal.

Tourism in the Southern Uplands is confined to the Galloway peninsula with sailing and activity holidays and tours of the Border country's abbeys, castles, and Walter Scott associations. The Central Lowlands contain the bulk of Scotland's population and industry. Edinburgh is the capital and cultural centre of Scotland, boasting tourist attractions which include Holyrood House, the Castle, and its famous summer festival celebrating music and drama. Glasgow is much larger and more industrialized, and it is the gateway to the Western Highlands, especially the Trossachs and islands of Arran and Bute. The Central Lowlands have fine beaches and golf courses in resorts such as Troon and Turnberry, and boating on the Firths of Forth, Clyde, and Tay.

The Highlands are the nearest to true wilderness in Britain, an area of mountains, lochs, and glens. The North West Highlands to the west of Glen More have a deeply indented coast with many islands. Transport is a problem and islands are reached by ferry or 'air taxi'. Skye is noted for the Cuillins, a challenge to rock climbers, Iona as a place of pilgrimage and Staffa for basalt sea caves. The Orkneys and Shetlands offer dramatic cliff scenery and relics of their prehistoric and Viking past.

To the east of the great rift valley of Glen More the Grampians are more accessible to the lowland cities. Loch Lomond and the Trossachs, Gleneagles, near Perth, and the Spey Valley were Victorian holiday areas and the legacy of hotels and development remains. The Grampians have well-developed winter sports at the purpose-built Aviemore complex and in surrounding areas. The Highlands and Islands Development Board which covers the area is an example of a government agency involved in tourism. Since the mid-1960s the Board claims to have generated some 30,000 jobs and invested over £3 million in tourism.

Ireland

Ireland's 'Emerald Isle' reputation is owed to the mild damp climate which favours the growth of lush vegetation and pasture. It is an essentially rural country with a distinctive culture and unhurried lifestyle.

The Dublin area contains over one-third of the population and Dublin itself is a business and tourist centre with fine eighteenth century buildings and the Wicklow mountains and glens within easy reach. The Government has encouraged tourist facilities in the poorer Gaelic-speaking West of Ireland and already 25,000 jobs have been created in areas like Donegal and Connemara where cottages, farm holidays, and handicrafts are important. Here too, coastal scenery is spectacular with small fishing harbours, inlets, and rugged headlands. Galway is the recognized capital of the West. Cork and Kerry in the south west are well known for the Lakes of Killarney with their mild climate and beautiful scenery, fishing villages (e.g. Kenmale and Dingle), and sailing (at Kinsale).

Northern Ireland is more urbanized than Eire, with over one-third of the inhabitants living in and around Belfast. As a tourist destination the Province offers scenery, fishing, and water sports, especially holidays based on the lakes and waterways of Fermanagh, or touring the plateau and glens of Antrim with its resorts and the Giant's Causeway, a unique geological feature of volcanic origin. However, since the late 1960s tourism has been severely hindered by social and political instability and terrorism.

The off-shore islands

The Channel Islands capitalize on their favourable climate, sunshine, and French flavour. Jersey and Guernsey are semi-independent States with their own parliaments and low rates of tax, which attract business, an influx of retired people and duty-free shoppers. The islands have attractive coastal scenery, fine beaches, and well developed tourist facilities in the town of St Helier (Jersey) and St Peter Port (Guernsey).

The Isle of Man is a microcosm of northern England with fells, coastal resorts (Douglas), and remains of industry (the Laxey Wheel). The island has its own parliament (Tynwald) and fiscal system. It is perhaps best known for its annual T.T. (Tourist Trophy) motorcycle races which take place in June using the island's road system.

Summary

The physical setting for tourism in the British Isles comprises the highlands, uplands, lowlands, and coasts. Climatically, conditions are unpredictable but remarkably mild for the latitude.

The British Isles are well endowed with all types of tourist attractions and an increasingly professional approach to their management is apparent. The location of accommodation in the British Isles is influenced by the concentration of stock into centres of demand such as the seaside or major towns and cities, and by the dispersal of accommodation along routeways and into rural areas. Britain's major airports handle around forty million passengers annually and attempts are being made to disperse traffic to regional airports. Similarly, sea ferry routes are now being developed away from the south east coast. The surface transport networks of the British Isles focus on the south east of England. Tourism is administered by a variety of public agencies, spearheaded by the country tourist boards and supported by regional boards and local authorities.

The British Isles comprise a variety of tourist regions, each with a distinctive blend of resources for tourism. Such resources include countryside, coast, towns and cities, and the heritage.

EIGHT

Scandinavia

LEARNING OBJECTIVES

After reading this chapter, you should be able to:

1 Describe the major physical regions and climate of the Scandinavian countries and understand their importance for tourism.
2 Understand the nature of Scandinavian economies and society, and their significance for tourist demand.
3 Outline the major features of demand for both domestic and international travel in Scandinavia.
4 Describe the major features of the Scandinavian tourism industry including transport, accommodation, and promotion.
5 Demonstrate a knowledge of the tourist regions, resorts, business centres, and tourist attractions of Scandinavia.

Introduction

Strictly speaking, Scandinavia is the peninsula shared by Norway and Sweden but is extended here to include Denmark, Finland, and Iceland. These countries have shared a similar cultural heritage from the time of the Vikings and have achieved some of the most prosperous economies in the world, with highly developed health and social welfare systems.

The climate of Scandinavia is influenced by three main factors: its northerly latitude (a considerable area lies within the Arctic Circle); the Atlantic ocean to the west; and the Kjolen mountains which form the border between Norway and Sweden. With the exception of Denmark and the Atlantic coastlands of Norway, the region experiences severely cold winters with long hours of darkness, icy winds, and frozen seas, but warm, sunny summers with up to 2100 sunshine hours per year in some areas.

The Scandinavian landscape still bears the imprint of the glaciers of the last Ice Age. These eroded the valleys of western Norway into deep troughs and scraped bare the ancient plateau surfaces of Finland and Sweden. Here the ice sheets left masses of boulder clay which are now covered by coniferous forest dotted with lakes and bare rock. The highest parts of Scandinavia are the Kjolen mountains which contain the largest glaciers of continental Europe. Iceland's landscape is also glaciated but has the added ingredient of volcanic activity with lava spreads, geysers, and hot springs. However, there are negative factors affecting tourist development in Scandinavia, notably the shortness of the summer season and the darkness of winter.

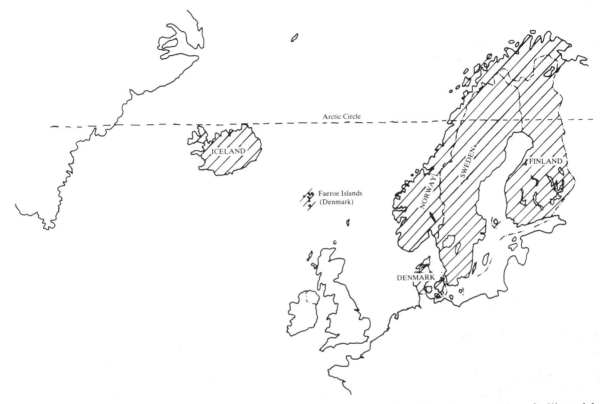

The Scandinavian countries have a combined population of 22.5 million, mainly concentrated in the southern regions. Social and economic conditions in Scandinavia have combined to make it one of the major generating areas in the world for holiday tourism, although the relatively high cost of living and strong currencies make it an expensive destination for inbound foreign visitors. Not only does the region have prosperous economies and a high standard of living, but at the same time emphasis is placed on leisure and quality of life; levels of education are high, and typical annual leave entitlement is five weeks or more. Add to this a well-developed, efficient travel trade throughout the region and it is no surprise that levels of both domestic and foreign holiday propensities are very high.

Much of the growth in holiday propensities throughout the 1970s took place in holidays abroad which now represent around one-third of all holidays taken by residents of Norway, Sweden, and Denmark. A large percentage of these holidays are to other Scandinavian countries, facilitated by the high degree of international co-operation in the region, including abolition of passport controls and promotion of inter-Scandinavian travel. Domestic holidays have grown as short, additional holidays have become popular (especially winter sports and activity holidays). In the future modest economic growth is expected in Norway and Finland and increased holiday entitlement and leisure time across the region will further increase travel propensities. Inbound tourism to Scandinavia stood at around eight million trips in the early 1980s, with the majority of trips to Denmark (almost 50 per cent). West Germany is the most important generator of trips to Scandinavia.

Denmark

Denmark is the smallest and most densely populated of the Scandinavian countries with over five million inhabitants. Copenhagen accounts for over one-fifth of the population and over 80 per cent of the population live in urban areas. Denmark has one of the highest gross national products per capita in the world and the high standards of living are reflected in demand for leisure, recreation, and tourism. Danes enjoy up to six weeks annual holiday entitlement and over half the population take a holiday away from home every year.

Almost 60 per cent of Danish holidays are domestic. In the domestic market staying with friends and relatives, staying in owned and rented summer homes, and camping are the most popular forms of accommodation in preference to serviced facilities. The Danes are increasingly taking more than one holiday away from home each year. Looking now at holidays abroad (40 per cent of all holidays) 10 per cent are taken in other Scandinavian countries and 30 per cent in other European countries, with West Germany and Spain the most important destinations. Inbound tourism to Denmark is dominated by neighbouring West Germany, with most visits concentrated between May and September. The absence of charter flights to Denmark, allied to good road and ferry links, means that surface travel is predominant, especially the private car. Denmark is promoted abroad by the official Danish Tourist Board while domestic tourism promotion is undertaken by regional and local authorities. Transport within Denmark is mainly by private car using a well developed internal and international road system with ferry connections to other parts of the country.

International ferry connections to Scandinavia, West Germany, and the UK are operated by companies such as DFDS Seaways. Public transport includes inter-city rail links, domestic air services, and buses, but the fact that these can be overcrowded and expensive, may depress the volume of internal travel by foreign visitors. The majority of Denmark's accommodation capacity is self-catering including summer homes and camp sites and this is where most of the growth of accommodation has occurred. Hotel and hostel capacity is also available with the highest occupancy levels in Copenhagen and in the peak season, on the island of Bornholm. Stays on Danish farms are popular among British families.

There are three main tourist regions in Denmark – the Jutland peninsula, the Danish Archipelago, and Copenhagen. Jutland is a flat, low-lying peninsula of heathland and pine forest. The east coast is less attractive than the North Sea coastline which has sand dunes for beach holidays and tidal creeks for sailing.

The Danish Archipelago consists of a large number of islands, of which Fano, Romo, and Bornholm (way out in the Baltic) live by tourism. The islands are linked by numerous ferries and have a landscape of farms and beechwoods with many hotels, restaurants, and bathing beaches. Odense, on the island of Fyn, attracts visitors for its associations with Hans Andersen, but the main centre for tourism (especially foreign visits) is Copenhagen on Zealand. Due to its strategic position between the North Sea and the Baltic, it is an important entrepôt handling a large volume of international passenger trade. Its airport (Kastrup) is not only the busiest in Scandinavia, but also a major gateway for the region. Major attractions include the Tivoli Gardens amusement park, Hamlet's Castle at Elsinore, and the Danish Royal Ballet. Nearby coastal developments include the new beach park complex at Koge Bay. Denmark has many open-air folk museums, where buildings and crafts are conserved in an authentic setting. Activity holidays are also available including cycling, angling, golfing, sailing, and nature study opportunities.

Norway

Norway is a remarkably elongated country extending almost 2000 kilometres from Kristiansand to the North Cape. It has over four million inhabitants, most of whom live in the coastal areas of the south. Although the population is small, holiday propensities are high, standing at over 75 per cent in the late 1970s. This is in part explained by Norway's prosperous economy, the continued growth of disposable incomes fuelled by oil revenue, and an increasing annual holiday entitlement.

Of Norwegians' holidays, almost five million were domestic holidays in the late 1970s, stimu-

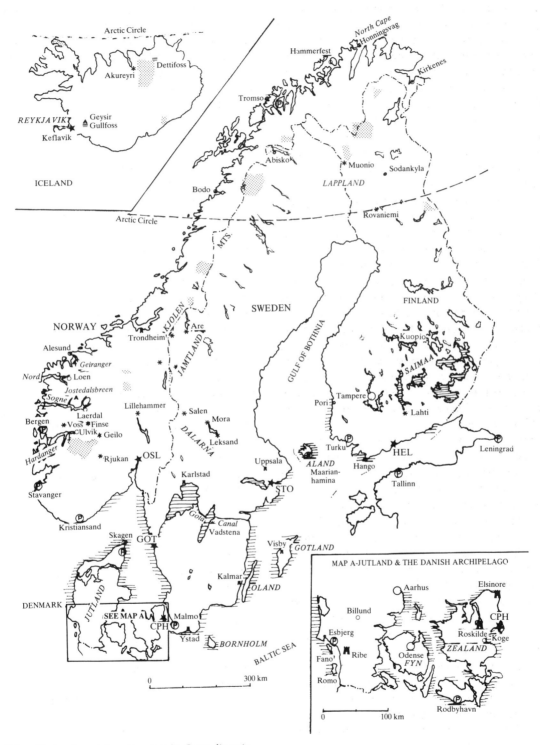

Figure 8.1 *Major tourist resources in Scandinavia*

lated by the widespread ownership of holiday chalets. The market is expected to grow further especially for winter holidays. Almost 30 per cent of Norwegians take a holiday abroad, leaving a deficit on the country's travel account. Only 13 per cent travelled to other Scandinavian countries; of the remainder over half visited the Mediterranean, North Africa or the Canaries, the rest mainly to other European countries. Business travel in Norway accounts for about half a million trips, the majority using hotel accommodation and most travelling by car (over 40 per cent) or air (around 40 per cent). Around four million foreign visitors come to Norway annually and the short season creates a marked summer peak. The major source areas are the rest of Scandinavia (65 per cent of visits), Germany, the USA, and the UK.

In such an extensive (almost 324,000 square kilometres) country transport can be a problem – it takes over a week to travel the length of Norway by car. The majority of foreign visits and domestic trips are car-borne, taking advantage of the improved 80,000 kilometre road system and ferry links across major fjords (though the ferries are crowded in the summer peak). The road and railway have opened up Norway for tourism. The 2400 kilometre railways system is run by Norwegian State Railways and offers efficient internal travel on often scenic mountain lines such as the Oslo to Bergen route. International air passengers are served by Oslo's two airports and domestic air services link forty destinations. Tourists can use the excellent coastal shipping services to the 'Land of the Midnight Sun' beyond the Arctic Circle as far as the Russian border. Norway has a large merchant shipping fleet and is important in the cruise market.

In the peak season, the majority of accommodation is in camping, though a decline in camping popularity is leading to a shortage of other forms of self-catering accommodation such as cabins. Hotels are more commonly open all year round. Other accommodation is available on farms and 'rorbus' (fisherman's shelters). Even so, there is an acute shortage of accommodation capacity in the popular tourist areas in the peak summer and Easter periods.

The main aim of the Norwegian Tourist Board is to attract foreign tourists to Norway and the Board is also now promoting domestic tourism. The Government is placing increasing importance on tourism for aiding local communities, transport operators, and accommodation proprietors, and is attempting to reduce the acute seasonal and geographical concentration of visits.

Norway contains some of the most spectacular scenery in Scandinavia and it has long been an important tourist destination for this reason. Norway's 55,000 kilometre coastline is deeply indented and the south west region with its fjords and many 'skerries' or islands is a major tourist region. The longest and most spectacular fjords are the Sogne and Hardanger extending over 200 kilometres inland, each with their own scenic resorts (Laerdal and Ulvik respectively, being the most important). On the southern coast coves and beaches are also popular. Temperatures on the coast are much milder than would be expected for the latitude due to the influence of the North Atlantic current.

Tourism is a mainstay of economies in rural areas, especially in the mountains with their waterfalls, lakes, forests, and picturesque villages. Holiday opportunities here include mountain rambles, orienteering, and summer skiing, and accommodation for visitors is available in mountain huts (saeters). Important winter sports centres, such as Lillehammer, are located along railways linking Oslo, Bergen, and Trondheim. Norway is also noted for its folklore and handicrafts, while the old fishing town of Bergen, and Oslo's Viking and maritime museums, attract cultural tourists.

Sweden

Sweden is the largest Scandinavian country with 450,000 square kilometres and over eight million inhabitants, the majority of whom live in urban areas, and in the southern half of the country. The Swedes have a very prosperous economy and, with high annual holiday entitlements (over 60 per cent have five weeks or more), Sweden has one of the highest holiday propensities in the world. In the early 1980s almost 90 per cent of those between sixteen and sixty-four years of age took a holiday of at least one night away from home. Holiday frequency is also high with additional holidays a particular growth market.

Of holidays taken by the Swedes, domestic trips have grown in the early 1980s. Car-borne holidays are the most popular (80 per cent of all trips), but escalating motoring costs have depressed touring holidays. Self-catering accommodation is favoured, especially summer cottages (some 600,000 are owned – often by those who have migrated to the cities but wish to retain a link with their rural homeland). Activity holidays are particularly popular, especially fishing, canoeing, and white-water rafting. Domestic business travel is focused on Stockholm, Gothenburg, and Malmo.

Thirty per cent of Swedish holidays are to other Scandinavian countries and almost 40 per cent to European destinations outside Scandinavia. The majority of these latter trips are to West Germany, Southern Europe, and the UK. In contrast to outbound tourism the volume of inbound tourism to Sweden is small, leaving a large deficit on the travel account. A shortage of hotel capacity delayed development of Sweden's foreign tourism industry but by the early 1980s six million nights were spent in registered accommodation, and devaluation of the krona in 1982 prompted an increase in inbound travel. The main generators are the rest of Scandinavia, West Germany, the UK, the Netherlands, and the USA.

Relatively little new development has taken place for a number of years in Sweden's serviced accommodation stock. For domestic tourism demand for hotel accommodation is small but business travel has created acute shortages in the cities and has led to the development of company flats in Stockholm, though new hotel capacity both under construction and planned should alleviate the problem. Self-catering accommodation is in demand for holiday tourism and time-sharing and multi-ownership schemes are being developed, as are high-quality camp sites. International air transport is serviced by three airports; however most holiday tourists arrive by car and ferry via the main routes from Denmark and West Germany. Car travel is expensive in Sweden and controls on the use of cars may prompt a switch to public transport. Swedish railways are being modernized with high-speed routes between cities.

The Swedish Tourist Board promotes both domestic and overseas tourism and is supported by an independent network of twenty-two regional organizations. At the national and regional level, assistance for tourism projects is available, though geared to job creation. Local authorities are involved in stimulating new hotel accommodation. Sweden's tourist resources include its large tracts of unspoilt forest and lake countryside, varied coastline, and the Swedish way of life. The central lake region contains many lakes – the two largest ones, Venner and Veter are linked by the 190 kilometre Gota canal. The southern Baltic coast enjoys exceptionally long sunshine hours and the islands of Gotland and Oland have fine holiday beaches. Facing the North Sea is the 'golden' coast, while the 1,400 kilometre 'midnight sun' coast along the Gulf of Bothnia is the gateway to Lappland, the largest unspoilt wilderness area in Europe. Swedish culture and crafts (especially glass) also attract tourism. The island city of Stockholm is a well-planned capital which provides a quarter of all Sweden's tourism employment. To the north west of Stockholm lies the picturesque Dalarna region – the Swedish Dales – where folk customs are preserved.

Finland

Finland is a spacious (over 337,000 square kilometres), sparsely populated country of almost five million inhabitants. Over 60 per cent of the Finns live in urban areas, of which the Helsinki conurbation is by far the largest with almost one million inhabitants. Around 50 per cent of the population take a holiday of four nights or more away from home; the majority of holidays are domestic, but almost 10 per cent are holiday trips abroad.

Finland has pursued an aggressive tourism policy aiming to attract both domestic and foreign tourists, spearheaded by the Finnish Tourist Board. International tourists are sought for their foreign exchange and tourism in general is seen as a means to regional development in the rural areas, and also for the diversification of Helsinki's economy. Inbound tourism numbers were around four million in 1980 making Finland the only Scandinavian country with a surplus on its travel account. The majority of arrivals are from Sweden (75 per cent) and Norway (10 per cent). Most come by sea through the main ports of Helsinki, Turku, and Maarianhamina (on the Aland Islands), though arrivals by road are increasing.

Air transport in Finland has grown steadily and was prompted by the modernization of Helsinki airport. Domestic transport arrangements are excellent with broad, surfaced highways, an improved railway system, and a network of domestic air services to twenty-one destinations. Motels and hotels are concentrated in the major towns (Helsinki, Turku, and Tampere) where business travel means that they can maintain a high annual bed occupancy (up to 75 per cent in Helsinki). Finland also offers holiday villages, concentrated in the Central Lakeland area, holiday cottages, farm accommodation, and camp sites. Seasonality is high, with the majority of foreign tourists arriving between May and October, with a peak in July. In consequence, roughly one quarter of Finnish accommodation is only open for part of the year. A conscious effort is now being made to extend the season by developing conference and winter sports tourism. Helsinki is developing as an important international conference centre with its Finlandia Hall and nearby international standard hotels.

For holiday tourism Finland's attraction is in the spacious natural resources of lakes and rivers (which cover 10 per cent of the land surface) and forests (almost 60 per cent of the surface). Finland is one of Europe's last wilderness areas and has capitalized on the emergence of environment-conscious tourism (or eco-tourism), which uses natural products and food from unpolluted sources. Other holiday opportunities include cross-country skiing, hiking, climbing, sailing, and spa tourism.

In the Finnish lake district of Saimaa cabins can be rented and many are owned by Finns. Here holidays and weekends are spent beside the unpolluted lakes which are heavily forested down to the water's edge. A more recent development here is low-density holiday villages of twenty or thirty cottages. The Finnish Archipelago consists of the south, south west, and west coasts with many islands, linked by luxurious ferry services. The Aland islands are especially popular with Swedish and Finnish holidaymakers alike. The main forest region bordering the USSR offers canoeing, hiking, and cross-country skiing. In Lappland (mainly inside the Arctic Circle) attractions include the way of life of the Lapps, winter reindeer safaris, and the winter sports complex in the Muonio Valley. Due to its neutral stance in world politics and its long association with the former Russian Empire, Finland is a convenient starting point for excursions to the Baltic coast of the USSR.

Iceland

Iceland's active volcanic landscapes contrast with snow and icefields. Despite an area of over 100,000 square kilometres, only 1 per cent of the surface is cultivated and the population is less than a quarter-million, leaving plenty of space for 'adventure holidays'. Iceland is anxious to expand its tourism industry in order to diversify the islands's economy which is dominated by the fishing industry. However, because Iceland is an expensive destination and relatively difficult to reach, inbound tourism is small (around 65,000 visitors per year, mainly from the USA, West Germany, and the UK). A small conference and incentive travel trade is now encouraged and measures are being taken to extend the season into May and September.

Air transport services to Iceland are comprehensive from Scandinavia and Western Europe with the island's own airline Flugleidir (Icelandair) and Scandinavian Airlines System (SAS) providing the bulk of the services. Iceland's international airport at Keflavik is often used as a stop-over on transatlantic flights. Access by sea comprises ferry services from the Shetlands, Bergen, and Hantsholm in Denmark. Internal transport is served by an extensive domestic air network (tourists can buy an air rover ticket), and bus services on the 9000 kilometres of road. Iceland's accommodation stock comprises hotels, guesthouses, youth hostels, farm holidays, and camp sites.

The main tourist attractions are scenic. The interior is rugged mountain and high plateau country averaging 500 metres in altitude. There are over 200 volcanoes with eruptions every five years on average. Volcanic activity also causes hot springs, geysers, and the abundant geo-thermal energy is harnessed to heat swimming pools, buildings, and greenhouses. Activity holidays include pony-trekking, bird watching, camping expeditions, and photographic safaris which are well suited to the crisp, unpolluted air. The island's capital, Reykjavik, is built on rolling hills and surrounded by mountains. With wooden houses, museums, and galleries of Icelandic culture and Viking heritage, its concentration of high-class accommodation makes it an important tourist centre. Winter sports facilities are available close to Reykjavik and near Akureyri on the north coast.

Summary

Scandinavia's climate is typified by severely cold, long winters and warm, sunny summers. The varied landscapes include forested countryside dotted with lakes; indented coastlines with fjords and islands; and the volcanic features of Iceland. Social and economic conditions in Scandinavia have combined to make it one of the major generating regions in the world for holiday tourism, although strong currencies make it an expensive destination for inbound tourists. Inter-Scandinavian travel has been particularly popular, facilitated by the abolition of passport controls.

Accommodation capacity in the short summer season is dominated by the self-catering sector as serviced accommodation is in short supply. The majority of international tourists arrive by car using the many ferry services available, though international air links are comprehensive. Internal travel is typified by rapid inter-city rail links; broad, surfaced highways; and extensive domestic air and sea links.

The most important of Scandinavia's tourist resources are: the uncrowded, unpolluted countryside; the spectacular scenery of the mountains and of the many coastal regions; islands and holiday beaches and the Scandinavian culture and outdoor way of life on show in the capitals and major cities of the region.

NINE

Central Europe: Austria, Switzerland, and West Germany

LEARNING OBJECTIVES

After reading this chapter, you should be able to:

1 Describe the major physical regions and climate of Austria, West Germany, and Switzerland and understand their importance for tourism.
2 Recognize that the strength of the economies of the three countries encourages demand for outbound tourism but their strong currencies deter inbound tourism.
3 Appreciate the volume and characteristics of demand for domestic holidays and trips abroad, particularly West Germany's position as the leading generator of international tourists in the world.
4 Understand the volume and nature of inbound tourism, particularly its importance to Austria and Switzerland.
5 Describe the main features of the tourism industries in Central Europe.
6 Demonstrate a knowledge of the tourist regions, resorts, business centres, and tourist attractions in the three countries.

Introduction

The countries of Austria, West Germany, and Switzerland occupy a key position in central Europe. This is particularly the case for West Germany whose present borders were determined after the Second World War and arbitrarily sever the country, stranding West Berlin as an enclave of Western democracy 160 kilometres inside East Germany (which is dealt with in Chapter 14).

Both Austria and Germany were historically great empires, whereas Switzerland has always been a small country owing much of its importance to its strategic location astride the major passes over the Alps. Apart from West Germany's short North Sea and Baltic coasts, the area under consideration in this chapter is landlocked. Three major physical regions can be identified. The first, the North German Plain and the coast are of relatively limited importance for tourism. More important are the Central Uplands which include the Rhineland and areas such as the Black Forest and the Harz Mountains. Finally, the three countries contain over 50 per cent of the Alpine area. This is of major importance for both winter and summer tourism and offers great variety of scenery from the high fretted ridges and peaks eroded by glaciation, snow-filled cirques and glaciers, to the lakes and forested lower slopes. Forests provide a major recreational resource throughout the region, especially in West Germany.

With the exception of the North Sea coast the region has a continental climate but inland winters become colder as a result of altitude. In the mountains the climate is bracing with clean air and brilliant sunshine, but the weather varies with aspect and altitude and fogs are frequent in some valleys during the winter. The cold winters bring the snow which made possible the development of winter sports, yet the resorts on the shores of the more southerly lakes bask in a Mediterranean warmth. The Föhn wind frequently blows down some of the south-facing valleys of the Alps bringing unseasonal warmth and excessive dryness during the winter months.

Despite their very different historical backgrounds, all three countries are Federal Republics, with considerable devolution of powers (including tourism responsibilities) to the states in West Germany, provinces in Austria, and cantons in Switzerland. In fact, Switzerland is more properly known as 'the Swiss Federation'. The combined population of the countries is over seventy-five million, with West Germany accounting for almost sixty-two million, followed by Austria with seven and a half million, and Switzerland with 6.4 million inhabitants. Major population concentrations include the Ruhr area of West Germany, the area around Vienna in Austria, and in Switzerland, Zurich, though not the capital, is the largest city. German is the dominant language but in Switzerland French, as well as Italian, and Romansh are also spoken and about one in eight of the population are foreign residents.

The economies of the three countries are highly developed and industrialized with a high standard of living. Demand for tourism and recreation is high, but the strength of the currencies does limit the number of inbound tourists. In Austria and Switzerland the annual holiday entitlement is four weeks or more, and in West Germany entitlement is five or more weeks. In Austria there is a thirty-five to forty hour working week, in West Germany forty hours is the norm, but in Switzerland working hours are relatively high and attempts are being made to reduce them.

Austria

Tourism is one of Austria's most important industries with spending by foreign tourists alone representing 8 per cent of the Gross National Product. Austria has the benefit of both a summer and a winter season – the winter season has grown steadily since the late 1950s and represents around 40 per cent of all visitor nights spent in the country. In fact Austria is the world's most popular skiing destination for residents of other countries.

Between fourteen and fifteen million visitors arrive in Austria's registered tourist accommodation annually giving Austria a large surplus on its travel account. The vast majority are on a holiday visit and there is no doubt that proximity to West Germany is important to Austria as that market accounts for around two-thirds of all nights spent by foreign tourists in registered tourist accommodation. The next two countries, the Netherlands and the UK, are also important sources of tourists but together only account for about 15 per cent of nights. In addition to its proximity, West Germans are attracted to Austria because there is no language barrier, their currencies have similar buying power, and yet Austria is sufficiently different from

West Germany to give a feeling of being in a foreign country. However, this reliance on one market does leave Austria vulnerable in times of recession and concentration of visits determined by holiday periods in West Germany causes congestion at the borders. In popular holiday areas many resorts become totally geared to the West German market.

Demand for domestic holidays in Austria grew slowly through the 1970s when the main increases in holiday taking were in the foreign holiday market. However, there is evidence of a temporary switch to domestic holidays in the 1980s, in part due to the cost of a holiday abroad, but also due to the promotion of Austria at home. Domestic holidays account for about one half of all holidays taken by Austrians and there is a move towards taking more than one holiday, particularly in the form of short breaks, and this is spreading the holiday pattern away from July and August. Vienna and the cities are gaining popularity amongst the Austrians, but there is still a concentration of holidays in the Tyrol. Austria is a major generator of international tourists on a world scale, though the majority of trips are to neighbouring countries, emphasizing Austria's favourable location in Europe. Almost one half of all holidays abroad are to Italy or Yugoslavia.

The majority of tourists arrive by car on the 18,000 kilometre road network and congestion on the roads is experienced at the beginning and end of the main holiday periods. The tortuous nature of some of the roads emphasizes the difficulty of transportation in this elongated and mountainous country, yet the network reaches into the most remote parts, and includes Europe's highest road to the summit of the Gross Glockner. There are over 6000 kilometres of railway including twenty private railway companies. There are six airports in Austria, but some argue that a restrictive policy on inbound flights to Vienna has held back the development of the tourism industry and compounded Austria's dependence on the West German market.

The majority of beds available are in serviced accommodation (over one million beds) and the authorities are improving the quality of accommodation as a means of boosting both domestic and foreign tourism. Although business travel is relatively unimportant in Austria, the small conference market is being developed, particularly in hotels in Vienna, Linz, Salzburg, Innsbruck, Graz, and Villach, as well as in the larger 'schlosshotels' – castles which have been converted into hotels.

Promotion of Austria at home and abroad is the responsibility of the Austrian National Tourist Organisation. The Austrian government provide grants and loans for tourist development, mostly in the accommodation sector. Provincial and local governments also promote and invest in tourism. The tourism authorities in Austria are upgrading tourist infrastructure generally, particularly in the area of sports and active recreation facilities, and extending the network of ski lifts and funiculars, which are rivalled in scope only by Switzerland.

Austria's 84,000 square kilometres contain 35 per cent of the Alpine area (compared to Switzerland's 15 per cent) and the country is famed for its lake and mountain scenery, winter sports facilities, and picturesque towns and villages. Trending east-west across the country and separated by the deep valley of the river Inn the mountains are Austria's main attraction. Here, tourism is often the only possible land use, and even though it often benefits only a few settlements, tourism is seen as a remedy for the problems of declining agriculture. However, this is not without the problems of forest hillsides and meadows scarred from ski-lift development or villages marred by insensitive building.

Each of the Austrian provinces can offer distinctive attractions. The Tyrol is by far the most popular destination for foreign visitors. Along with its neighbour Vorarlberg it contains the most spectacular Alpine scenery and the greatest number of ski resorts. Most of these have been developed from villages situated in the tributary valleys of the Inn – the Otztal and the Zillertal for example – at altitudes of between 1000 and 1800 metres. Traditional building styles and folklore provide a pleasant ambience for holidays. Innsbruck is an important cultural centre with many Renaissance buildings, and has twice hosted the Winter Olympics. In addition to the villages nearby, other important ski resorts include Kitzbühel – the

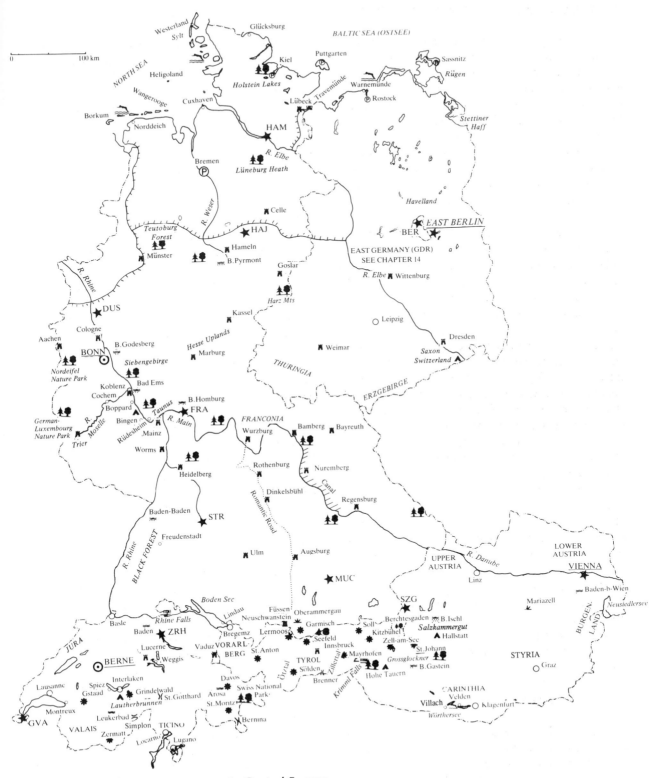

Figure 9.1 *Major tourist resources in Central Europe*

largest, Mayrhofen, Söll, and St Anton. Summer activities in the Tyrol include hiking and gliding.

The Austrians themselves prefer the less commercialized resorts of Styria, the forested 'green province', and Carinthia. The latter is chiefly known as a summer destination where the warm sunny climate and lakes are the main attractions. The province of Salzburg and the adjoining Salzkammergut is a region of lake and mountain scenery, spas, hunting reserves, and caves. Completely different in character is the Burgenland, the low-lying province to the east of Vienna. Here the scenery around the shallow Neusiedlersee is reminiscent of the steppes of Hungary. Monasteries, castles, and vineyards line the Danube in the provinces of Upper and Lower Austria.

The towns and cities of Austria are important tourist centres, particularly Vienna and Salzburg. Vienna, the former capital of the great Hapsburg Empire and a port on the Danube, attracts over five million tourist nights every year and has a handsome townscape with parks, palaces, museums, and a heritage of art and music. Salzburg's attractions include the castle, cathedral, Baroque architecture, and its international music festival.

Switzerland

The Swiss have one of the highest holiday propensities in the world with around 75 per cent taking a holiday of at least four nights. Holiday taking is at its highest amongst upper income groups, the middle aged, and those living in the larger towns or cities. Demand for domestic tourism has remained static at around five million trips (over one half of all trips taken by the Swiss). The high frequency of holiday taking means that most domestic holidays are second or third holidays.

Domestic holidays contrast with those taken abroad as they tend to be winter sports or mountain holidays, many taken in the months of January to March. Swiss holidays abroad are concentrated into the summer months of July to September and the most popular destinations are Italy and France (over 50 per cent of trips).

In the early 1980s foreign visitors to Switzerland exceeded nine million arrivals in registered tourist accommodation, keeping the travel account in surplus. The strength of the Swiss franc gives Switzerland a reputation as an expensive country to visit, and this is reflected in the increasingly short lengths of stay of foreign visitors. As in Austria, West Germans account for the majority of visitors (about one-third of the total). Around 40 per cent of bednights occur in the winter season (November to April), a figure boosted by the Swiss participating in winter sports.

The private car dominates travel in both the domestic and foreign travel markets. There are 66,000 kilometres of roads, including 1550 kilometres of motorway. As in Austria, the transport networks are tortuous and the topography often demands major engineering feats – the eighteen kilometre tunnel under the St Gotthard being an outstanding example, while the roads over the Alpine passes are spectacular. Even so, roads in the high Alps are often blocked by snow from November to June. While the road network brings many remoter parts of the country within reach of day visitors this has created congestion in holiday areas. Recent imposition of tolls may alleviate this congestion. Swiss Federal Railways and the private railway companies operate 5000 kilometres of track (1400 kilometres are narrow gauge) and there are many mountain railways, funiculars, and rack-and-pinion systems which are often tourist attractions in themselves. Although the cost is high, tunnels and snowploughs allow the railways to operate throughout the year. There are three international airports – at Zurich, Geneva, and Basle. The national carrier is Swissair. Other features of the Swiss transport system include the postal coaches – which penetrate the remotest villages, bicycle hire at many rail stations, and the lake ferries.

About one-third of the serviced accommodation capacity is only available in the winter season, particularly in the high ski resorts (such as St Moritz and Arosa). Most hotels are small with the few larger hotels found mainly in Zurich and Geneva. 'Supplementary accommodation' includes chalets, apartments, holiday camps, and camping and caravan sites. This lower cost supplementary accommodation has flourished as foreign visitors offset the high cost of a Swiss holiday but it is also popular with domestic holidaymakers.

The Swiss Tourism Service is responsible to the Federal Department of Public Economy and formulates and implements national tourism policy. It is assisted by the Swiss National Tourist Office (founded in 1917) which oversees promotion, and the Swiss Tourist Federation which is responsible for tourist development. Switzerland's maturity as a destination is reflected in the long tradition not only of hotel service but also of tourist associations and information services at local and regional levels. There are also many specialist organizations such as the Swiss Travel Saving Fund which was founded to give less privileged workers the chance to go on holiday.

The Swiss Plan for Tourism (1979) established a national policy framework for action by the cantons. The plan envisages Switzerland as a destination for individual and small-group tourism. It also sees the development of the supplementary accommodation sector and new infrastructure development in less developed tourist regions, such as the foothills and the Jura, in a bid to spread the benefits of tourism and take pressure away from the established areas.

Switzerland's tourist industry became established in the latter half of the nineteenth century when wealthy visitors sought the magnificent scenery and fresh alpine air of the mountains and the sporting challenges of skiing (introduced from Norway) and mountaineering (a British sport). The most popular area is the Alpine zone attracting over half of all visitor arrivals. Here lie the majestic snow-capped peaks, glaciated valleys, and winter sports developments which are Switzerland's trademark. However, tourist development has placed pressures on the society and environment of the area and the integration of tourism into the agricultural and forest economies has needed sensitive handling.

Within Switzerland's 41,000 square kilometres each of the Swiss cantons has its own range of attractions, but several major tourist areas stand out. The most spectacular Alpine scenery is found in the Bernese Oberland south of the lake resort of Interlaken. An excellent network of funicular railways and ropeways provide access to the snowfields and glaciers, the most famous ascending the slopes of the Jungfrau and Eiger. At Lauterbrunnen there is a classic example of a glaciated valley with spectacular waterfalls. Important winter sports developments are also found in the Pennine Alps of the Valais, which contains Zermatt with its views of the Matterhorn. Lake Lucerne is the centre of the country and perhaps the most beautiful body of inland water in Europe. In the south there are many resorts adjoining Lac Leman, (Lake Geneva) and Lugano which enjoy both a winter and summer season due to their sheltered location. The Grisons canton in the east contains a number of health resorts, the Swiss National Park, and the world famous ski resort of St Moritz.

Most of the Swiss people live outside the Alps in the plateau region to the north and west, where the major cities are located. Of these, Geneva is the headquarters of many international organizations and a conference centre, Berne is the Federal capital, Basle is the only port, while Zurich is the commercial and financial centre. All these cities provide a wealth of sightseeing as well as facilities for the business traveller.

The western boundary of Switzerland is formed by the forested Jura mountains. Less spectacular than the Alps this region receives fewer tourists. It is famous for Swiss crafts such as watchmaking.

West Germany (The Federal Republic of Germany, or BRD)

The West Germans have been the world's greatest spenders on travel and tourism for many years and they attach great importance to their annual holiday, even in times of recession. For holidays of five days or more, holiday propensities reach around 55 per cent, though this does vary according to age, socio-economic status, and place of residence. Domestic holidays have remained stable at around 40 per cent of the total number of trips (over thirty million in the early 1980s), with most of the growth occurring to satisfy the Germans' desire for holidays abroad. Even so, the domestic market accounts for the vast majority of bednights spent in the country and so dominates the industry. Domestic holidays are particularly concentrated into the summer months and in the south of Germany (around one half of trips), and on the coast (around one-third of trips). Business travel is important in the domestic market accounting for around a quarter of nights spent in West Germany. Germans are very health conscious and spa resorts based on abundant mineral springs have long been developed to meet this demand. Most of these are located in the uplands of the Mittelgebirge. Hiking is also popular and Germany was the first country to provide a nationwide network of youth hostels.

West Germany is the most important generator of international tourists in the world, and there is no reason to expect this situation to change over the 1980s. Around 60 per cent of all holidays are taken abroad, and the majority of trips are to other European countries, particularly Italy, Austria, and Spain. Around a quarter of all trips are package tours sold by West Germany's highly organized travel industry which has grown up to meet the demand for holidays abroad. Spain is by far the most important package holiday destination.

The high volume of travel abroad keeps West Germany's travel account in deficit, even though around nine million foreigners arrive in registered tourist accommodation annually. In the early 1980s the main origin countries were the Netherlands, the USA, and the UK. However, average lengths of stay are short – around two days – and this does mean that foreign visitors contribute less than 10 per cent of the bednights in the country. Business travel is important in the inbound market, exceeding the volume of holiday traffic from abroad.

Domestic business travellers, and most foreign visitors are accommodated in hotels in towns and cities. Demand for self-catering accommodation exceeds supply, as does demand for most types of accommodation in the peak season. The majority of accommodation is concentrated in Bavaria and Baden Württemberg.

The car is the most important form of tourist transport. The road network is excellent with over 7000 kilometres of autobahns and also specially designed scenic routes for visitors. A major problem is seasonal congestion both en route to and in the popular holiday areas. Rail travel is the second most popular form of travel with promotional fares and inclusive package holidays available. The larger cities have a fully integrated public transport system of trams, buses, underground, and 'S Bahn' (fast suburban trains). Air travel is served by eight international airports, all well connected by rail with the urban areas they serve. The national carrier, Lufthansa, is based at the main gateway of Frankfurt. Arrivals by sea can enter via Hamburg from Harwich and from Rodby Havn in Denmark to Puttgarten. Cruises on the Rhine, and the other major rivers, canals, and on Lake Constance are also popular. Transportation in West Germany was truncated by the new post-war boundaries, particularly communications with West Berlin where surface travellers need visas to cross into East Germany.

The German National Tourist Organization promotes West Germany abroad and is mainly financed by the Federal government. The German Tourist Federation is made up of state, city, and other organizations and is responsible for domestic promotion and tourist development. Although these central organizations are important, tourism powers have devolved to the cities and states, who have considerable independence to promote and develop tourism. A German Convention Bureau now promotes West German conference facilities. Tourism is low on the list of government economic priorities and little Federal aid is available for the industry. The aid that is available is mainly used to boost accommodation in less-developed areas, and to stimulate farm tourism. The states provide funds for both upgrading accommodation, and for season-extension developments (such as indoor swimming pools) in resorts.

Within West Germany's almost 250,000 square kilometres each of the states has its own distinct attractions, although it must be said that the lowland scenery of Schleswig Holstein and Lower Saxony suffers by comparison with the mountains of Bavaria. The Baltic coast includes the yachting centre of Kiel, the picturesque old seaport of Lübeck and the resort of Travemünde. On the North Sea coast the outlying island of Heligoland and the sandy beaches of the North Frisian Islands are popular with Germans, particularly Sylt, which was the first to encourage naturism as part of the holiday scene. Inland there are large areas of forest and heathland dotted with numerous small lakes.

To the south of the North German Plain rise the forested mountains of the Mittelgebirge, of which the best known are the Harz region with its waterfalls. This area contains many spas and picturesque medieval towns such as Goslar. The uplands of Hesse and the Weser Valley are particularly rich in legendary associations, made famous by the Grimm Brothers.

The Rhineland is a major attraction for foreign tourists, particularly the stretch of the Rhine between Bingen and Koblenz where it is confined in a narrow gorge. Here the river, followed closely by the autobahn and railway, meanders between terraced vineyards and steep crags topped by romantic castles. The Moselle offers similar attractive scenery and is likewise a major wine producing region. Cologne, Aachen, Bonn, and Trier are the main tourist centres of the Rhineland.

To the east of the Rhine lie the forested uplands of the Black Forest which contains Germany's most noted spa – Baden Baden – and ideal opportunities for skiing in winter and hiking in summer. Heidelberg in the Neckar Valley is a famous old university town.

Bavaria is the most popular state with domestic and foreign tourists, since it contains a great variety of attractive scenery. The northern part of the state is noted for its well-preserved ancient cities – of which Rothenburg is perhaps the best example – and the musical centre of Bayreuth. In the south the Bavarian Alps provide more spectacular scenery, including the Zugspitze, Germany's highest mountain. Garmisch-Partenkirchen is the leading ski-resort while the village of Oberammergau is famous for its religious play. Near Fussen are the romantic castles created by King Ludwig of Bavaria. All these attractions are within easy reach of the Bavarian capital, Munich, which has a wealth of Renaissance buildings as well as modern facilities developed for the 1972 Olympics. Its beer gardens and annual Oktoberfest are renowned throughout Europe.

Unlike most European countries, West Germany is not dominated by one major city, in fact Bonn the Federal capital is relatively small. As a result of Germany's former division into many states there are six major cities, each with a full range of theatres and other cultural facilities as well as being major centres of commerce and industry. They account for the majority of business travellers and over a quarter of the nights spent by foreign visitors. In the north Hamburg is Germany's major port, famous for its uninhibited nightlife centred on the St Pauli district and for its conference facilities. Hanover has an important trade fair, Dusseldorf is the major city of the Ruhr industrial region, while Frankfurt is the banking centre located at the cross-roads of Germany. West Berlin is exceptionally interesting, since this divided city was the former capital of Germany and it provides the opportunity for foreign visitors to glimpse the very different lifestyle of East Berlin by taking an excursion across the Berlin Wall. West Berlin is renowned for its museums and art galleries and the impressive International Conference and Exhibition Centre; less well known is the fact that it contains more parkland and lakes within its boundaries than any other European city.

Summary

Apart from the short German coast, Austria, Switzerland, and West Germany are landlocked countries. Physically, three regions can be identified: the coastal lowlands; the central uplands; and the Alps. The combined population of the three countries is over seventy-five million, and with highly developed economies and standards of living, demand for tourism and recreation is high. Of particular note is the importance of West Germany as the world's leading generator of international tourists. Austria and Switzerland are both major destinations for tourists from the rest of Europe.

Transportation in the three countries is well developed but has to overcome problems such as the disruption caused by the division of Germany and the harsh physical conditions and topography of the Alps. The Federal organization of the three countries has led to considerable devolution of tourism powers to the states in Germany, provinces in Austria, and cantons in Switzerland.

The main tourist regions are: the coasts of northern Germany with its islands and resorts; the central uplands of Germany, including the Rhineland and the Black Forest; and the Alpine area of all three countries with its opportunities for both winter and summer tourism. The towns and cities of all the countries are also important for sightseeing, and as business travel centres.

The Benelux countries

Introduction

Physically, the Benelux countries are made up of lowland plains adjoining the North Sea and flat-topped uplands. Much of the Netherlands and the north west of Belgium comprise flat plains and polderlands reclaimed from the sea. This reclamation, and the constant battle against the sea, is proudly told in exhibitions and museums, as well as in the many engineering works (such as the Delta Project) which are tourist attractions in themselves. Areas of heathland separate the coastal lowlands from the Ardennes, a broad upland area of southern Belgium and northern Luxembourg, rising to over six hundred metres. The region has a temperate climate. Near the coast the cloudy weather is unpromising for tourism with moderate rainfall throughout the year. Inland the maritime influence begins to fade and winters tend to be colder (with enough snow for skiing in the Ardennes) while summers are warmer.

Culturally the Benelux countries are interesting for their wealth of historic buildings and the heritage of the fourteenth to the sixteenth centuries when their textile industries were the most advanced in Europe. Belgium in particular, also contains many battlefields, a reminder of the numerous occasions when this region was the 'cockpit' as well as the crossroads of Western Europe. After the Second World War, Belgium, the Netherlands, and Luxembourg joined together in a customs union, with the result that restrictions on movement between the three countries are minimized. With a combined population approaching twenty-five million and total area of only 74,000 square kilometres the countries of Benelux are not only some of the smallest in Europe, but also some of the most densely populated. This leads to intense competition for land use and places pressures upon the environment to the extent that any proposed tourism developments are very closely scrutinized. The economies of the three countries grew steadily over the 1970s giving rise to increased demand for both domestic and foreign tourism, and the ownership of leisure equipment. However in the early 1980s there is evidence that the region's stagnating economies have led to a temporary emphasis on domestic holidays. Annual holiday entitlement averages four or more weeks and a typical working week is less than forty hours.

The Netherlands

Holland is the name commonly given to the country, although it really applies to only two of the constituent provinces, albeit the most important historically. The Netherlands was once a major colonial power and overseas trade remains vital to the economy.

Around 40 per cent of the Dutch population took part in domestic tourism in the early 1980s – a slight increase on the position in the 1970s when holidays abroad grew rapidly at the expense of holidays at home. Over 80 per cent of domestic holidays are concentrated in July and August, leading to congestion in popular holiday areas. A nationwide programme to stagger holidays was introduced in 1983 to help ease seasonal congestion, while a trend to more winter holidays may also help combat the problem. Most people taking domestic holidays use the private car and tend to stay in self-catering accommodation (such as summer houses, caravans, or holiday villages) rather than in hotels. Despite the prevalent use of the private car the Dutch rarely take touring holidays, preferring instead single-centre stays in their small and crowded country.

Business and conference tourism is an important sector of the domestic market. Good quality conference facilities are dispersed throughout the country in both purpose-built centres and in hotels, motels, and holiday villages. International conferences are seen as a growth area, especially given the Netherland's central position in Europe.

The Dutch have some of the highest holiday propensities in Europe, and, as they take more holidays abroad than in their own country, the Netherlands are a major generator of international tourists on a world scale. The small size of the country encourages cross-border trips (around two-thirds of all foreign trips are to neighbouring countries). The Netherlands also receive large numbers of visitors (around four million foreign tourists in the early 1980s). The majority of tourists are from Western Europe (75 per cent). Inbound tourism to the Netherlands has been declining and the Dutch tourism authorities are implementing promotional campaigns to attract business travellers, and also short-break holidaymakers. This short-break market is important in the Netherlands with most foreigners only staying for two to three nights on average. Foreign visitors are concentrated into a few centres; Amsterdam alone accounts for around 50 per cent of the nights spent in the country.

Tourists can enter the Netherlands through Schiphol, Amsterdam's international airport. The

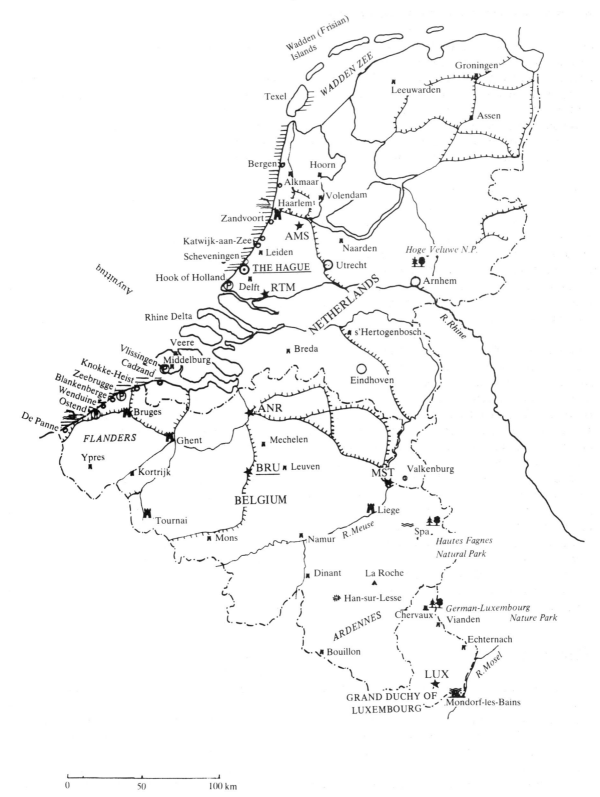

Figure 10.1 *Major tourist resources in the Benelux countries*

national airline is KLM which together with its subsidiary NLM carries domestic passengers and those travelling to neighbouring countries. Martinair and Transavia are the main tourist charter airlines. Other international gateways are Maastricht airport, and the ferry terminals at Vlissingen, Europoort, and the Hook of Holland, mainly handling passengers from the British Isles. Surface transport arrangements are excellent both throughout the Netherlands and also into neighbouring countries with 90,000 kilometres of road and a comprehensive inter-city rail network. This system is augmented by a fully integrated public transport network of buses, trams, and trains.

Accommodation in the Netherlands is dominated by self-catering with campsites, holiday villages, and a new network of trekker's huts for cyclists and walkers. This sector of the accommodation market is well developed in the Netherlands to meet the demand for inexpensive family holidays. Overall, serviced accommodation capacity is declining, particularly in the boarding house sector.

Tourism promotion, both domestic and international, is the responsibility of the Netherlands National Tourist Office, sponsored by the Ministry of Economic Affairs. The Office is backed by regional, provincial, and local promotion, as well as by the Netherlands Congress Bureau. The Government have increased the budget for tourism in an effort to improve the Dutch balance of payments situation – the Dutch spend far more abroad than foreigners spend in the Netherlands. The Government are also improving tourist infrastructure by investing in bungalow parks, hotels, marinas, and tourist attractions.

Amsterdam ranks among the world's top five tourist centres. It is the cosmopolitan, financial, and cultural capital of the country, famous for its canals, architecture, art galleries, and liberal atmosphere. Amsterdam is a focus of both business tourism (which accounts for around one-third of all trips to the capital) and holiday tourism and contains almost half the country's first-class hotel beds. Other important tourist cities are the Hague – the diplomatic capital – and Rotterdam, the country's major port at the mouth of the Rhine.

These three cities attract the majority of hotel visitors, but other regions are also important for tourism, particularly for caravanning and camping. The North Sea resorts from Scheveningen to the Wadden Islands (particularly Texel) attract domestic and foreign visitors alike. In a particularly ambitious scheme the resort of Scheveningen has been transformed from decline into a successful conference and day-trip centre with a casino and new pier. The Dutch coast is now well protected against inundation by the sea but the dunes are vulnerable to tourist pressure and are protected by conservation areas between the resorts. In the sandy heathlands to the east and the south camping and general outdoor recreation is important, especially in the Veluwe area and at Valkenburg. Other attractions include the distinctive Dutch landscape of polders and windmills, the spring bulbfields around Haarlem, and the traditional flower and cheese markets.

Belgium

Belgium is culturally divided between the Dutch-speaking Flemings of the north and the French-speaking Walloons of the south. Almost half of the Belgian population take an annual holiday away from home. As in the Netherlands, domestic holidays registered some growth in the early 1980s at the expense of those abroad, after a period of growth of foreign holidays in the late 1970s. For domestic holidays the most popular form of transport is the car (80 per cent of trips), and self-catering accommodation (holiday villages, caravans, and camping) is becoming increasingly used as serviced accommodation declines in popularity. Social tourism is important in the Belgian domestic market. The Ardennes and the coast are the most popular holiday regions.

Belgium is an important generator of international tourists. In the early 1980s the majority of main holidays were taken abroad (over 60 per cent). Threequarters of trips are to neighbouring countries but Italy and Spain are also important destinations. As in the Netherlands, the high number of trips abroad leaves a deficit on the

THE BENELUX COUNTRIES 83

tourism account, even though over thirteen million nights are spent annually in Belgium by foreign tourists (excluding those visiting friends and relatives). This figure represents an increase on the position in the late 1970s when demand was depressed by high prices due to the strength of the Belgian franc.

Over 80 per cent of foreign arrivals are from other European countries (around one-third from the Netherlands alone). However, visits from neighbouring countries tend to be short compared to visits from, say, the UK or the USA where stays are considerably longer. Business trips are concentrated into Brussels and Antwerp and international conferences are attracted to the seaside resorts of Ostend and Knokke, as well as to new facilities in Liege and Bruges. Apart from these business travel centres, visits elsewhere in the country tend to be for holiday purposes. In the serviced accommodation sector low occupancy rates mean that few new hotels are being built and, despite government assistance schemes, little investment is occurring in the existing hotel stock. Most hotel guests are business travellers while demand for self-catering accommodation comes from holidaymakers. Campsites, holiday villages, chalets, and apartments are available.

Both international access and internal transportation are highly developed. There are international airports at Ostend, Antwerp, and Brussels and passenger capacity has been increased on the ferries from the UK to Ostend and Zeebrugge, and on the hovercraft services to Antwerp and Brussels. The road network contains one of the best motorway systems in Europe (1250 kilometres) while the railway network is focused on Brussels.

The small size of the tourism industry in Belgium has meant that government tourism policy lacked clear objectives. However, in 1983 the organization of tourism underwent a major change with the establishment of promotional commissions for both the French and Flemish communities, whilst the Belgian National Tourist Office continues to oversee the promotion of Belgium abroad.

Belgium has three main areas of tourist attraction. Brussels is both a business and diplomatic centre (as the seat of the EEC) and a handsome city for sightseeing with medieval guildhouses, museums, and art galleries. The art cities of Flanders attract international sightseers. Pre-eminent is Bruges – a well-preserved medieval city with canals, picturesque bridges and quays, and museums, and churches. Antwerp is a business travel centre and also a historic city with its Flemish Baroque architecture. Other important towns include Liege and Ghent.

The North Sea coast is the second area of tourist interest. It has over sixty kilometres of sandy beaches, dunes, and resorts which reach saturation point in the peak season. Ostend, Blankenberg, and De Panne offer a sophisticated holiday product with nightlife, casinos and, in Ostend, a marked English atmosphere. Knokke-Heist, by the Dutch border, is more exclusive with its elegant avenues and villas, while family resorts include Zeebrugge and Wenduine. The coastal area is particularly popular with West Germans, while many Dutch prefer the third area, the Ardennes.

The Ardennes are a rolling forested upland area in the south of Belgium. Here, self-catering holidays are popular, as are activity holidays such as skiing, mountaineering, and watersports. Attractions include the caves and grottos of Han, Rochefort, and Dinant; the castles at Namur and Bouillon; and the spas and health resorts of Liege province. The Ardennes do suffer severe tourist pressure in the summer months and, to help manage the area, the National Park of the Upper Ardennes has been designated.

Luxembourg

The Grand Duchy of Luxembourg is closely linked to Belgium, sharing the same currency. Due to its small size (only 2586 square kilometres), inbound tourism is of far greater importance to Luxembourg than it is to Belgium. The annual number of foreign visitor arrivals is three times that of the population of Luxembourg and the impact of tourism on the society and environment of the Grand Duchy are correspondingly great. However, length of stay is short and many arrivals are business travellers to Luxembourg city. Others are transit passengers taking advantage of Luxembourg's low-cost international flights, while holidaymakers tend to be campers from the neighbouring conurbations of France, Belgium, the Netherlands, and West Germany.

Tourism also has a major impact on the economy and is Luxembourg's third foreign currency earner. The majority of visitors are from Europe with almost half from Belgium and the Netherlands. Seasonality is also marked with most visitors arriving between June and September.

The majority of Luxembourg's accommodation capacity is in campsites. Although more nights are spent in campsites than in hotels, it is the latter which are most important in terms of tourist spending. Transport facilities include Luxembourg airport itself, close to the city, and even in such a small country the railway network covers 270 kilometres, and there are over 5000 kilometres of road.

Tourism promotion is the responsibility of the Ministry of Tourism (backed by the National Tourism Office). The Ministry of the Economy oversees tourism's role in the Luxembourg economy. Plans for the 1980s include promoting rural tourism, improving accommodation facilities and general tourist infrastructure, developing the cultural heritage, and promoting congress tourism.

Luxembourg has two major areas of tourist attraction – Luxembourg city itself, and the variety and scenery of the countryside. The city is an important business and finance centre as well as being a seat of the European Parliament and other EEC institutions. It is historically important as one of the great fortresses of Europe. To the north of the city lie the Ardennes with Vianden, the country's most famous beauty spot, and the Germano-Luxembourg nature park which extends across the border into West Germany. As in Belgium, the Ardennes are popular with the Dutch. To the south of Luxembourg city lies an area of scarpland – the Bon Pays – with spas such as Mondorf-les-Bains.

Summary

Physically, the Benelux countries comprise three regions – the lowlands of the coast, the intermediate plateaux zone, and the uplands. The climate is unpromising for tourism. The Benelux countries were joined by a customs union in 1947 and they are closely integrated. Demand for tourism and recreation is high, but this does place pressures on the environments of these small, densely populated countries.

In the early 1980s the recession gave a temporary boost to the demand for domestic holidays at the expense of holidays abroad. Inbound tourism is on the increase after a period of decline in the 1970s. The majority of foreign tourists are from Western Europe. Transport facilities are comprehensive and the region's position in Europe attracts many transit passengers. Accommodation provision is dominated by self-catering capacity, particularly campsites and holiday villages.

There are three main areas of tourist attraction. Firstly, the historic towns and cities attract business and holiday tourists alike, secondly the resorts of the North Sea coast are major holiday and day-trip centres, and thirdly the uplands and countryside are important holiday centres for campers and day recreationists.

ELEVEN

France

LEARNING OBJECTIVES

After reading this chapter, you should be able to:

1 *Describe the major physical regions and climate of France and understand their importance for tourism.*
2 *Appreciate the changing social and economic conditions of post-war France and understand the implications for tourism.*
3 *Understand the major components of the French holiday market and the scale of inbound tourism to France.*
4 *Outline the organization of tourism in France.*
5 *Be aware of recent initiatives in French tourism planning; demonstrate the regional development role of tourism in France and be familiar with the major tourism development schemes.*
6 *Demonstrate a knowledge of the tourist regions, resorts, business centres, and tourist attractions of France.*

Introduction

The fact that France is the world's most popular international tourist destination is not surprising given the diversity of tourist resources available in its half million square kilometres. These range from the historical and cultural attractions of Paris or the Loire chateaux, to the Mediterranean resorts of Nice and St Tropez, or the winter sports centres in the Alps and Pyrenees, as well as the internationally famed cuisine and French way of life. France is also an important generator of both domestic and international tourism. The scale of tourism in France thus has far-reaching geographical implications and deserves consideration as a single chapter.

Spectacular scenery is provided by the relief of France which is dominated by four upland areas (the Ardennes, Vosges, Massif Central, and Armorican Massif), with intervening basins between these uplands, linked by a series of lowland corridors. Beyond, to the south east and south west lie the frontier mountain ranges – the Alps and Pyrenees. The country is drained by five major rivers: the Loire, The Garonne; the Rhone; the Seine; and the Rhine – themselves important tourist resources.

The latitudinal and altitudinal range of France gives rise to a variety of climatic features. Mediterranean conditions are found along the Languedoc-Roussillon and Riviera coasts, and in Corsica. Here summer sunshine hours are at their highest and continue through the autumn and winter to give a prolonged tourist season. A long dry summer confirms the region's climatic advantages for tourism. The Atlantic coasts have less sunshine and precipitation is likely in summer. In the mountains snow cover is uneven and variable, especially in low or middle altitude winter sports centres, hence the development of new centres above 2000 metres.

The demand for tourism in France

The changing economic and social geography of post-war France has implications for participation in tourism. Post-war growth has boosted the population by thirteen million (to around fifty-three million), restored the imbalance between males and females, and replenished both the low numbers of young people and the toll of two world wars. However, by the 1970s France was experiencing an increased number of old people and, paradoxically, a decrease in average family size. At the same time, France was transformed from an essentially rural society into an industrial economy with population leaving the countryside for urban manufacturing and service centres. Accompanying these changes has been a growth in the numbers

employed in the service sector, increased car ownership, and rapid rises of both disposable and discretionary incomes. This has led to an expansion of leisure spending as recreation and tourism have become significant in French life.

In this respect an important enabling factor has been the increased leisure time available to the French. Successive reductions of working hours have left a statutory working week of less than forty hours. Also, the minimum school-leaving age has been raised to sixteen years, and there is continuing pressure for early retirement. Since its introduction in 1936, annual holiday entitlement has grown to five weeks, and many workers have six or more weeks. The fact that at least two of these weeks have to be taken between May and October has led to congestion in this peak holiday period.

The Second World War delayed any expansion of holiday taking and, as recently as 1958, only 25 per cent of French people took a holiday. Both domestic and foreign tourism increased through the post-war years and is expected to continue to do so through the 1980s. Well over 50 per cent of the population took a holiday away from home in the early 1980s. In 1983 the stagnating French economy led to currency restrictions and 'condemned' many to holiday at home rather than abroad. At the same time, recession checked the growth of international tourists visiting France.

France has a very high proportion of domestic holiday taking (around 85 per cent of all holidays). French domestic holidays demonstrate a number of characteristics. Firstly, they are lengthy – often three or four weeks, though there are signs that the traditional month away in August 'en famille' is decreasing. Secondly, they are concentrated into the peak summer months (over 90 per cent of holidays are taken in July and August), although efforts are being made to spread the load with promotional campaigns, the timing of school holidays, and growth of winter holidays. In a country with such varied holiday opportunities, a wide distribution of holiday destinations is evident, though a general movement from north to south, as well as to the periphery, can be discerned with a concentration in the mountains and at the coasts.

The car is the most common means of domestic

holiday transport and self-catering accommodation, second homes, and visiting friends and relatives account for the majority of holidays – simply because their cost commends them to families in peak season. The majority of holidays are arranged independently, but works councils and other non-profit-making organizations play an important role. These range from professional organizations who own fully-equipped holiday accommodation and rent to members at competitive rates, to those involved in social tourism (over twenty million French people do not take a holiday in any one year). Examples of initiatives in social tourism include children's hostels (colonies des vacances), family holiday villages (villages vacances familiales (VVF)), and the Mitterand government's schemes to boost holiday opportunities for the old, the handicapped, and for women. The scale of social tourism in France contributes to the high volume of domestic tourism.

Around 15 per cent of French holidays are taken abroad, mainly in Spain or Italy. This represents a growth in foreign tourism since 1945 which is rooted in the changing social and economic circumstances of France. Spending abroad by French nationals is low compared to receipts from inbound tourists and France therefore runs in surplus on its travel account and has done so consistently throughout the 1970s.

In the early 1980s France received around thirty million international tourist arrivals and ranked as the world's most popular international tourist destination. Arrivals grew throughout the 1970s and are expected to continue to grow in the 1980s. The majority (around 85 per cent) of visitors are from Western Europe. West Germany, Belgium, the Netherlands, and the UK account for almost 70 per cent of visits to France, attracted by the ease of road and ferry access and the range of French tourist resources. North America accounts for 5 per cent of total visits, often as part of a European tour. Over half of international tourists arrive in June, July, or August to exacerbate the already acute concentration of French domestic holidays. However, winter holidays, and the West German trend to take second holidays in France in the off-peak may help to alleviate the problem.

France has always been popular for conventions and sales meetings. Business travel has increased over the 1970s, typically concentrated in major urban centres, and using serviced accommodation. Paris is especially important here, well served by national and international communications, it is the centre of French commercial life and has the added incentive of a possible weekend or short-break holiday at the beginning or end of the business trip. In 1980 a government office of conferences was established to co-ordinate the promotion and development of conference activities.

The organization of tourism in France

Tourism is a fragmented industry in France, comprising many small, often family-run enterprises. It is therefore difficult to gauge levels of employment in the industry. Official figures estimate over 400,000 jobs in hotels and catering, official tourist offices, and agencies, but this figure clearly falls short of the real total.

In the accommodation sector there is an increasing trend for holiday travellers to demand self-catering accommodation, while business travel is using serviced accommodation. Camping and caravanning are popular in both the domestic and inbound markets and the number of sites (especially three and four star) increased during the 1970s. In addition there are holiday villages, youth hostels, and gîtes – privately owned self-catering cottages, houses, or flats in or near small country villages. Self-catering accommodation is concentrated in Provence/Côte D'Azur, Languedoc, Aquitaine, Brittany, and the Pays de Loire (Loire Valley). The hotel beds in France account for less than 10 per cent of domestic holidays so hotels are increasingly reliant on business and foreign markets. Despite this, hotel building, especially in the two star and budget categories, has continued – both to attract the foreign market and also under social tourism schemes. Hotel capacity is concentrated in Paris, the Rhone Alps, and Provence/Cote d'Azur.

Transport by car dominates tourism in France,

accounting for two-thirds of inbound tourists and almost 80 per cent of domestic holidays. This reflects the demand for self-catering and informal holidays, as well as the well-developed road system with its 3000 kilometres of motorway, (some linking Paris and the Mediterranean coast), and international connections, and 80,000 kilometres of first class roads. There are few long-distance bus services in France as the 9000 kilometre rail system handles lengthy surface journeys. French railways (SNCF) has invested in main line services (most are electrified) and is now expanding its 270 kilometre per hour TGV service (initially from Paris to Lyon) to Brittany and the Atlantic seaboard. French railways are concentrated on Paris, but an overnight through-train runs between Calais and the Riviera all year round, and between Calais and Languedoc in the summer. International air connections are comprehensive and enhanced by the opening of a third airport for Paris. Air-Inter is the domestic national airline flying between Paris and thirty regional centres. There are over twenty ferry connections to Great Britain and further ferries from Marseilles, Nice, and Toulon to Corsica. Finally, the 7500 kilometres of inland waterways have become a tourist attraction in themselves, the most well-known being the Canal du Midi between Toulouse and Sete.

The French travel trade is made up of many small tour operators and travel agents. For example, the top ten tour operators generate one-third of total turnover of the sector, compared to say, Britain, where the equivalent figure is well over two-thirds. The lack of organization means that technological development is less advanced than in the UK and most of the business is done by post.

Tourism in France demonstrates strong central government control. A French national tourist office was established in 1910, an early recognition of the importance of tourism in France. Since 1910, the office has undergone changes of name and function of which the most recent occurred in 1981. Tourism is now the responsibility of the Ministry of Free Time and is under the Secretary of State for Tourism.

Regional and local tourist offices also exist and receive strong central support. Regional boards are cooperative local authority and private sector ventures, controlled by the government regional tourist delegate. At the local level, in most French towns 'Syndicat d'Initiatives' provide information for travellers (there are over 5000 offices nation-wide). Where resorts have development potential but lack private initiative in tourism, a government 'office du tourisme' can be established to run the resort. In effect, this represents a government 'take-over' of promotion and development in these 'scheduled' resorts.

In 1980, an action plan for tourism was launched with five themes; to understand and monitor tourism's contribution to the French economy; to promote France; to encourage investment in tourist facilities; to increase tourism's role in regional development; and update tourism management and training. This plan was endorsed in 1981 by the French President's definition of the principles of tourism policy in France: tourism must be for the benefit of all citizens; development must be accompanied by the improvement and creation of facilities; and tourism must be profit-making, earn foreign exchange, and create jobs.

Tourist resources and planning in France

The richness and diversity of the human and physical geography of France is reflected in the range of tourist resources available. Tourism in France gravitates to the periphery – to the coasts and rural areas. The Cote d'Azur – or Riviera – runs from Toulon to Italy. This naturally endowed south-facing coastline is sheltered by maquis and garigue-clothed mountains and is home to such famed resorts as Nice, Cannes, St Tropez, and Monte Carlo (in the Principality of Monaco). The coast is well served by rail, air, and road communications (including the three contour-hugging Corniches). The Riviera's very popularity has brought problems. It has a fast growing population, a growing second home and retirement industry, and now has an almost continuous linear development of apartments, villas, and studios along the coast, and encroaching inland to villages like St Paul de

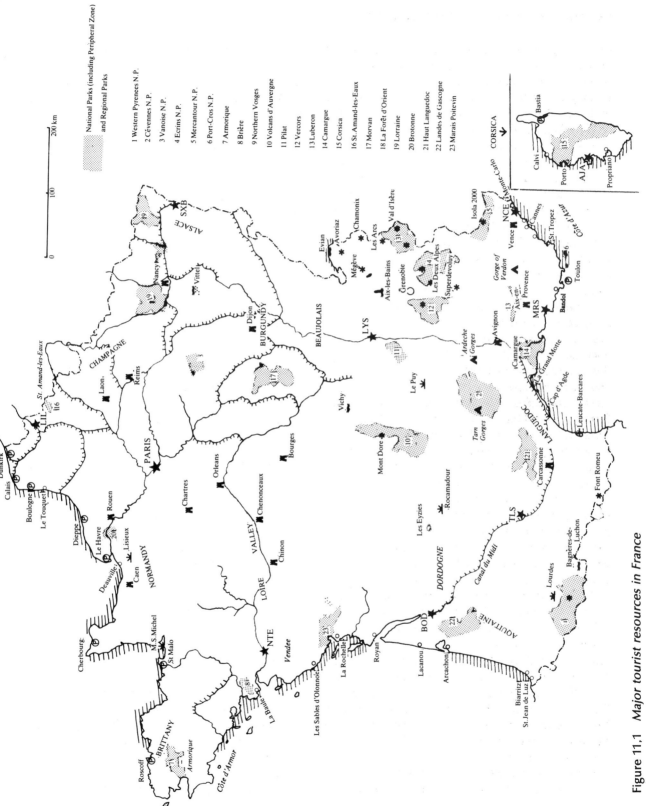

Figure 11.1 Major tourist resources in France

Vence. At the same time, pollution has closed beaches, and seasonal congestion and water shortages are a major problem. The Riviera is also facing problems adjusting to new forms of holidaymaking (caravanning and camping) and is vulnerable to competition from Spain and Italy.

In some respects the success of the Riviera has been at the expense of the Channel coast. This coast comprises a number of physically contrasting sections from the cliffs of the Cotentin Peninsula to the dunes of Flanders. Proximity to Paris and northern industrial conurbations has led to extensive second home development. The resorts (such as Deauville, Trouville, and Le Touquet) face competition from self-catering complexes along the coast and suffer from a relatively short season, a surplus of hotel accommodation, and changing holiday tastes. The most popular tourist centre for British day-visitors is Calais.

The interior of France shares in the prosperity of tourism to a greater extent than is the case in Spain. This is because the French countryside is a significant tourist resource, boasting accessible attractive scenery, and historic towns and villages. Touring holidays are especially suited to areas such as Burgundy and Beaujolais with their terraced slopes and noted cuisine; the northern provinces of Champagne – an area of plains and wooded valleys, and Alsace with the historic town of Strasbourg. The Loire valley is a well-known touring area, famed for its palaces and chateaux, though much tourism is concentrated on the coast at the south-facing Cote d'Armor and along the beaches of the Vendee coast.

In rural areas tourism's regional development role is important. In general terms, 'green tourism' is growing in popularity with holiday cottages, riding, walking, and children's holidays. Brittany has long been peripheral to the mainstream of French economic and social life. Yet, the rugged coastline, Breton culture, and distinctive rural landscape have considerable tourist potential. Currently, efforts are being made to disperse tourism from established centres (such as St Malo), to extend the season, and ensure tourism complements the rehabilitation of agriculture and industry. Tourism is also seen as aiding the regeneration of the Massif Central, a vast upland area in south central France. Here, declining economic fortunes in agriculture have allowed tourism to be integrated with rural development in the form of second homes and holiday villages. Other forms of tourism are also important. Over a third of French spas are found in the region, and winter sports have generated modest investment.

Winter sports, of course, form the basis of tourism in the Alps and Pyrenees, though spas are also important in the latter area, and second homes, lakeside holidays, and camping are popular in the Alps. While some Alpine winter sports complexes are based on existing villages (Chamonix), many are recent, high-altitude, purpose-built developments (as at Chamrousse) providing evidence of the thriving tourist economy of the Alps. Because tourist developments are localized and many less accessible areas are still economically stagnant, the French government is considering new management schemes to assist the dispersal of tourist development and benefits in the mountains.

Paris is an important tourist centre, offering a complete range of cultural attractions from the Louvre, to Montmartre, the Eiffel Tower, and the Arc de Triomphe. Equally, it offers the possibility of excursions to the nearby former royal palaces of Versailles and Fontainebleau, or to the historic towns of Orleans, Chartres, or Beauvais. Paris is particularly popular with business travellers and foreign tourists and this is reflected in the availability of modern conference facilities and top quality hotels. (Up to 50 per cent of the top 'luxe' class of French hotels are located in Paris.)

Tourism plays an important regional development role in France, enabling, in particular, the economic regeneration of stagnating rural areas in the West, South West, and Massif Central. Government grants, loans, and subsidies not only encourage such tourist development as the upgrading of accommodation and the redevelopment of thermal spas throughout France, but they have also concentrated upon major regional schemes as at Languedoc-Roussillon, Aquitaine, and Corsica; and have helped establish national and regional parks.

National Parks date from 1960, and include

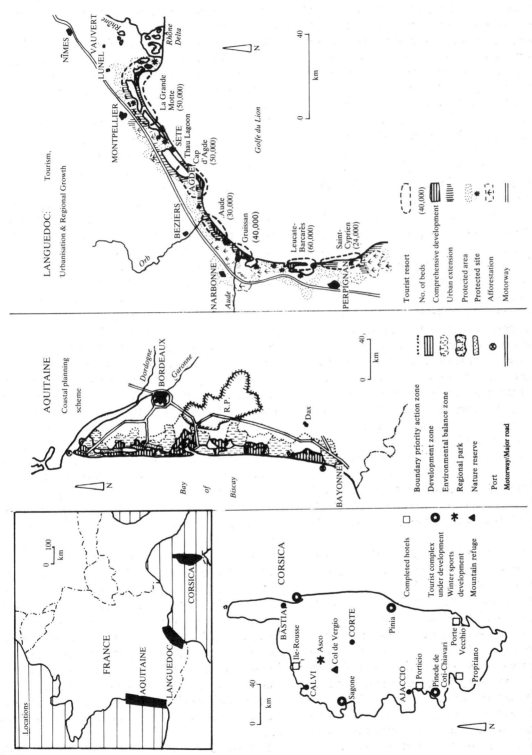

Figure 11.2 *Tourism development projects in France*
Sources: Clout, H. D., *The Geography of Post-war France*, Pergamon, 1972; House, J. W., *France: An Applied Geography*, Methuen, 1978; Thompson, I. B., *Modern France: A Social and Economic Geography*, Butterworths, 1970.

parks in the Cevennes; the Alps (adjacent to the Italian Gran Paradiso National Park); and the Pyrenees (linking with the Spanish National Park of Ordesa). The parks are managed to conserve the natural flora and fauna but, in order to encourage tourism and recreation, the parks are zoned. Tourism is encouraged in the outer zone with information points and accommodation. A second zone is subject to regulations on hunting and detrimental activities, and an inner zone is reserved for research and often includes a nature reserve. Regional nature parks are found close to major cities. Examples include Armorique Park in Brittany; the Camargue; and St Amand-les-Eaux in northern France.

The Corsican regional nature park has the triple aims of nature conservation, providing for tourism, and preserving rural life and traditions. The park aims to attract tourists away from the coast and into the rural interior of the island (Figure 11.2). This attempts to redress the imbalance caused by the previous, somewhat disorderly, coastal development of hotels and water-based recreation which has encouraged rural depopulation. Development plans for the island place tourism in a key role and already up to a quarter of the island's jobs are in tourism. New transport links to the mainland and the growth of inclusive tours will ensure tourism's increased role in Corsica.

Regional development schemes are also underway at Languedoc-Roussillon and Aquitaine (Figure 11.2). The Languedoc-Roussillon project began in 1963 with the establishment of an interministerial commission to coordinate the involvement of government, local authorities, and chambers of commerce. The project is designed as both a safety valve for the congested Cote d'Azur, and also an intervening opportunity to divert holidaymakers who might otherwise go to Spain. Tourism plays a major role in the rehabilitation of the area with eight new resorts planned along a thirty kilometre coastal strip. The eight resorts are grouped into five tourist units: La Grande Motte, with its ziggurat-like apartment blocks; Thau Lagoon; Leucate Barcares; Canet Argeles; and Gruissan. Languedoc-Roussillon is one of the most ambitious tourist projects in the world with government investment totalling almost one billion francs to 1980. By 1980, Languedoc-Roussillon attracted 3.7 million visitors, however, despite substantial employment creation many jobs are seasonal or in construction and there is a danger that Languedoc-Roussillon could become over-dependent upon tourism.

The second development involves 280 kilometres of the Aquitaine coast begun in 1967. The administrative organization is similar to that at Languedoc-Roussillon. Based on the tourist resources of pine forest, sandy beaches, fresh-water lakes, and a planned recreational canal, the project plans a capacity of almost 760,000 in hotels, guesthouses, campsites, and pleasure-boat berths. This capacity is in both newly created resorts (as at Moliets) and restructured existing resorts (as at Arcachon).

Summary

The changing economic and social conditions of post-war France have encouraged participation in tourism. The majority of French tourism is domestic, characterized by long-stay holidays concentrated into the peak summer months. Domestic holidays are widely distributed throughout France, and tend to be organized independently, although social tourism is important. The majority of French holidays abroad are in Spain and Italy. France is the world's most popular tourist destination, dominated by Western European tourists.

The tourism industry in France is fragmented, comprising many small businesses. In the accommodation sector, there is an increasing trend for business travel to demand serviced accommodation, while holidaymakers seek self-catering accommodation. Internal and international transport links are comprehensive. Tourism is strongly centralized at government level with a national tourist office and both regional and local organizations.

Tourist resources in France are diverse, ranging from winter sports in the Alps, through the landscapes of Brittany and the Massif Central, to the contrasting coasts of the Riviera, and the

English Channel, and the cultural heritage of Paris or the Chateaux of the Loire. Tourism plays an important regional development role in France, and encompasses major schemes such as regional and national parks, and those at Languedoc, Aquitaine, and Corsica.

TWELVE

The Iberian peninsula

LEARNING OBJECTIVES

After reading this chapter, you should be able to:

1 *Describe the major physical features and climate of the Iberian peninsula and the Spanish and Portuguese holiday islands and understand their importance for tourism.*
2 *Trace the development of Spanish tourism and understand the reasons for Spain's success as a tourist destination.*
3 *Appreciate the nature of inbound tourist demand to Spain and Portugal.*
4 *Outline the major features of the tourist infrastructure in Spain, Portugal, and Gibraltar and contrast the different nature of development between Spain and Portugal.*
5 *Outline the main features of the administration of tourism in Spain and Portugal.*
6 *Demonstrate a knowledge of the tourist regions, resorts, business centres, and tourist attractions of Spain, Portugal, and Gibraltar.*

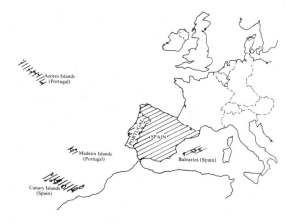

Introduction

The Iberian peninsula and the Spanish and Portu-
guese islands have been favourite holiday destinations for northern Europeans since the availability of inclusive tours in the 1960s. By the mid-1980s tourist arrivals to Spain and Portugal approached thirty million. Spain was one of the first countries in the world to enter the mass inclusive tour market, capitalizing on its advantageous combination of an extensive Mediterranean coastline and proximity to the European tourist–generating markets. To an extent Spain is now attempting to move away from its image of mass tourism, but this may be difficult given the established orientation of much of the Spanish tourist development and facilities and also Spain's image as a holiday destination in the popular culture of northern Europe. Portugal in contrast was a later entrant

into tourism and has not only made a determined effort to avoid some of the worst excesses of Spanish tourist development but has also attempted to both control tourism's impact on the country and attract the more affluent tourist from the outset. A major development of the 1980s has been the relaunching of Gibraltar as a holiday destination with the opening of the border with Spain.

Spain

Introduction

In area, Spain is only slightly smaller than France and most of the country is contained in the Iberian peninsula, stretching 800 kilometres from north to south. Outside the Peninsula are the Balearic and Canary Islands, as well as Ceuta and Melilla on the North African coast. Spain is dominated by a high central plateau – the Meseta – surrounded by mountain ranges and fringed with narrow coastal strips where most of the tourist development has taken place. Spain has a highly distinctive culture due to her relative isolation from the rest of Europe and old traditions still persist. In the north the Pyrenees are crossed by a handful of roads and railways from France and in the south Spain is separated by only a narrow stretch of water from North Africa and its Islamic culture.

Spain has achieved outstanding success in international tourism, and ranks with France and Italy as a leading tourist destination. It now has one of the largest tourist industries in the world and there is no doubt that tourism has contributed greatly to the transformation of the Spanish economy since the Second World War. This has not been without its costs however; uncontrolled resort developments mar parts of the coast and bring pollution, Spanish lifestyles have been affected, and tourism has exacerbated regional contrasts – particularly between the developed coastal areas and the interior. Yet the basic Spanish beach tourism product, allied to Spain's proximity to the generating countries of northern Europe, guarantees a ready market and tourism continues to represent a vital sector of the economy.

Spain's success in tourism is due to a variety of factors. Firstly, there was a growth in demand for holidays in the sun from countries in northern Europe once they had recovered from the effects of the Second World War. Secondly, Spain benefited from the development of civil aviation and changes in the structure of the travel industry, especially from the introduction of air inclusive tours. Thirdly, Spain's relatively late entry into the European tourism market allowed it to evaluate the competition and offer lower prices than those of existing destinations such as France or Italy. Finally, the Spanish government encouraged tourism strongly by providing incentives to developers, regulating the industry in order to protect the consumer, and in other ways.

The demand for tourism in Spain

Before the 1960s only the Spanish middle and upper classes took holidays. Residents of Madrid escaped the summer heat by visiting centres in the mountains, the beaches of the east coast, or the northern coastal resorts such as Santander or San Sebastian. During the 1960s and 1970s the Spanish economy was transformed from that of a developing country into an industrialized market economy, and in 1986 Spain joined the European Community. This economic progress has increased disposable incomes and boosted car ownership, thus allowing a greater participation in domestic tourism. By the early 1980s domestic holiday propensities approached 50 per cent of the population (of almost forty million). The pattern of domestic holiday-taking contrasts with that of foreign visitors; although the coasts are popular with both, many Spaniards visit the interior rural areas, often retracing their family roots and staying with relatives, in houses left to them by parents, or in second homes. The number of foreign holidays taken by Spaniards is limited (less than 10 per cent of main holidays) and those that do venture abroad commonly go to Portugal or France.

Spain received small numbers of foreign visitors before the Second World War and these were attracted by the country's unique cultural heritage and not by sun, sand, and sea, unlike many of today's tourists. The spectacular growth of arrivals began with large increases each year throughout the 1950s. Devaluations of the peseta encouraged further growth throughout the 1960s and the air-inclusive tour industry supplied low-priced holidays to its increasingly affluent northern European clients. By the early 1970s Spain was a leading holiday destination for most of the European generating countries. However, this has made Spanish tourism strongly dependent on the economies of northern Europe. The recessions of the mid-1970s and early 1980s checked the growth of visits to Spain and prompted the search for new markets such the USA, Japan, and Latin America – which has strong cultural affinities with Spain as two hundred million Latin Americans are Spanish speaking.

In the early 1980s Spain received over twenty-five million staying visitors and a further fifteen million or more excursionists annually, the latter particularly from neighbouring France and Portugal. Otherwise the most important generating countries are the UK and West Germany, reflecting Spain's popularity with air-inclusive tour clients.

The organization of tourism in Spain

The large number of excursionists means that around two-thirds of all visitors arrive by surface transport, especially by road through the eastern Pyrenees. The inclusive tour market ensures a constant supply of tourists by air, using Madrid and the main gateways for the holiday areas (Barcelona, Alicante, Malaga, Palma, Ibiza, Las Palmas, and Tenerife). Spain recognizes the importance of airport provision for tourism and a new airport is proposed for Algeciras to relieve Malaga and to encourage tourist development at the western end of the Costa del Sol. Surface transport is also being developed. The motorway network is fragmented, but the eastern coastal route – the Autopista de Levante – is being extended to Cartagena and there are plans to link Madrid with Seville, Valencia, and Zaragoza. The railways are tightly focused on Madrid and differ from most European tracks in being broad gauge so that delays are common at frontiers.

Spain offers a variety of accommodation, mainly concentrated in Madrid and Barcelona, at the coast, or on the islands. In fact, over two-thirds of total capacity is in the Balearics and the Canaries. Modern accommodation is also found in the winter sports resorts of the Pyrenees. Hotels and apartments are concentrated in the major resorts and cities. Camp sites are related to road accessibility from France and are focused on the Catalan coast and down the east coast as far as Alicante. As early as 1928 the Government began to set up a chain of state-run inns (albergues) and hotels (paradors) offering a high standard of accommodation away from the main tourist centres and in traditional Spanish style (often in old castles, monasteries, or palaces).

This early involvement of the Government reflects the importance of tourism to Spain. Indeed, Spain's tourism organization has attracted attention from countries around the world and many have adopted the Spanish model. Tourism became the responsibility of a cabinet minister in 1951 and the national tourism plans since 1953 have set the institutional and public sector framework for Spain's growth and continued presence in the world tourism market. By the early 1960s it became clear that with the steadily increasing air-inclusive tour business Spain needed a programme of expansion of accommodation and amenities. This was assisted by the formation of a Ministry of Tourism in 1962 and the gradual removal of administrative barriers to tourist development. At the national level the Ministry of Transport, Tourism, and Communications is now responsible for tourism policy and co-ordinates tourist developments and transport infrastructure. Generally, the government is anxious to provide an environment within which tourism can flourish and a variety of grants and incentives are available for developers in addition to government's direct investment. Yet, despite the depth of government involvement, provision has often lagged behind demand and the private sector has been left to fill the gap. There are also two specialist national agencies; one to promote conferences, and one to manage state-owned accommodation, restaurants, hunting grounds, and tourist routes.

Until 1978 tourism was firmly administered by central government from Madrid. The Spanish constitution of 1978 introduced democracy to Spain after a long period of authoritarian rule under Franco and gave the regions the right to govern themselves. Tourism is administered by the seventeen regional governments who have the power to approve developments and determine policy. At the local level, councils have powers to grant planning permission for tourist development and to impose local taxes. This may mean that tourism receives more favourable treatment in some areas than others. In the more developed tourist localities there are also associations of business people – centros de iniciativas – who promote their destinations and local facilities.

Tourism in most of Spain is highly concentrated both seasonally and geographically. Well over half of foreign visitors arrive between June and September coinciding with domestic holiday demand and creating congestion in the resorts. The Canaries do not have this problem because of their subtropical climate but others, particularly inland spas and ski resorts, have a season of only a few months. Seasonality creates a problem for businesses as many find it uneconomic to remain open out of season or, if they do stay open, they reduce their staffing and add to seasonal unemployment. The public sector too, is affected as services – such as water and sewerage – must have the extra capacity to cope with peak demand, but are under-utilized at other times of the year.

Geographically, most tourist development is concentrated into a few coastal areas, and on the islands. In fact, the Balearics alone have almost as many bed spaces as Greece and twice as many as neighbouring Portugal. Apart from some development in the Pyrenees, and in Madrid, the great majority of tourist development is at the coast. This means that the benefits of tourism are not spread evenly and it has led to a migration of labour from the less developed areas to the resorts.

Spain's economy is very dependent on tourism for foreign exchange, regional development, and employment. Tourist consumption represented around 10 per cent of the gross domestic product in the early 1980s, and tourism employs 9 per cent of the work force. But this dependence on tourism leaves Spain vulnerable to changes of holiday tastes or recession in the generating countries. Also, the very nature of tourism to Spain has reduced the economic benefit. Spanish tourism is dominated by the demands of the large European tour operators who provide high volumes of visitors but demand low-priced accommodation. This encourages low cost high-rise hotel and apartment development at the coast and reduces the economic benefit of each tourist to Spain.

Although the mass inclusive tour market for sun, sea, and sand represents the majority of demand for Spain, there are attempts to develop new holiday styles in order to reduce seasonality, spread the geographical load of tourism, and encourage higher-spending visitors. Conference and activity holidays are promoted, winter sports facilities are being built in the Pyrenees and the Sierra Nevada, and undeveloped coastal areas such as the Costa de la Luz along the Atlantic and the Costa de Almeria in the south east are being opened up for international tourism.

Tourist resources in Spain

The coasts

The coastlines of northern Spain are more popular with domestic holidaymakers than with foreign tourists, largely because of their climate which brings cool summers and heavy rainfall. This is particularly true of Galicia, the rugged green misty region in the far north west, where the people speak a language closely related to Portugese and have a Celtic cultural heritage. Galicia has an important fishing industry based on the numerous 'rias' or drowned estuaries which provide excellent harbours and there are a number of fine beaches facing the Atlantic. The most important tourist centre is Santiago de Compostella, an inland town visited by pilgrims from all over Europe because of its religious significance. Further to the east lie Asturias and Cantabria with their apple orchards, the beaches of Gijon and Santander, the prehistoric cave paintings at Altamira, and the spectacular scenery of the Cantabrian mountains. Within easy reach of the French border is the resort of San

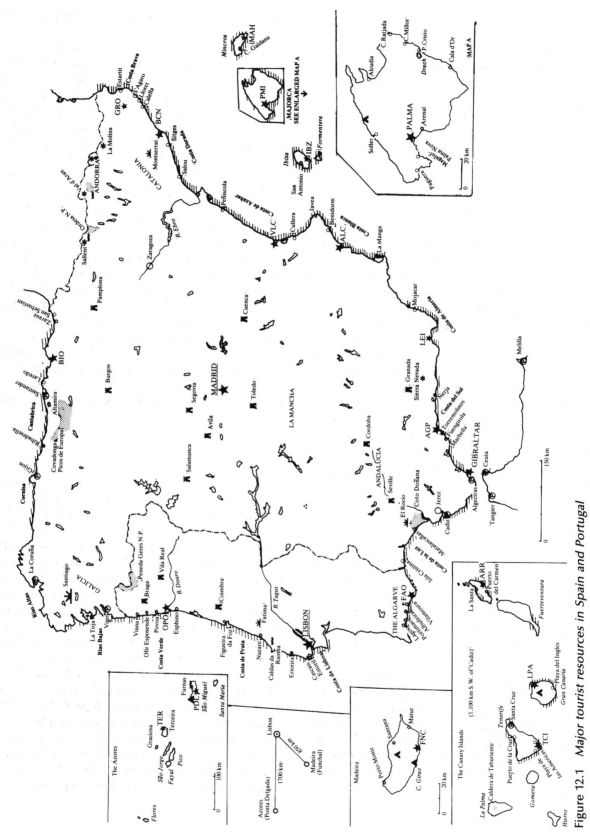

Figure 12.1 *Major tourist resources in Spain and Portugal*

Sebastian which was developed in the last century by fashionable society and was for many years the summer capital of Spain. It has suffered a decline recently because of political unrest among the Basques who form the majority of the population of this region. The northern coast can be reached directly from Britain by using the car ferries from Plymouth to Santander.

The majority of foreign tourists visit the various costas and islands of the Mediterranean where summer sunshine is almost guaranteed. The first area to be developed for mass tourism was the Costa Brava, the rugged coast between Blanes and Port Bou on the French border. Some resorts, such as Tossa and S'Agaro, were fashionable in the 1920s but the bulk of development took place in the 1950s and 1960s particularly at Lloret, San Feliu, and Estartit. So popular has this coast become that its natural assets of pine-covered hills, red cliffs, and sheltered coves have been spoiled by overcrowding and unsuitable development. The Costa Brava forms part of Catalonia where the people speak Catalan, a language which has more in common with French than Spanish. The regional capital is Barcelona, Spain's second city. It is one of the great seaports and industrial centres of the Mediterranean and has a wealth of entertainment.

There has been considerable development of the flatter sandy coast between Barcelona and the delta of the river Ebro, notably at Calella north of Barcelona and at Salou and Sitges to the west. This area known as the Costa Dorada has problems of industrial pollution. South of Valencia the next concentration of tourist development is the Costa Blanca. This is one of the driest regions of Spain enjoying over 3,000 hours of sunshine annually. The main resort is cosmopolitan Benidorm with the advantages of a sheltered south-facing position, two good sandy beaches, and proximity to Alicante airport. Elsewhere on the Costa Blanca holiday villas and apartments are being built along the coast, particularly around Javea and Denia, catering for both Spanish and northern European clients. In this region tourism is often in direct competition with the important citrus industry which has developed using sophisticated irrigation techniques.

In the extreme south, the Costa del Sol enjoys a climate which allows winter sunshine holidays. The coast is almost continuously developed from brash Torremolinos close to Malaga airport to Marbella, further from the airport and a more sophisticated resort. East of Malaga development is mainly in the form of villas as larger developments are constrained by high land values in the very narrow coastal strip and the transport bottleneck of Malaga itself. Much of the development on the Costa del Sol is in the form of holiday villages, often financed by West German, Scandinavian, or British investors. A large variety of sports facilities have been provided to attract higher income groups – these include tennis, yachting, riding, and golf. The Costa del Sol also has the advantage, not shared by the other costas, of being able to offer skiing facilities in the nearby Sierra Nevada where the snow cover lasts from December to June, and easy access to an extensive hinterland which includes Granada, Seville, Cordoba and some of the greatest cultural attractions in Spain. The Costa del Sol is also able to offer excursions to Morocco and Gibraltar.

The islands

In addition to mainland Spain are the Spanish islands which fall into two groups – the Balearics in the western Mediterranean, and the Canaries in the Atlantic. The Balearic islands of Majorca, Minorca, and Ibiza are of limestone formation so that water has to be obtained from wells, and windmills are a characteristic feature. On Majorca the caves of Drach attract large numbers of excursionists from nearby resorts. The islands are well cultivated, mainly with tree crops such as almonds, olives, and citrus. Climatically, Ibiza is the driest of the three main islands, while Minorca is the coolest.

Tourism has been extensively developed, especially on Majorca, which is much larger than the other islands, and the economy depends heavily on foreign tourism for income and employment. Palma, capital of the Balearics, is one of the main seaports of the Mediterranean and its airport handles the largest amount of holiday traffic in Spain. Most of the high-rise hotels and apartments are concentrated in the south-facing coastal strip extending from Paguera to Arenal, while the west is little developed. The east coast of Majorca is given mainly to villa developments. Ibiza is reaching saturation point as regards visitors due to problems of water supply and the scarcity of good accessible beaches. Here development is spilling over onto neighbouring Formentera. Minorca is less developed, catering more for higher income visitors, with well-planned holiday villages at Binibeca and Fornells.

The Canary Islands are situated almost 1000 kilometres from the Spanish mainland and are much closer geographically to the coast of Morocco. They are of volcanic origin and contain some magnificent scenery, including the peak of Teide on Tenerife, the lunar landscape of the Fire Mountains on Lanzarote, and the crater of Caldera de Taburiente on La Palma. The islands have a subtropical climate; winters are pleasantly warm, while summer temperatures are moderated by the cool Canaries current. The Canaries are now a year-round destination, whereas before the 1950s they were visited mainly in winter by wealthy British people. Large numbers of cruise ships still call at the ports of Santa Cruz and Las Palmas, but most holidaymakers now arrive by air and come from a much wider market. Since the islands are regarded as a free port, duty-free shopping is an important attraction for many visitors.

Tenerife is famous for its variety of scenery, including the banana plantations of Orotava, the craters of Las Cañadas, and the desert-like south. These are all accessible from Puerto de la Cruz, the most popular resort on the island, but which lacks natural beaches and suffers from a misty climate. However, there are good beaches on the sunny south coast as at Los Cristianos. Gran Canaria has more to offer mass tourism with fine sandy beaches in Las Palmas and along the south coast at San Agustin, and Maspalomas. Lanzarote is becoming an important winter-sun destination with some development at Puerto del Carmen and the sports complex at La Santa, although the beaches are mainly of black volcanic sand. Fuerteventura has a very dry climate but is fringed by magnificent white beaches and is in the early stages of

developing tourism. The three smaller islands – La Palma, Gomera, and Hierro offer attractive scenery but lack infrastructure.

The interior

Despite the dominance of the costas and the islands in Spain's tourist product, the interior has much to offer and is being promoted by the Spanish tourism authorities. The heartland of Spain is the high central plateau of the Meseta which has an average altitude of 600 to 1000 metres, making Spain the second highest country in Europe (after Switzerland). The Meseta has a rather extreme continental climate and a harsh landscape quite different from the tourist image of Spain. To some extent its aridity has been modified in recent decades by reservoirs created primarily for irrigation which provide an important recreational resource for the region's population. Culturally the Meseta is important as it contains Castile, whose language became modern Spanish. Castile has a number of tourist centres the most important being Madrid, the national capital, important for business tourism, and a touring centre for the ancient cities of Toledo, Avila, Segovia, and Salamanca, which contain a wealth of art treasures. The area south of Toledo, the arid plain of La Mancha, is associated with Don Quixote, Spain's most well-known literary figure.

In northern Spain the Pyrenees have winter sports developments especially in the Aran Valley as well as a number of historic towns. High in the Pyrenees is Andorra, a tiny nation almost completely dependent on revenue from its budget winter sports tourism and low-duty shopping (around twelve million crossed into Andorra each year in the early 1980s).

Southern Spain is quite different in character containing the only extensive area of fertile lowland and having a warm sunny climate. This region, known as Andalucia, was ruled for eight centuries by the Moors, and they have left their mark on the local architecture and folklore. Andalucia is the home of flamenco and a land of large estates given over to the cultivation of olives – one of Spain's staple cash crops or the raising of fighting bulls for the corrida, Spain's best known national sport. The most important tourist centres are Seville – famous for the spectacle of its Holy Week religious processions and the exuberance of its Easter Fair, and Granada and Cordoba which contain important relics of their Moslem past. Jerez is the centre of the sherry producing area.

Gibraltar

Gibraltar, the famous limestone rock commanding the entrance to the Mediterranean, towers over 400 metres above the harbour with the town on its western side. Despite its size – only 6.5 square kilometres and 24,000 people, Gibraltar's strategic importance has left a legacy of invasions and cultural influences in the city. The British claimed it as sovereign territory in 1713, and it has remained a Crown colony ever since. However, Spain disputed Britain's claim to the Rock and in 1969 the border with Spain was closed, along with the ferry link to Algeciras, and telecommunications links were severed. This closure of the border affected tourism as Gibraltar relied on its Spanish hinterland for excursions, and on the land border for arrivals (40 per cent of all visitors came overland) before closure. However, in 1985 the border was reopened and communications restored, and Gibraltar is once again easier to reach from mainland Spain. This will encourage day visitors from Spain, as well as providing a gateway to the Spanish hinterland, and the possibility of two centre holidays; Gibraltar and Spain or Morocco.

Accommodation in Gibraltar consists of a small number of hotels, guesthouses, and self-catering complexes but, given a major expansion of tourism, the accommodation stock may need to be upgraded and extended. Gibraltar offers a Mediterranean climate but with British currency and language. There are a few small beaches but Gibraltar also offers the historic attractions of the Castle, the military and naval heritage, as well as the natural history of the Rock. Excursions to Morocco are possible using the hydrofoil or ferry link to Tangier.

Portugal

Introduction

Portugal has a population of over ten million, little more than a quarter of that of Spain. It is also a much smaller country in area than Spain and in contrast, the development of tourism has not only been geared to the more affluent sections of the travel market but has also been more carefully controlled. Due to its long Atlantic coastline, Portugal's climate is milder and more humid, and the landscape greener, than that of Spain. The Portuguese built up a vast Empire in the sixteenth century with the result that Portuguese is spoken in Brazil, some African countries, and parts of Asia. These overseas contacts are reflected in the ornate architecture of many of Portugal's churches and country houses.

The demand for tourism in Portugal

Agriculture is still the dominant sector of the Portuguese economy and Portugal has the lowest standard of living of all the countries of the European Community, which it joined in 1986. This is reflected in the holiday propensities of the population which are lower than those of Spain since 40 per cent or less of the population took a holiday away from home in the mid 1980s and less than 10 per cent of these went abroad. Arrivals of foreign tourists to Portugal grew throughout the 1970s and passed four million in the mid-1980s. However, if excursionists are included in the figures – Spaniards crossing into Portugal for shopping or to visit friends or relatives, or cruise passengers (mainly to Funchal or Lisbon) – then around ten million visitors crossed into Portugal. This is reflected in the high percentage of visitors arriving by road (80 per cent). However, for tourists from northern Europe, air transport still dominates, and the major scheduled and charter airlines operate flights into Lisbon and Faro (the Algarve) on the mainland and to Madeira, the major holiday areas. Spaniards are by far Portugal's most important market, usually short-stay and travelling independently. This contrasts with Portugal's other main markets, that of Britain, West Germany, and France, with air-inclusive tours the norm, a marked summer peak, longer stay, and spending per tourist higher than for the Spanish visitors. As in Spain, villas used as second homes or retirement properties have created a long-stay market, particularly on the Algarve and Madeira.

Around two-thirds of visitors to Portugal use hotel accommodation, although an increased preference for cheaper forms of accommodation has become evident as more Spaniards visit Portugal and camp or stay with friends. Nonetheless, Portugal's accommodation is well developed, with a concentration of larger hotels in the Algarve, at Estoril, and on Madeira (both catering for inclusive tour clients), and in Lisbon, where business travel is important. The government own a chain of hotels – Pousadas – similar in concept to the Spanish Paradores. Camping and caravanning are important on the Algarve, especially around Faro, and attract West German, French, and Spanish visitors, whilst the many sites around Lisbon are a popular cheaper alternative to the capital's hotels. The British and Dutch patronize apartments, again mainly in the Algarve.

The organization of tourism in Portugal

The Portuguese economy is very reliant on the success of the tourism industry, both as a source of foreign exchange (accounting for almost 20 per cent of Portuguese exports of goods and services) and employment. But tourism also provides a safety net against changes in demand for Portugal's traditional products in agriculture, fisheries, and textiles.

The importance of tourism is reflected in the fact that Portugal has a General Directorate for Tourism, which reports to the Secretary of State for Tourism. The Directorate co-ordinates the various sectors of the industry and is attempting to create an environment in which tourism can flourish. Although the government does make loans and other incentives available for tourist development, the bulk of investment is from the private sector. Investment in hotel developments has been encouraged particularly on the Algarve, around Lisbon, and on Madeira and the Azores.

Portugal is anxious to control the impacts of tourism on both the environment and Portuguese society. There are a number of national nature reserves and management plans exist for the estuaries and coasts in the more popular recreational and tourist areas. Impact is also reduced by Portugal's emphasis on the upper and middle sectors of the tourism market, in contrast to Spain's predominance of the mass market, and this is reflected in the generally higher quality of the Portuguese tourism product compared to Spain. Portugal is also attempting to spread the load of tourism more evenly, both seasonally and geographically (well over a half of foreign arrivals are between June and September). The Algarve is already nearing saturation in terms of tourist development, and contrasts with many interior or remoter provinces which see few tourists. Counter-attractions are being developed in the Porto-Espinho area in the North, and at Setubal, south of Lisbon. Finally, Portugal is diversifying its tourist product by encouraging activity holidays – 'Sportugal' – and conference tourism.

Tourist resources in Portugal

The most popular holiday region is the Algarve, in the extreme south, which has an exceptionally sunny climate, fine sandy beaches, rocky coves, and picturesque fishing villages with a strong Moorish influence. The area was undeveloped for tourism until the mid-1960s when Faro airport was opened and the bridge across the Tagus from Lisbon greatly reduced travel times by road. Many of the resort developments, as at Lagos, Albufeira, and Portimao, are in the form of self-contained holiday villages, often with sports facilities.

The main tourist area in central Portugal is Lisbon, a great port city and the commercial and national capital and offering a wealth of cultural attractions. The strip of coast to the west, known as the Costa de Lisboa and contains a number of fashionable resorts such as Estoril (with its casino) and Cascais. To the south, the coastline around Setubal and the Serra da Arrabida is being developed for tourism. In the north Oporto is the second largest city in Portugal and is expanding its international airport as the gateway to the resorts and countryside of northern Portugal. Oporto has a picturesque riverside area, cathedral, and many historic buildings. To the south of Oporto lies the Costa de Prata with seaside resorts and fishing harbours such as Figueira da Foz and Nazare, and inland there are a number of spas and historic towns such as Coimbra.

Tourism north of Oporto is less developed, though there are major resorts (as at Espinho) and a number of very fine beaches are found in the Minho region, particularly at Viana, Povoa de Varzim, and Ofir, but these are mainly visited by the Portuguese themselves. Inland, the Douro Valley around Vila Real is famous for its vineyards producing port and a variety of table wines. There is a national park in the mountains of Peneda Geres.

In addition to mainland Portugal, there are two groups of Atlantic islands – Madeira and the Azores – both of volcanic origin and with autonomous tourist organizations. The climate of Madeira is subtropical, but without the aridity of the Canaries in summer. The main island is scenically very attractive and the capital, Funchal, has long been a port of call for cruise ships. The island's airport, opened in 1964, has allowed tourism to become one of the island's main industries. However, Madeira lacks sandy beaches, which are to be found on the smaller island of Porto Santo. The nine islands of the Azores 1500 kilometres west of Lisbon are little developed for tourism due to their remote location in mid-Atlantic. They receive less sunshine than Mediterranean resorts but their scenic attractions, including hot springs and the crater lakes of Sao Miguel, compensate.

Summary

The Iberian peninsula and the Spanish and Portuguese holiday islands are among the major tourist destination areas in the world. This is partly due to Spain's early entry into mass tourism in the 1960s based upon its holiday resources of an extensive Mediterranean coastline and proximity to northern Europe. Portugal was a later entrant into the tourism market and is attempting to avoid mass tourism, focusing instead upon more affluent markets.

Tourist accommodation is concentrated at the coast, on the islands, and in the major cities. The major resort areas are served by a well developed transport infrastructure. However, in Spain uncontrolled resort development has caused environmental damage, exacerbated regional contrasts, and affected Spanish lifestyles to such an extent that many countries in the world – including Portugal – are anxious to avoid these negative effects of tourism. The attractions of the countries are based on the Mediterranean coastline and there are major resort concentrations on the islands, on the Costa Brava, Costa Blanca, Costa del Sol, and the Algarve coast. Other attractions include winter sports in the Pyrenees and the Sierra Nevada, the cultural attractions of the Spanish and Portuguese cities, and the natural attractions of the peninsular and island landscapes.

THIRTEEN

Italy, Malta, Greece and Yugoslavia

LEARNING OBJECTIVES

After reading this chapter, you should be able to:

1 Describe the major physical features and climate of the region and understand their importance for tourism.
2 Appreciate the tradition of tourism in Italy and Greece and the more recent entry of Malta and Yugoslavia into the market.
3 Appreciate the nature of inbound and domestic tourist demands.
4 Outline the major features of tourist infrastructure in the region, notably the highly developed tourism industry of Italy.
5 Demonstrate a knowledge of the tourist regions, resorts, business centres, and tourist attractions of the region.

Introduction

Both Italy and Greece have a long tradition of tourism, attracting tourists seeking culture for centuries, while Yugoslavia and Malta did not seriously enter the tourism market until the 1960s. In the case of Yugoslavia, a Western style of tourist development was adopted to encourage tourists.

Cultural tourism is still important in Italy and Greece, and to a lesser extent in Malta, but all the countries in this chapter have developed a sizable tourism industry based to a great extent on Mediterranean beach holidays serving the European market.

Italy

The 300,000 square kilometre peninsula of Italy is separated from northern Europe by the high mountain barrier of the Alps and has a long coastline facing both the Adriatic and Western Mediterranean. The country is divided physically and culturally into a number of distinct regions. Firstly, in the north the south-facing slopes of the Alps are much warmer than would be expected. Here winter sports and the scenic attractions of lake and mountain scenery attract many tourists. Secondly, the vast fertile plain of Lombardy contains some of the largest industrial cities in Europe, as well as many of Italy's historic towns and cities. Thirdly, peninsular Italy is dominated by the rugged Appennines, which form a major obstacle to east-west communications and in the south, which includes the islands of Sicily and Sardinia, is found one of the poorest regions of Europe.

Italy has been central to international tourist

traffic since Victorian times and has a long established tourism industry. But domestic tourism in Italy goes back to Roman times when the wealthier citizens of Rome took their holidays at their seaside villas around the Bay of Naples. With the Renaissance, Italy again became the centre of European civilization. At this time the country was politically divided into a number of city states, and the most important of these – Venice, Florence, Genoa – had grown rich on the profits of banking and trade. The rulers of these cities used their wealth to build and decorate with art treasures churches, palaces, and public buildings and it is this cultural and architectural heritage which was the mainstay of Italian tourism. From Shakespeare's time wealthy young English men habitually visited Italy on the 'Grand Tour' to complete their education and even today much tourism to Italy is cultural. Italy was the most popular tourist destination in the Mediterranean until the 1960s when it was overtaken by Spain.

In the mid 1980s Italy received each year around fifty million foreign visitors at its frontiers, but less than half of them were staying visitors and more than half were on day visits. Holidays are the main reason for visiting Italy, particularly for beach holidays and sightseeing in the historic towns and cities. Almost one-third of tourists are West Germans, an increasingly important market to Italy on account of the improved road links (most arrive by car) and the strength of the mark against the lira. The most popular area for West German tourists are Veneto, the Trento Alto Adige region for skiing, and Campania (the region around Naples and Sorrento) for camping. Other important generating markets are neighbouring France, Switzerland, and Austria, the USA, and the UK. The French, Swiss, and Austrians typically arrive by car and visit the beaches and the historic cities. In contrast, about half of the UK visitors arrive by air, with the remainder driving or using the train. For UK visitors, Veneto, Tuscany, Campania, and Emilia Romagna are the most popular regions. Visitors from the USA are commonly touring Europe and consequently only spend a short time in Italy, which is only one of the countries visited.

The main attractions for Americans are the historic towns and cities.

Despite Italy's appeal to the international tourist, it is the domestic market (drawn from the population of over fifty-six million) which dominates the Italian tourism industry, accounting for between two-thirds and three-quarters of all Italian bednights. Italians have a legal minimum of four weeks annual holiday and the bulk of their holidays are taken within the country. The Italian tourist typically stays in hotels, pensions, or at campsites. The most popular holiday areas are Tuscany, Emilia Romagna, Lombardy, Veneto, and Latium, with the Ligurian coast attracting long-stay villa holidaymakers. A number of factors keep Italians at home for their holidays. These include the weakness of the lira, and foreign currency travel restrictions, but also the fact that the wealth of Italy's tourist resources mean that most holiday motivations can be satisfied at home. In consequence Italy has a surplus on its travel account.

Surface travel to Italy dominates because of the good European road and rail links. The Italians were the first to build motorways (autostradas) in Europe, completing the link between Milan and Como in 1925. There are almost 6000 kilometres of autostrada, and users pay a toll. The most important is the Autostrada de Sole which carries many domestic and foreign tourists from the north to the sunny coasts of Campania, Calabria, and Sicily. Italian State Railways also own the major tour operator (CIT) and, by catering for both holiday and business travellers to Italy, it has sponsored a revival in rail travel by tourists, Alitalia, the national airline, also actively promotes tourism to Italy and works closely with both CIT and the national tourism organization. Few tourists arrive by sea but there are numerous ferries to Yugoslavia, Greece, Tunisia, Malta, and France, as well as to the Italian islands of Sardinia and Sicily.

Luxury hotel accommodation is concentrated around Rome, Venice, and Florence, but throughout the country serviced accommodation is available in various grades of hotels, pensions, or inns (locande) which are popular with domestic tourists. In the domestic market there is a switch away from serviced accommodation to self-catering holidays and the use of second homes. Campsites are concentrated in Campania, and villas in Veneto, Liguria, and Abruzzi. In 1981 the government established a fund for the modernization of accommodation, to be administered by the regional authorities.

Italy's long tourism pedigree is reflected in the fact that the Italian State Tourist Office (ENIT) was set up in 1919. ENIT's main purpose is promotion and research and it is responsible to the Ministry of Tourism and Entertainment. ENIT is promoting new styles of holiday, attempting to diversify Italy's tourism product away from the historic cities and beach holidays. These new products include sport holidays and spa tourism. At the same time ENIT is hoping to achieve a more equitable spread of tourism in the country by including lesser known cities in the classical tours, promoting the ski resorts in Trento Alto Adige, and developing tourism in the less developed regions of the south. In consequence the share of total tourism in the traditionally popular regions of Piedmont, Tuscany, and Lombardy has fallen since the 1960s.

As in Spain, each of Italy's twenty regional governments has responsibility for tourism. ENIT is represented in each region and has powers to coordinate the regions' planning and overseas promotion. Tourism's role in regional development is clearly recognized by central government. In particular tourism is playing an important role in the regeneration of the poorer South – the Mezzogiorno – where investment in infrastructure and accommodation has attracted tourists. More generally, rural tourism is also encouraged in a bid to stem depopulation and sustain the rural landscape and services. With help from the EEC 'Agriturist' has been formed to develop farm tourism and promote rural tourism.

The Italian Alps are becoming increasingly popular for winter sports as they are very competitive in price compared to other European destinations. The best known area is the Dolomites, a group of spectacular limestone mountains with the important resort of Cortina d'Ampezzo. Many of the villages in this region, which is close to the Austrian border, have German-speaking popula-

Figure 13.1 *Major tourist resources in Italy and Malta*

tions. In the Western Alps around Aosta, French is spoken. Here the main resorts are Sestriere, Sauze d'Oulx Val'veny, and Breuil-Cervinia. The national park of Gran Paradiso adjoins the Varnoise in the French Alps.

The central section of the Italian Alps is crossed by long north-south valleys which end in a number of large lakes. This Italian lakes region is sheltered from northerly winds and has a milder, sunnier climate than the plains further south. Many resorts have developed on the shores of Lakes Maggiore, Como, and Garda, all quite close to the industrial cities of Lombardy and Veneto. A number of ski resorts have developed near the Swiss border, the most popular being Livigno and Bormio.

In contrast, the North Italian Plain stretching from Turin to the Adriatic is rather featureless. It has a continental rather than a Mediterranean climate with cold winters and hot, humid summers. The main tourist attractions are in the many historic towns, where, despite industrialization, the art treasures and buildings of the Middle Ages have been preserved – especially in Mantua and Verona. Venice, built on many islands and bisected by the Grand Canal is world famous as a tourist centre, but is suffering from subsidence and industrial pollution from the urban area of Mestre on the mainland. Not the least of its attractions is the lack of vehicles – all transport is on foot or by water. Other islands in the Venetian lagoon include Murano, noted for its glass, and Burano, for lace making. The long sandy beaches of the Adriatic coast are especially popular with both domestic and foreign inclusive-tour holidaymakers. Here the most important resorts are Grado and Lido de Jesolo to the north of Venice, and Rimini and Cattolica to the south.

South of the Appennines the landscape changes. The resorts of the Ligurian coast near Genoa have a rocky shoreline and picturesque mountain background, quite different from the flatter beaches of the Adriatic, and traditionally they cater less for mass tourism. The regions of Umbria and Tuscany are hilly and less fertile than those of the North Italian Plain, but the scenery is much more attractive. The most important tourist centres are Florence – which has one of the finest art collections in Europe – Pisa, Siena, Assisi, and Urbino. Further south is Rome, an international gateway and pilgrimage centre of worldwide significance, containing within it Vatican City, a tiny independent state ruled by the Pope.

In Southern Italy the summers are dry and hot, while torrential rain falls in the autumn and winter months, especially in mountain areas. The best known holiday region in the south is located in the Campania region around the Gulf of Naples, including Sorrento and the islands of Capri and Ischia. The region is subject to volcanic activity and in Roman times the towns of Pompeii and Herculaneum were destroyed by an eruption of Vesuvius. The island of Sicily has a great deal to offer, with good beaches and cultural attractions. The island was ruled by the ancient Greeks, Arabs, Normans, and Spaniards – all of whom left their mark. The most important resorts are Cefalu on the north coast and Taormina on the slopes of Mount Etna. Sardinia has fine white beaches and high interior mountains and is developing an exclusive tourism industry. The rugged north eastern corner, named the Costa Smeralda, is a resort area for higher income groups.

Malta

Malta's 350,000 population live on a group of small islands – Malta, Gozo, and Comino – strategically located in the central part of the Mediterranean. Malta was acquired by Britain to defend the vital trade routes through the Mediterranean and it became independent in 1964. The islands are of limestone formation, the landscape is characterized by a patchwork of small terraced fields, and the deeply indented coastline with unpolluted seas is suitable for water-sports, but there are few sandy beaches. The capital, Valletta, is situated on the finest natural harbour in southern Europe and now has a new conference centre. Malta is rich in historical associations including the prehistoric temples at Tarxien, the medieval walled town of Mdina, and the 'Three Cities' built on the south side of the Grand Harbour by the crusading Knights of St John as a defence against the Turks.

The climate is generally pleasant, except when the Scirocco blows from North Africa, bringing with it high temperatures and humidity.

Before independence Malta was not a major tourist destination but, with the departure of the military in Malta, tourism became an important part of the island's economy and now employs around 5000 people. Tourism to Malta boomed in the 1970s, reaching 700,000 arrivals by 1980, but in the early 1980s arrivals fell to about half a million, emphasizing Malta's dependence on the British market and hence her vulnerability to recession in the UK, or simply the changing tastes of holidaymakers and the fierce competition in the holiday market. This slump in visits has prompted a search for new markets, particularly the USA and other European countries.

Tourism in Malta is spearheaded by the Ministry of Tourism and its main agency, the Malta Government Tourist Board. The government is anxious to maintain Malta as a competitively-priced destination but also have to solve the problems which the 1970s tourism boom has left on the island. These include water shortages, poor standards of accommodation and transport infrastructure – the roads and inter-island ferry system can barely cope with peak demand, and the added pressure on land on an island with one of the highest population densities in the world. These problems have led to restrictions on accommodation development in St Paul's Bay, Sliema, and in the south east of the island. There is also the realization that, if Malta has reached its saturation point in terms of tourist development, then the only way the industry can expand is to use the spare capacity in the off-peak months.

Greece

Greece was the birthplace of Western civilization and for centuries travellers have been fascinated by the art, philosophy, and literature of Classical Greece and the Greek legends of 'gods and heroes'. However, unlike Italy, tourism did not take place on any scale in Greece until the 1950s. One reason for this was distance, before the introduction of

rapid air travel. More important perhaps was the low level of development and the poor communications of a country which had been under the rule of alien conquerers, especially the Turks, for centuries. To achieve independence from Turkey, Greece fought a series of wars from 1821 to 1913. Since then there has been much political instability and a lack of good relations with her neighbour on the other side of the Aegean.

Before the Second World War, foreign visitors to Greece only numbered a few thousand cultural tourists. However, along with other Mediterranean countries, Greece developed its tourism industry rapidly throughout the 1960s and by 1970 arrivals reached one and a half million. By the mid-1980s this figure was between five and six million foreign tourists annually. However, this growth has been uneven, and was particularly affected by political uncertainties in the late 1960s and early 1970s. Most visitors originate in Europe, with the UK, West Germany, France, and Italy the major generators. The USA is also a major source of visits to Greece.

Around two-thirds of visitors arrive by air, but a significant minority arrive by road, often driving through Yugoslavia, and Greece also receives about 10 per cent of its visitors from cruises. Most holiday tourists fly into Athens in the south (a second airport is planned for Athens), Thessaloniki in the north, or into the airports on the Greek islands of Corfu, Rhodes, Crete, Mykonos, Zakynthos, Kefalonia, and Kos. Rail communications (run by Hellenic Railways) within Greece are poor but are being improved. The Greeks do have excellent coastal shipping services linking the mainland ports and islands, and there are domestic flights operated by Olympic Airlines.

The National Tourist Organization of Greece is faced with a number of problems brought about by both the nature of tourism to Greece and the sensitivity of many of the country's tourist resources. Firstly, the emphasis on holiday tourism to Greece does mean that there is a severe seasonality problem with around half of all arrivals in the third quarter of the year. Secondly, tourist development is geographically concentrated, mainly in Athens, the coastal resorts, and on the islands. This makes

Figure 13.2 *Major tourist resources in Greece*

it difficult to spread the benefits of tourism, and to provide adequate accommodation and other facilities to cope with demand. It has also led to the view that Greece will become saturated with tourists and that damage will be done to the environment and cultural heritage in the more popular areas. Already the environment has suffered from haphazard, uncontrolled building, and pollution of the sea, and the flora and fauna are being affected by waste disposal.

In a bid to solve these problems the National Tourist Organization of Greece is overseeing a programme of accommodation building and upgrading, and hotels are being sited with care. Some areas of cultural interest are being preserved from development and others are being restored and conserved. There is an emphasis on decentralizing tourism to the regions of Greece, promoting the off-peak months, and developing alternative types of tourism such as working holidays or visits based on ecological attractions. These measures are being taken because tourism is important to the Greek economy as a source of foreign exchange, an employer of some 100,000 people, a contributor to

ITALY, MALTA, GREECE AND YUGOSLAVIA 111

economic development, and a regional development tool – especially on the islands where tourism has stemmed depopulation and stimulated handicrafts.

In Greece the sea and the mountains are never far away. The country is at the end of the Balkan peninsula and is deeply indented, mountainous, and has a large number of islands (comprising 20 per cent of the surface area of over 130,000 square kilometres) with the result that it has one of the longest coastlines in Europe – over 15,000 kilometres. About 80 per cent of the country is mountainous and the landscape in many areas has been devastated by soil erosion. The climate is typically Mediterranean, although the mountains of Northern Greece experience severe winters. Summers tend to be drier and hotter than in the Western Mediterranean and autumn is warm and sunny in the Aegean Islands.

Continental Greece is mountainous with numerous valleys and plains. Holiday resorts have developed along the shores of the Saronic Gulf near Athens, and along the Bay of Marathon. In the north the wooded Halkidiki peninsula contains some good beaches and has been developed for tourism, particularly at Kassandra. It is close to Thessaloniki, the second largest city in Greece. In addition to beach tourism Greece is rich in historical and archaeological sites. Apart from Athens, which is now a modern city, the most significant sites are the theatre at Epidaurus, and the temples at Delphi and Olympia. From the more recent past there are many Greek Orthodox monasteries such as the religious community of Mount Athos in the Halkidiki, and the monasteries of Meteora in Thessaly perched high on rock pinnacles.

Insular Greece is characterized by thousands of islands with persistently blue skies and attractive landscapes with whitewashed fishing villages. The islands are popular for cruises, sailing, and all activities associated with sea and shore. The wooded island of Corfu has been developed for mass tourism attracting over half of all British tourists to Greece. Crete offers more scope for adventure holidays, with a mountainous spine separating the north coast, which contains a number of major resorts such as Aghios Nikolaos

and historic cities, from the less developed south. This island, together with Santorini to the north contains many remains of the Minoan civilization, the oldest in Europe. Of the Aegean islands, Rhodes is the most popular, followed by Mykonos and Kos.

Yugoslavia

The socialist federal Republic of Yugoslavia has an area of a quarter of a million square kilometres and is composed of six republics and two autonomous provinces. The country has many cultural groups – such as the Slovenes, Serbs, Croats, and Montenegrins who form part of the population of twenty-three million. Yugoslavia's ethnic diversity means that there are three official languages and two main cultural centres – Zagreb and Belgrade – which cater for the two major groups, the Serbs and the Croats. Like Greece, most of Yugoslavia was under Turkish rule for several centuries and this has left its mark on the cultural heritage.

Yugoslavia has developed as an important seaside destination for northern European tourists, as well as a popular holiday area for Eastern Europe and the USSR. Growth of foreign arrivals was rapid throughout the 1960s when the government decided to adopt a Western style of tourist development rather than follow the model of other Eastern European countries. Entry restrictions and barriers to internal travel were eased and by 1973 6.2 million arrivals were recorded at registered tourist accommodation. By the mid-1980s Yugoslavia received over seven million tourists annually at registered accommodation. However, if tourists who stay with friends or relatives, or in unregistered accommodation are included, then the total number of foreign tourists rises to around ten million annually. West Germans and the British are the most important market, attracted by the resorts on the Adriatic, but neighbouring Italy and Austria are also a significant source of arrivals, as are the Netherlands and France. Since the early 1970s Eastern Europe and the USSR have become increasingly important generators of tourists to Yugoslavia, whose combined arrivals are second only to those from West Germany.

Surface transport dominates arrivals to Yugoslavia, particularly as the country also receives transit traffic en route to Greece or Turkey. These visitors mainly arrive overland by road or rail. Italians, West Germans, and Austrians commonly drive to the Adriatic resorts. This was made easier by the construction of the Adriatic Highway, a scenic coastal route running the length of the country and giving access to the Adriatic resorts. Other surface transport includes the old 'Orient Express' route also running the length of Yugoslavia but inland towards Istanbul, and regular ferries to the islands and Italy. Inclusive tour clients normally arrive by air to Pula, Split, Belgrade, or Dubrovnik. Yugoslavia's national carrier is JAT but there are also two charter airlines – Inex Adria Airways and Aviogenex.

Although Yugoslavia has developed as an international destination, domestic tourism is also important, accounting for almost twice the number of foreign arrivals at registered tourist accommodation. Domestic tourism grew after the Second World War, encouraged in the first instance by the socialist principle of organized holidays as a right and later, in the 1970s, by rising incomes and aspirations. However, Yugoslavs spend less on holidays and also have shorter lengths of stay than foreign tourists.

Yugoslavia began to develop a tourist infrastructure in the 1960s, catering mainly for transit traffic who stayed for one or two nights. Early developments were in the north, in Slovenia, but soon spread southwards and, by the late 1960s, a concerted programme of tourist development was underway along the Adriatic coast. In consequence, Yugoslavia's accommodation stock is concentrated along the coastal strip. The majority of serviced accommodation is in hotels, but self-catering provision includes camp sites which line the main routes through Yugoslavia, cluster around the provincial capitals, and have developed along the coast. The accommodation industry suffers acutely from Yugoslavia's seasonality as the great majority of foreign visitors arrive between June and September. In the peak season rooms are at a premium and any expansion in capacity is designed to meet summer demand, yet in the off-peak months occupancy rates plummet and many establishments are closed.

Much of the accommodation development has been assisted by cheap government loans to Yugoslav companies. Although the individual republics and provinces have responsibility for tourism, overall policy is the responsibility of the Federal Secretariat for the Market and General Economic Affairs which is assisted by the Tourist Association of Yugoslavia. The Association promotes the country abroad and co-ordinates the activities of the many local tourist associations and societies. This highly structured approach to tourism is reflective of Yugoslavia's socialist politics and the fact that the government recognizes the importance of tourism as an earner of foreign exchange. The five-year plan framework is attempting to maintain Yugoslavia's position in the international tourism market, better utilize existing tourist infrastructure, and spread the load of tourism both seasonally and geographically. In fact, it is recognized that many areas have potential for development, including some coastal sites and, to avoid the worst effects of tourism at these sites, an environmental protection programme is under way with measures including an environmental plan for the Adriatic coast and the designation of new national parks.

Most tourism is concentrated on the rocky Adriatic coast with its many islands and shingle beaches. The coast also has many old ports in historic settings. Most of the coast is within the republic of Croatia and it is here, between the major ports of Split and Dubrovnik, that most development has taken place. In fact, this coast already received tourists in the late nineteenth century when it was popular with French and Czech travellers and Grand Hotels were built in Dubrovnik and Opatija.

Adjacent to Northern Italy is the Istrian peninsula with its many coves and islands for bathing. The peninsula has a mild climate and many historic towns and fishing villages which are now resorts. These include Opatija – Yugoslavia's premier resort, Pula, Rovinj, and Porec. The Dalmatian Riviera lies between Split and Dubrovnik. The main resorts are Split itself and Zadar as well as developments on the large off-shore islands,

Figure 13.3   *Major tourist resources in Yugoslavia*

which are linked to the mainland by ferries and hydrofoils. Further south the Dubrovnik Riviera is focused on this historic and cultural town, though most of the hotel development has taken place on the Babin Kuk peninsula. Tourism south of Dubrovnik, in the republic of Montenegro, has been hampered by poor communications, and in 1979 an earthquake destroyed much of the accommodation stock. Despite these problems, Montenegro is scenically attractive with great tourist potential. It has sandy beaches and rugged interior mountains which have some winter sports development. There is a luxury island tourist complex at Sveti Stefan.

Inland, Yugoslavia offers splendid remote scen-

ery, historic towns and cities, spas, and hunting and fishing opportunities, but despite winter sports development and some business tourism few travellers spend much time away from the coastal strip. Winter sports complexes have been developed in the Julian Alps in the northern republic of Slovenia. Here the main resorts are Kranjska Gora, Bled, Pogla, and Vogel. Slovenia is also developing year-round tourism based on the lakes and mountains around lakes Bled and Bohinj. Further south in neighbouring Bosnia Hercegovina, Sarajevo now has a major skiing complex after hosting the 1984 Winter Olympics. Serbia is a completely landlocked republic but its cities – including Belgrade – attract business travellers and the development of motels and restaurants has persuaded transit travellers to stay longer in Serbia to enjoy the monasteries, rivers, mountains, and spas. Elsewhere, the provincial capitals, particularly Zagreb and Ljubljana attract business and conference tourism.

Summary

Both Italy and Greece have a long tradition of tourism while Yugoslavia and Malta are more recent entrants to the industry. All the countries in the region have benefited from proximity to the tourist-generating markets of northern Europe and have taken the opportunity to develop a sizable inbound holiday industry, based on attractive islands and coastlines and a Mediterranean climate.

Both Italy and Greece are also important cultural tourism destinations. Domestic tourism is particularly important in Italy.

With the exception of Malta, the region's tourist infrastructure is well developed though existing facilities in Greece are almost at saturation level. Italy's long tourism pedigree has produced a mature tourist infrastructure which contrasts with Yugoslavia's modern, planned developments. Tourism is also seen as an important regional development tool and is helping to boost the economies of southern Italy, provincial Greece, and parts of Yugoslavia. Tourist attractions are varied and range from the developed beach resorts and islands; to winter sports complexes in northern Italy, Yugoslavia and Greece; and the world famous cultural attractions of Greece and Italy.

FOURTEEN

Eastern Europe and the USSR

LEARNING OBJECTIVES

After reading this chapter, you should be able to:

1 *Describe the major physical features and climate of the region and understand their significance for tourism.*

2 *Appreciate the role of Communism in promoting economic and social change in Eastern Europe and the USSR, and promoting increased demand for recreation and tourism.*

3 *Recognize that domestic tourism dominates and tends to be organized by public institutions.*

4 *Show that outbound tourism is small in volume and dominated by other Communist destinations.*

5 *Appreciate the role of inbound tourism in boosting the economies of the region.*

6 *Demonstrate a knowledge of the major national organizations controlling tourism in the region.*

7 *Demonstrate a knowledge of the tourist regions, resorts, business centres, and tourist attractions of the countries of Eastern Europe and the USSR.*

Introduction

The countries of Eastern Europe have a combined area of one million square kilometres, and since the Second World War have adopted the Soviet political and economic model and consideration of tourism has to take this into account. Communism, which entails the state ownership of the means of production and distribution, colours both the demand for, and the supply of, tourism in the countries considered in this chapter. Governments for example, have virtual monopoly control of all aspects of tourism from strategic planning to owning and managing accommodation. Public institutions are closely involved in 'social tourism' by subsidising workers' holidays and providing tourist facilities. Generally, the role of the private sector is limited to very small enterprises, and commercial advertising is virtually absent.

Concern for leisure and tourism arose in the 1960s when the political and economic restructuring following the Second World War was well under way and considerations of housing, education, and health were less pressing. Inhabitants of Communist countries (or Socialist Peoples' Republics) have the constitutional right to leisure and tourism. Pressure for longer holidays and two-day weekends has coincided with growing urbanization and the production of leisure goods (including cars). These trends have fuelled demand for

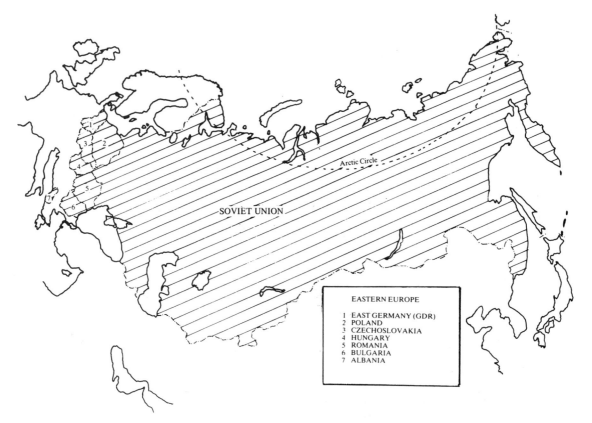

EASTERN EUROPE

1 EAST GERMANY (GDR)
2 POLAND
3 CZECHOSLOVAKIA
4 HUNGARY
5 ROMANIA
6 BULGARIA
7 ALBANIA

recreation and tourism facilities. Traditionally, domestic holidays have been spent at the seaside or spas, but new holiday formulas and diversified facilities at established resorts are now encouraged. Even so, many still do not take holidays, especially the elderly and those in rural areas.

Demand for international travel is slowly increasing, despite currency and other restrictions. Inevitably, the majority of outbound tourism is to other Communist countries, and its volume is regulated by bilateral agreements between countries. Inbound tourism from the West is now actively sought as it earns hard currency (particularly from shops which only accept foreign currency) and also encourages sympathetic consideration of Communist achievements.

Burgeoning domestic and international tourism has triggered considerable investment in tourist facilities. There is no doubt that low standards of service, outdated infrastructure, and red tape have inhibited the growth of international tourism while the simple lack of bedspaces has held back domestic tourism. However, current five-year plans, which cover every aspect of social and economic development, give tourism top priority.

Hungary

Hungary's two main geographical regions are firstly, the hills and mountains of the Central Range running across the northern half of the country, and the Great Plains. Hungary is drained by the Danube, itself a major tourist resource. The climate is predominantly continental, with hot, sunny summers, cold, cloudy winters, and a summer maximum of rain.

The present People's Republic was inaugurated in 1949. Over half of the eleven million population live in cities and around two million live in the capital, Budapest. Demand for recreation and domestic tourism has increased as living standards have risen and work-free Saturdays have been

Figure 14.1 *Major tourist resources in Eastern Europe*

introduced. Annual holiday entitlement averages twenty days. The majority of Hungarians take a domestic holiday, either staying with friends or relatives, or at weekend cottages in the countryside. Almost four million Hungarians take a holiday abroad, although this type of travel is subject to visa and currency restrictions. Most visit other Communist countries (over 90 per cent of trips) especially Yugoslavia, whose Istrian coastline is readily accessible.

Inbound international tourism contributes to Hungary's balance of payments, with almost nine million visitors in 1980 (although many more arrive on day excursions) and the average length of stay is short. Most international tourists arrive by car as Hungary is a land-locked country, with a good primary road network which includes 500 kilometres of motorway. The gateway for air travellers is Budapest's Terihegy airport. Large numbers of tourists and excursionists use the hydrofoil service from Vienna. The state-owned Ibusz company handles both inbound and outbound tourism. Accommodation ranges from campsites and self-catering villas to major international hotels such as those in Budapest. However, a shortage of accommodation has held back the development of tourism in Hungary and reflects the under-capitalization of the industry. The government is attempting to remedy this problem with an investment programme in the five-year plan framework using the National Tourism Fund.

Hungary's primary tourist attraction is Budapest. Formed from the twin cities of Buda – the old royal city on the hilly left bank, and Pest – the commercial centre on the right bank of the Danube, it boasts magnificent buildings as well as a nightlife which is exuberant by East European standards. The second area is Lake Balaton, seventy-seven kilometres in length and rarely over four metres deep. The lake is fringed by beaches, modern hotels, campsites, and nature reserves. In the summer, swimming and water-sports are popular, while in winter, visitors can skate or sledge. In common with the rest of Hungary, Balaton has an acute accommodation shortage in summer and an accelerated development plan is under way to alleviate the pressure.

A third group of attractions focus around Hungary's spas and health resorts. Over 545 hot springs exist, including some in Budapest itself and many more on the shores of Lake Balaton (the most important being Heviz). A current UN/Hungarian project is upgrading over thirty spas to increase the capacity of their facilities. Hungary's natural and cultural heritage form a fourth group of attractions, particularly its gypsy and peasant folklore. A large number of rural villages are to be developed as tourist centres. Many of these are situated in the pusztas, the treeless steppes to the east of the Danube.

Czechoslovakia

Physically Czechoslovakia is an elongated country and, like Hungary, it has no coastline. There are three main physical regions. The first two – Slovakia and Bohemia – are mainly upland or mountainous areas, important to tourism for their spectacular scenery. Bohemia is an ancient massif characterized by deep, forested valleys and gorges. It is fringed to the north east by the Giant Mountains, one of Czechoslovakia's three national parks. Slovakia lies in the Carpathians where the high Tatra Mountains are an area of over 300 peaks reaching altitudes of 2500 metres. This is a major winter sports area, where clear lakes and historic towns are complemented by modern resort developments. Moravia, the third region, is relatively low lying and its capital Brno is a major trade centre. The climate of Czechoslovakia is continental, with much of the rainfall occurring in summer.

Over a quarter of Czechoslovakia is covered by deciduous and coniferous forest and although the timber industry is important, the forests are extensively managed for recreation and tourism with nature reserves and way-marked trails. Czechoslovakia is an advanced industrial nation compared to most other Eastern European countries. This has given rise to a comparatively high standard of living with increased demand for domestic tourism and recreation amongst its fifteen and a half million inhabitants.

Czechoslovakia's long history of tourism has ensured that the industry is correspondingly well developed. Spearheaded by Cedok, the Republic's largest hotel and travel company, tourism ranges from city, lakes and mountains, touring, or spa holidays. International tourists can enter by two international airports at Prague and Bratislava, or by rail and road links. Internal flights serve the major resort areas. The political disturbances of 1968 reduced the number of international tourists and Czechoslovakia now recognizes that marketing and information services need to be improved in order to attract an international market.

The country has long been famous for its therapeutic springs and spas (such as Karlsbad and Marienbad), which are now diversifying into activity and sports holidays. Czechoslovakia's cultural heritage is also an important tourist attraction, with castles, chateaux, and many small towns and villages which are in protected conservation areas. Prague itself is a major tourist centre boasting an impressive Baroque heritage of music and architecture.

Rumania

Rumania's boundaries and Communist government date from the end of the Second World War. However, it has followed a more independent policy and its twenty-three million people, with a Latin language and temperament, differ from their Eastern European neighbours. It is dominated by the high mountains of the Carpathians, which are aligned horseshoe-fashion with a fringe of low, rolling plains. Rumania has an extreme continental climate with warm summers and cold winters although the coast enjoys milder conditions.

Rumania has urbanized and industrialized rapidly since 1947 and demand for domestic tourism almost trebled between 1965 and 1972. The Communist Party has a long-term commitment to improving holiday and leisure conditions and demand for travel abroad is growing among Rumanians. The Ministry of Tourism was formed in the early 1970s to increase the numbers of tourists from both socialist countries and the West (currently accounting for around 20 per cent of tourists), through the State company called Carpati.

The Ministry is overseeing a major investment programme in tourism initially aimed at the Black Sea resorts fringing a 250 kilometre arc of coast around Constanta where broad, gently shelving sandy beaches ideal for bathing are backed by extensive lagoons. New hotels, parks, and infrastructure are planned for Mamaia, and a string of new resorts are already flourishing (Neptune, Jupiter, Saturn, and Venus). The Black Sea resorts are the premier tourist attraction of Rumania, accounting for 75 per cent of bedspaces and attracting Western package holiday companies.

The mountain resorts have yet to benefit from this somewhat unevenly distributed investment, but they too have a long tradition of tourism. Today, the cooler resorts attract the affluent residents of Bucharest in the hot summers. The main Carpathian resort is Poiana Brasov, fully equipped for winter sports but also offering hiking and adventure holidays. In the Transylvanian Alps the tourism industry has exploited the lucrative legend of Count Dracula.

Other tourist resources of Rumania include the capital, Bucharest, a garden city of churches and ornate buildings; the teeming wildlife of the Danube Delta nature reserve; the historic towns of Moldavia and Transylvania with their monasteries and folk cultures; and over 160 spas and health hydros, some (such as Eforie on the Black Sea) specializing in rejuvenating mud treatments.

Bulgaria

Bulgaria has a central mountainous belt separating two plains. In the south west lie the high Pirin and Rila ranges, an important winter sports area. Climatically, the north has a continental climate of cold winters and hot, stormy summers. To the south Mediterranean influences bring milder winters and longer summers.

Bulgaria was one of Europe's poorest and most under-developed countries before the Second World War. Today, its developing industrial economy is increasing the demand for recreation and tourism. The introduction of the two-day weekend has meant that the nine million Bulgarians can travel further afield for their recreation. Weekend cottages are popular, as well as forest parks and amenity zones around major towns and resorts to cater for this increased demand.

International tourists are encouraged for their hard currency, and can enter via international rail links, by the airport at Sofia, or by road or sea. Balkan Tourist organizes international travel to Bulgaria by special offers, such as favourable exchange rates and off-peak bargains. A further incentive is the fact that government price controls ensure stable holiday prices and good value for money. A recent initiative is the formation of the Bulgarian Association for Recreation and Tourism to co-ordinate tourism and recreation across the country. Despite a late start in tourism, Bulgaria now offers over 200,000 bedspaces and has developed its own 'Inter' hotels chain.

The coastal and mountain resorts are the major tourist areas of Bulgaria. A string of seven resorts and many rest homes has developed along a twenty kilometre stretch of coast around Varna, the chief seaport. The resorts include Golden Sands, Drouzhba, Sunny Beach, and Albena. As in Rumania, the Black Sea resorts attract both domestic and international tourists and fears of damage to the forest have prompted careful zoning and management. In order to reduce peak-season congestion, a programme of off-peak tourism is planned and the southern part of the coast is being developed with new vacation settlements such as Dyuni. The mountain resorts, set in thick forests, provide respite from summer heat and also include major winter sports centres such as Vitosha near the capital, and Pamporovo and Borovets in the south.

Poland

Poland's physical structure neatly delimits its tourist regions; the coast is by far the most popular, followed by the mountains and then the lakes. Poland has an extensive coastline along the Baltic, with excellent sandy beaches and resorts such as Miedzydroje and Sopot which are popular with Swedes as well as Poles. The historic seaport of Gdansk is a major business centre. The southern third of Poland consists of the Sudet Mountains, the Carpathians (Beskids), and in the far south, the Tatra. The economy of the mountains is benefiting from tourism with Zakopane the major winter resort complex in the Tatra offering ski lifts and trails, museums, and organized walks. The Beskids are also an important winter sports area and a centre for spa tourism. The northern two-thirds of Poland is a plain of glacial drift, a landscape of low hills and lakes which are the major focus for such recreational activities as canoeing, camping, boating, and hostelling.

In 1952 the Polish Communist Party formed the Polish People's Republic. Poland's fifty-two million population has the right to rest and leisure in the constitution and industrialization has ensured that demand for leisure is high. The majority of Poles holiday within Poland and domestic tourism is supported by both the State and worker organizations. The General Committee for Tourism encourages international tourists via the Polish travel office, Orbis, but they tend to be short-stay tourists from neighbouring socialist countries.

The old towns of Poland have a rich architectural heritage which, though destroyed during the Second World War, has been meticulously restored, above all in Warsaw, the capital, which is a centre of music and culture. In the north the historic city of Cracow is a major cultural centre, while Czestochowa nearby is one of Europe's most important shrines.

The German Democratic Republic (GDR)

The GDR (East Germany) is a fragment of Germany cut off from the rest in the post-war political division of Europe in 1945 which culminated in the construction of the Berlin Wall in 1961. The seventeen million population of the GDR is an ageing, declining one, and this has depressed demand for domestic tourism and recreation, although both are actively encouraged and provided for. International tourists can enter via four international airports. However, this area was always the crossroads of Europe and surface transport includes the longest rail network in Eastern Europe, and a network of autobahns inherited from Hitler's Reich.

The majority of the GDR forms part of the North European Plain, a low lying area of lakes, marshes, and heaths. This unpromising landscape includes the lake district of the Havelland north of Berlin, with boating and camp sites. The remainder of the GDR is an area of uplands and valleys to the south. The Harz Mountains are the main tourist attraction rising spectacularly from the plains to 1000 metres. The other major mountainous region is Saxon Switzerland and the Erzgebirge Mountains, both the focus of excursions organized by Berolina, the tourist office of the GDR. The tideless low Baltic coast and its many haffs (lagoons), nehrungs (spits), and islands is being developed for tourism with small resorts backed by forests. In East Berlin attractions include the State Opera, theatres, and the restored old city. The literary and architectural heritage of the towns of the GDR also attract tourists, notably to Dresden, with its Baroque architecture, and Weimar, which has associations with Goethe, Germany's greatest poet. Leipzig has an important trade fair.

Albania

Albania is undoubtedly the poorest and least developed Eastern European country, especially for tourism. It is a small country, separated from the rest of Eastern Europe by Yugoslavia and its government has consistently pursued a hard-line isolationist policy. Access is limited to infrequent air services via Yugoslavia to the capital Tirana as the land frontiers are closed; the only tourists permitted entry are those in groups invited by the State agency Albtourist, and visitors are subjected to many restrictions. Nevertheless, Albania does possess considerable tourist potential. It has a fairly extensive Mediterranean coastline, with fine beaches near Sarande in the south, a warm sunny climate, and high mountain and lake scenery to the north and east where it borders Greece and Yugoslavia.

The USSR

It is difficult to conceive of the vastness of the USSR; it covers 22.4 million square kilometres; it is three times the size of the USA; has a latitudinal range from 78° North to 36° North; and spans eleven time zones. Physically, the USSR can be divided into its two stable continental platforms and its mountain ranges. The East European platform forms much of European Russia to the west of the Urals and contains Moscow and Leningrad. To the east of the Urals the vast Siberian platform stretches to the Pacific coast. Mountainous zones fringe the USSR to the south and west but from a tourism point of view, the most important are the Caucasus, the Crimea, and the Central Asian Ranges.

As would be expected, the climates of the USSR are also varied. The dominant influence is a continental one with extreme temperature ranges and low precipitation – which falls as snow in winter. In the west the Atlantic has a moderating maritime influence but distance weakens the effect. Climatic variety is provided by the warmer tourist areas of the Crimean coast, the Transcaucasian region, and the southernmost part of Central Asia. In these areas even the coldest months have average temperatures above freezing, and summers are warm, or in the case of Central Asia, hot. From this mosaic of physical environments, some are suited to tourism, others less so, but many provide barriers to tourist development. These 'anti-resources' include permafrost, aridity, frozen rivers and seas, mountains, and vast marshes.

Socially, the USSR is equally diverse. A population of almost 275 million contains a mix of races all with their own history, culture, and language. The Soviet Union was formed after the 1917 Revolution on the ruins of the old Russian Empire. Theoretically at any rate, it is a quasi-voluntary union of fifteen constituent republics, including Estonia,

Latvia and Lithuania, which were formally incorporated after the Second World War. The Russian Federated Socialist Republic is in effect dominant although Ukraine and Byelorussia have separate representation in the UN.

The new constitution of the USSR gives the population the right to one holiday a year, to rest and leisure, and espouses the principle of tourism as a medium for mutual understanding and co-operation between nations. Since the early 1960s the Soviet population has enjoyed a rise in prosperity, reduced working hours, and has been able to buy an increased range of leisure goods (skis, canoes etc.). Since the Second World War the population has been concentrated in urban settlement and car ownership is predicted to rise to fifteen or twenty million by 1985. These developments have created a burgeoning demand for tourism and outdoor recreation, especially in rural areas.

By 1981, thirty-three million Russians took a domestic holiday, and 177 million went on excursions. In the Moscow area alone, almost four million people relax outdoors on a summer weekend. This demand has placed great pressure on the recreational resources of the USSR. These include the Parks of Culture and Rest for mass recreation, and green 'wedges' of parkland stretching out from the cities into the forests beyond. Many cities are surrounded by forest-park zones, with accommodation facilities for active recreation. Forest parks surround Moscow on all sides. Second homes – or dachas – are also popular, usually cottages for weekend or holiday use, they cluster along railway lines running out of cities.

Despite restrictions, 2.7 million Soviets travelled abroad in 1977, mainly to other Communist countries (66 per cent of trips) such as Yugoslavia and Bulgaria. Until the early 1960s facilities for foreign tourists were limited, but from 1966 onwards the five-year plans invested in tourism infra-structure and staff training. This boosted the number of foreign visitors to five million by 1980 (including all purposes of travel). Attracting foreign tourists is now a priority, not only for international relations, but also for the hard currency generated.

Foreign travel by Soviets and inbound travel are handled by Intourist. Formed in 1929, Intourist has twenty-eight offices worldwide; acts as agents for Aeroflot; owns and manages accommodation, carhire, and coach companies; and organizes excursions and information services. Tourists can enter the USSR by surface or air transport. There are sixty-seven international airports, and Aeroflot carries over 1000 million passengers annually. Travellers to the USSR need a visa and are debarred from many parts of the country, nevertheless they are free to explore cities without a guide or drive the 11,000 kilometres of tourist routes. Because prices are set administratively, they are stable and often guaranteed for the terms of the five-year plans. However, there are problems such as poor standards of service, the language barrier, a lack of late-night entertainment, and restrictions on photography.

Overseas tourists are concentrated into five main areas. The most popular area for overseas visitors is the central part of European Russia which includes Kiev, Moscow, and Leningrad; each historically have served as national capitals. Moscow is the showplace of the Communist world, containing the Kremlin, the ancient inner city, as well as many impressive modern buildings. The tourist circuit from Moscow includes the Byzantine churches of Suzdal and Yaroslavl, and cruises on the river Volga to Ulyanovsk (Lenin's birthplace) and Volgograd. Moscow's nearest rival is Leningrad which as St Petersburg was the Western style capital and port built by Peter the Great with its classical palaces and boulevards. The fine beaches of the Baltic coasts of Estonia and Latvia can be visited from Leningrad.

The second most important area for both domestic and international tourism, is the Black Sea coast, especially the Crimea which enjoys Mediterranean sunshine and a mild winter climate. The main resorts are Yalta and Sochi (the largest resort in the USSR) and expansion of spas and resorts in the area include Dagomys, a major new holiday complex to boost the accommodation capacity of this region.

To the east of the Black Sea is the Transcaucasian area bounded by the snow-capped Caucasus

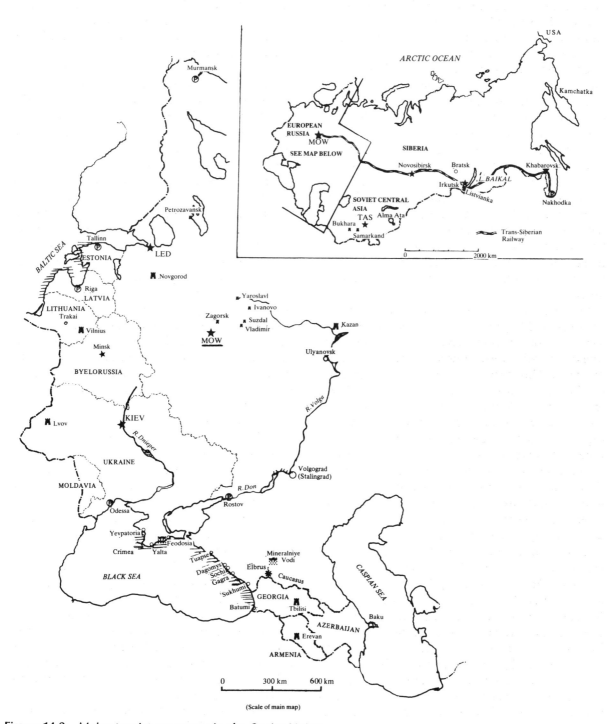

Figure 14.2 *Major tourist resources in the Soviet Union*

mountains which contain many spas and ski resorts. Georgia is noted for its wines, tea plantations, and a culture which has little in common with that of European Russia. Further east still, beyond the Caspian Sea, is Soviet Central Asia, which has an ancient Islamic culture. Cities such as Samarkand and Tashkent (an important stopover on trans-Asian flights) are now on the tourist circuit. Finally Siberia – or rather that part of it adjoining the Trans-Siberian railway – has been opened to Western and Japanese tour operators. The main centres are Novosibirsk and Irkutsk, adjoining Lake Baikal, the world's deepest freshwater body. Some interesting projects are taking place in Siberia which is Russia's 'land of tomorrow' but large areas with tourism potential, such as volcanic Kamčhatka, remain off-limits to Western visitors.

Summary

Communist social and economic planning has urbanized and industrialized Eastern Europe and the USSR and demand for tourism and recreation has risen. Indeed citizens of all these countries have the constitutional right to rest and leisure. Domestic tourism dominates, and social tourism is also important with subsidized holidays on offer to workers. Even so, there is still a large number who do not take holidays. Demand for international tourism is increasing, though at the moment actual numbers are small. Most international tourism is to other Communist countries. International tourists from the West are encouraged for their hard currency and the opportunity to win sympathetic consideration of Communist achievements.

The tourist resources of Eastern Europe and the USSR can be classified into four main types. Firstly, the major cities and culture of each country are a major attraction in themselves. Secondly the resorts of the Black Sea and the Baltic are a focus of both domestic and international tourism and are now receiving considerable investment. Thirdly, the mountains and resorts of the Carpathians, the Tatra, the Harz, the Caucasus, and the Crimea offer both winter sports and cool respite from the hot dusty summers of the plains below. Finally, the spas and health resorts are a major feature of both Eastern Europe and the USSR.

FIFTEEN

Africa

LEARNING OBJECTIVES

After reading this chapter, you should be able to:

1 *Describe the major physical regions and climate of Africa and understand their importance for tourism.*
2 *Understand the relevant social and economic background to the most important tourism countries in Africa.*
3 *Recognize that, aside from developments in North Africa, Africa's tourism potential is largely unfulfilled.*
4 *Describe the main dimensions of inbound tourism to the major African destination countries.*
5 *Describe the major international gateways and relevant features of internal transport for tourism in Africa's major tourist regions.*
6 *Outline the organization of tourism in the major tourism countries in Africa.*
7 *Demonstrate a knowledge of the tourist regions, resorts, business centres, and tourist attractions of Africa.*

Introduction

It will be explained in Chapter 16 that Egypt is included in the Levant region. Africa is a very extensive landmass. Most of the continent south of the Sahara consists of plateau and block mountains with only a narrow coastal plain separated from the interior by high escarpments. There is also a degree of cultural unity among the nations of 'Black

Africa' who have only recently emerged from a period of colonial rule by Europeans.

The sheer size of Africa is at once an asset and a hindrance to developing a tourism industry. On the one hand, most of Africa is sparsely populated offering wide open spaces, a wealth of wildlife, spectacular scenery, and tribal cultures that have always fascinated armchair travellers. Yet, apart from North Africa which has taken advantage of proximity to European generating markets, Africa's tourist potential is largely undeveloped. This is in part due to the fact that before the advent of air travel much of the interior of the so-called 'Dark Continent' was virtually inaccessible. Even today air services are poor and many consider this is holding back tourism in Africa. The same is true for surface transport. There are very few harbours along the coast and even penetration up the largest rivers – the Zaire (Congo) or Zambesi for example – is blocked by rapids and waterfalls inland. Road and rail infrastructure is generally inadequate so that touring holidays can be a major undertaking, although some ambitious projects will improve the situation. Nor is transport the only reason for Africa's undeveloped tourism potential. Most countries have a low level of industrial development and are rural in character, with tourism low on the list of economic priorities. Although some countries do see tourism as an important source of foreign currency and a stimulus to the economy, others place bureaucratic obstacles in the way of travellers. Add to this a generally poor level of organization of tourism, particularly at the regional level, and it is clear that tourism in Africa is still a fledgling industry. This is borne out by the statistics; for the whole of the continent international tourist arrivals are estimated at seven and a half million in 1984. Out of more than fifty countries considered in the region less than half have developed significant tourism industries. In the remaining countries hotel accommodation is rarely found outside the national capitals so that tourism is largely restricted to 'expeditions'.

In contrast to most of Africa south of the Sahara, the North African countries, with the exception of Libya, have developed a sizable tourism industry based on beach holidays and inclusive tours for north Europe. In fact, this represents an extension of Mediterranean coastal developments, facilitated by improved air transport technology and this region now accounts for 60 per cent of foreign tourist arrivals to the African continent. Morocco was the first country to enter the market in the 1950s and both Tunisia and Algeria soon followed. Libya is the wealthiest country in the region due to its petroleum resources but tourism is not encouraged by its strongly Islamic and socialist government, though business travel is of some significance.

North West Africa

Introduction

North West Africa takes the lion's share of tourism in Africa and contains the majority of the continent's tourist infrastructure – particularly accommodation. Yet the countries of North West Africa – Morocco, Tunisia and Algeria – are quite distinct culturally and physically from those of 'Black Africa' south of the Sahara. The desert has for long acted as a formidable barrier and physically areas north of the Sahara form part of the Mediterranean region, and much of the scenery resembles that found in Greece, Spain, or Southern Italy. The dominant feature of the region is a system of high, intensely folded mountains – the Atlas. South of the Atlas, the Sahara and its peoples provide the region with its best known tourist 'image', but in reality the nomadic tribes now constitute only a small minority of the population, while the camel caravan has been largely superseded by motorized transport.

Culturally, Morocco, Algeria, and Tunisia have more in common with the Arab countries of South West Asia than with either Southern Europe or West Africa. They have formed an important part of the Islamic world ever since their conquest by the Arabs in the eighth century AD. Arabic is the official language and Arabs form the majority of the population, especially in the cities. However, the earlier inhabitants, the Berbers, still carry on their traditional way of life in the more remote, mountainous areas of Algeria and Morocco. During the first half of this century, most of the region was under the rule of France with the result that French is the second language. The French were also responsible for constructing a good highway system and well-planned European-style cities adjoining but distinct from the Arab Medinas with their congested maze of narrow streets, souks – or covered markets, and fortified kasbahs. Religion plays a major part in the life-style and the skyline of the cities is dominated by the minarets of the mosques.

Morocco

Morocco exemplifies the tourist advantages of North Africa, close to the markets of Europe, but with the attraction of an exotic culture quite different from the European experience. On offer are excursions to the desert or medieval cities like Marrakesh. Also unlike either Algeria or Tunisia, Morocco has been an important independent monarchy for many centuries, with the exception of a brief period from 1912 to 1956, when it was divided under French and Spanish rule. It has a large number of ancient cities, four of which – Fez, Meknes, Marrakesh, and Rabat – have, at various times, acted as the capital.

The core of Morocco's half million square kilometres is a plateau (similar to the Spanish Meseta) which is bounded to the north and east by the high Atlas mountains. Large numbers of Berbers live in the mountain regions and in the 'deep south' of the country, where the landscape is dotted with fortified villages. Morocco is also fortunate in having an extensive coastline on both the Atlantic and the Mediterranean. The climate of the Atlantic coast is particularly attractive, largely because of the influence of the cool Canaries Current. Winters are warm and sunny, while the summers are free of the excessive heat and dust found elsewhere in North Africa at this season.

Tourist arrivals to Morocco stood at around one and a half million in the early 1980s. As in Algeria a major source of visitors are expatriates returning for their annual holiday. Europeans make up around two-thirds of foreign visitors, notably the French, Spanish, British, and West Germans. This is not surprising given the development of air-inclusive tours to Morocco, and the convenient ferry links from Spain.

Two-thirds of Morocco's accommodation capacity is in hotels and the rest in self catering. This represents considerable investment in tourism by the government, particularly in the middle and luxury priced hotels. The Ministry of Tourism co-ordinates a number of government bodies with responsibility for tourism, notably the promotion of tourism and the financing and development of tourist projects. However, the Moroccan government is now encouraging private investment in the tourist industry by attractive incentives and reducing its own involvement by simply influencing the location and type of tourist developments, but not the detail of its construction. This has meant identifying a number of schemes for development – for example on the Atlantic coast at Agadir, at Tangier, and Taghazoute where well planned and designed developments are in the traditional Moroccan style.

Clearly, the Moroccan government recognizes the importance of tourism to both the economy and for employment. After a period of poorly organized promotion and development (and underfunding) the Moroccans are now attempting to widen the appeal of Morocco and to attract inclusive tours from Spain, and develop conferences and activity holidays.

The Moroccan government has also encouraged the development of a number of international resorts along the Atlantic coast, especially around the modern city of Casablanca in the north, and at Agadir in the south. Morocco's leading tourist destination, Agadir, is a modern resort, purpose built after being destroyed by an earthquake in 1960. The resort has a core of high-rise hotels and apartment blocks which contrast with the more recent low-rise developments in traditional Moroccan style.

The French tour operator Club Mediterranee has done much to promote the country as a 'winter sun' destination, with holiday villages at Malabata (near Tangier), Smir, Al Hoceima, and Yosmina on the Mediterranean coast, as well as inland at Mar-

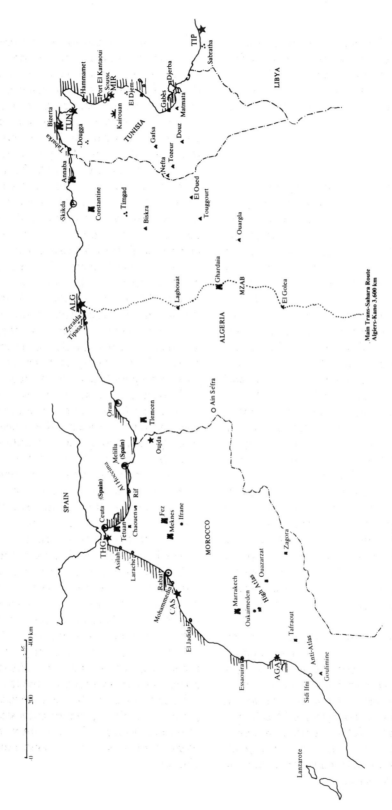

Figure 15.1 Major tourist resources in North Africa

rakesh and Ouazarzat. From the coastal resorts the historic cities of Morocco can be reached fairly easily, and even the formerly inaccessible High Atlas and Rif mountains are being opened up by the construction of scenic highways and skiing resorts.

Tunisia

Tunisia has developed as a holiday playground for Europeans seeking sun, sea, and sand, not only on account of its superb beaches and good winter climate, but also because tourist development has been encouraged and carefully managed. Tunisia caters for the mass market, and this is reflected in the arrivals figures – around three-quarters of the two million arrivals are European, concentrated into the summer months, though successful promotion of Tunisia as a winter-sun destination has boosted arrivals between October and March to a third of the total in the early 1980s. The most important markets are France, Germany, and Britain, and from North Africa – Algeria. However, Tunisia's dependence on the European market leaves it vulnerable to recession in the generating countries, and also to the changing political relations between her North African neighbours – Algeria and Morocco.

As would be expected in a country dependent on the mass travel market, the majority of arrivals are by air, mostly through Tunis, or Monastir – on the coast, which was specially built to handle charter flights. La Goulette and Bizerta are the ports of arrival for cruise passengers. Tunisia's increasingly professional approach to tourism includes upgrading the welcome facilities for travellers at the major gateways.

Tunisia had a period of hotel construction throughout the 1970s and, in order to aid competitive holiday pricing, increased the average size of hotels – particularly around Sousse, Hammamet, and on Djerba. Most are low-rise developments, often in the local architectural style and blending in with the environment. Hotel accommodation is concentrated on the coast, and in the capital, Tunis. Other forms of accommodation include youth hostels and camp sites.

Tourism accounts for almost one-fifth of Tunisian exports and is the second most important source of foreign exchange after petroleum products. Given tourism's importance to the economy, government involvement is extensive. The National Ministry of the Economy formulates the policy context of tourism in Tunisia but the day-to-day implementation of the policy is done by the Tunisian National Tourism Office (ONTT). By the mid-1980s, Tunisia plans to have boosted hotel capacity and to have diversified the tourism product away from the sea, sun, and sand image. Plans include a prestigious new marina and sports complex at Port El Kantaoui, north of Sousse. Also a new product 'Saharan Tourism' is being developed to open up the south as a tourist region. Tunisia has been fortunate in being able to learn the lessons of uncontrolled tourist development from other countries and has adopted a positive approach to protecting the environment, regulating tourist development, and yet at the same time encouraging and supporting tourism investment.

Tunisia is a country of over 165,000 square kilometres where the tourist resources are based on the contrasts between the coast, where most tourists stay, and the opportunities for excursions into the Saharan region to the south. South of Tunis is fertile Cap Bon with its flower gardens and intensive agriculture. The coast offers good beaches and tourist complexes stretching from Hammamet, Sousse, and Monastir, to the Gulf of Gabes with the island of Djerba.

North of Tunis lies Carthage, the old pirate port of Bizerta, and the 'Coral Coast' where the Atlas mountains meet the sea. The Tunisian authorities have nominated this coast as an area for tourist development. Tunis has much to offer the tourist and features on many excursions from the coastal resorts. It is a modern city of spacious leafy boulevards, set around the medieval Arab medina, a maze of narrow twisting streets.

Inland, most of Tunisia consists of semi-arid plain – the Sahel, where excursions by jeep and camel are available. But even here tourism development is planned for the area around Gafsa and Tozeur.

Algeria

Despite its strategic position close to the tourist markets of northern Europe, Algeria receives only a small number of international tourists annually, compared to the other North African countries. The majority of visitors are from France, Tunisia, Italy, West Germany, and countries of Eastern Europe. Friends and relatives are an important market, particularly Algerian emigrants now resident in Western Europe, who return home for their annual summer holiday.

The majority of international tourists arrive by air, though most Tunisians arrive overland. Algeria has five international airports and scheduled flights are operated by the major European airlines as well as Air Algerie – which also serves the domestic air network, so important in a country the size of Algeria, and allowing tourists access to the remoter parts. Surface transport links to Algeria include car ferries to France; (operated by French Societe Nationale Maritime Course Mediterranee (SCNM)) and the Algerian state-owned shipping line. The 4700 kilometre rail and 70,000 kilometre paved road network (with an excellent bus service) allows visitors to travel throughout Algeria and into the neighbouring country of Tunisia. The rail link with Morocco was closed in 1975 with the beginning of the Western Sahara dispute, though foreign visitors can cross into Morocco by road.

Algeria's tourism industry has suffered from an acute shortage of accommodation, exacerbated by the need of many foreign companies to house their employees in hotels, owing to the shortage of housing. At the same time, service standards are poor. The problem is at its worse in the capital, Algiers, where accommodating delegates attending conferences, and tourists attending other events, is a continual headache. Most hotel beds are concentrated at the purpose-built tourist centres on the coast and in the Saharan oases.

Like other sectors of the economy, tourism is closely controlled by the State. Tourism policy is decided by the Ministry of Tourism, which also oversees a number of tourism agencies. These include the Office National Algerien du Tourisme (OWAT) which oversees promotion and development; the Enterprise des Travaux Touristiques (ETT) which implements development schemes, and three other agencies which are responsible in turn for running most of Algeria's hotels, camp sites, and health spas.

Algeria recognizes the contribution of tourism in both earning foreign exchange and also fostering good international relations. However, the country's economic priority is to build a sound industrial base and consequently few resources are left for tourism. In fact only 3 per cent of the area of this vast country (almost two and a half million square kilometres) is cultivated land, and the majority is desert, but fortunately Algeria has immense reserves of oil, natural gas, and iron ore to bring in the foreign currency she needs. Industrialization may however, increase Algerians' demand for both domestic tourism and travel abroad.

Algeria's vastness offers a diversity of scenic and cultural resources to the tourist. In the north lies Mediterranean Algeria with 1200 kilometres of unspoilt coast. The fertile but narrow coastal plain known as the Tell, contains the main centres of population, including the capital, Algiers, which became a modern cosmopolitan city under French rule. Near Algiers a number of seaside resorts (Tipasa, Zeralda and Sidi Ferruch) have been developed to cater for European tour operators. Some of these resorts have been planned as self-contained towns in Arabic style, demonstrating high standards, and complete with souks (covered markets), and entertainment and sports facilities. Between the coastal plains and the south lie the Atlas mountains, offering respite from the heat of the plains and where skiing is possible from December to March.

Between the two Atlas ranges are semi-arid plains, containing large numbers of salt lakes, known as the Plateau of the Shotts, reaching the true desert at Laghouat, some 400 kilometres inland. From here the Trans-Sahara Highway, the most important of the desert routes, runs 2400 kilometres to Kano in Northern Nigeria. Only a small proportion of the Sahara is actually sand dunes or 'erg', and there is considerable scenic variety, including the volcanic rock formations of the Hoggar rising to 3000 metres, and eroded badlands criss-crossed by a network of dried-up rivers or wadis. Each oasis town has a distinct character, the most interesting being those of the M'zab region, while Tamanrasset is the main centre of the veiled Tuareg nomads. Prehistoric rock paintings at Ain Sefra and in the Tassili Mountains show that the Sahara once enjoyed a more humid climate. Winter is the best time to visit the desert, as average maximum temperatures in summer usually exceed 40°C, and their effect is intensified by the dusty winds.

East Africa

Contrasts in scenery, climate, and culture are particularly evident in East Africa and form the basis of a flourishing tourism industry. Most of East Africa consists of an undulating plateau over 900 metres in altitude, but it also contains the most spectacular scenery to be found anywhere on the continent. Part of the Rift Valley – a deep gash in the earth's surface extending from the Dead Sea to Lake Malawi – cuts through the region as two branches. The western branch contains Lakes Mobutu and Edward in Uganda, and Lake Tanganyika, while the eastern branch is bounded by a high escarpment in western Kenya. The earth movements which formed the rift also raised the high mountains of volcanic origin on either side, notably Mount Elgon, Kenya, and Kilimanjaro. The valley floor is littered with a number of craters, (the most famous being Ngorongoro which is a spectacular wildlife sanctuary), and there are numerous lakes. Some of these, like Naivasha, contain fresh water and are rich in fish, whereas others – like Nakuru, Magadi, and Natron – contain deposits of salt and soda which have attracted the attention of mineral developers, as well as of conservationists who wish to protect the millions of flamingos which breed there.

Most of East Africa has a tropical wet-dry climate, but because of its position astride the Equator, the region has two dry seasons and two rainy ones. The coast is also influenced by the seasonal shift in wind direction caused by the Monsoon over the Indian Ocean. Altitude too has an important effect. Conditions in Nairobi at 1800 metres are ideal for Europeans with daytime temperatures between 20°C and 25°C all year round. The main tourist seasons for East Africa's big game areas are December to early March, and July to early October as these correspond to the dry seasons when the animals are concentrated around the water-holes. Travel is also easier then, whereas the dirt roads are often impassable at the height of the rains.

East Africa contains a large variety of habitats for wildlife, ranging from the semi-deserts of Northern Kenya and Somalia which support herds of antelope and gazelle, to the dense rain forests of the Ruwenzori on the Uganda-Zaire border and the Kagera Mountains in Ruanda which shelter the chimpanzee and gorilla. The dominant type of vegetation is thorny scrub in the drier areas, alternating with open plains or savanna where the tall grasses dotted with umbrella-shaped acacia trees support large herds of grazing animals and the great predators such as the lion. In most other parts of Africa these animals have become scarce as the result of man's interference with the natural environment.

Wildlife is the basis of East African tourism and the organization of big-game safaris dates from the late nineteenth century, though the first national parks were designated in the 1940s. Kenya, Tanzania, and Uganda have devoted large areas to wildlife conservation, either as national parks, where the protection given to animal life and vegetation is absolute, or in game reserves. In some game reserves the local nomadic tribes, notably the Masai, have the right to use the land as they have always done as pasture. Poaching for skins and ivory receives wide publicity but a more serious long-term problem is the encroachment of the human population (growing at a rate of 3 per cent annually) on what is perceived by Africans as potential agricultural land. Most of the best land is given over to the production of cash crops for export and not to food staples.

Tourists now come to East Africa to photograph the wildlife, as hunting expeditions are a thing of the past – especially in *Kenya*. The term safari has

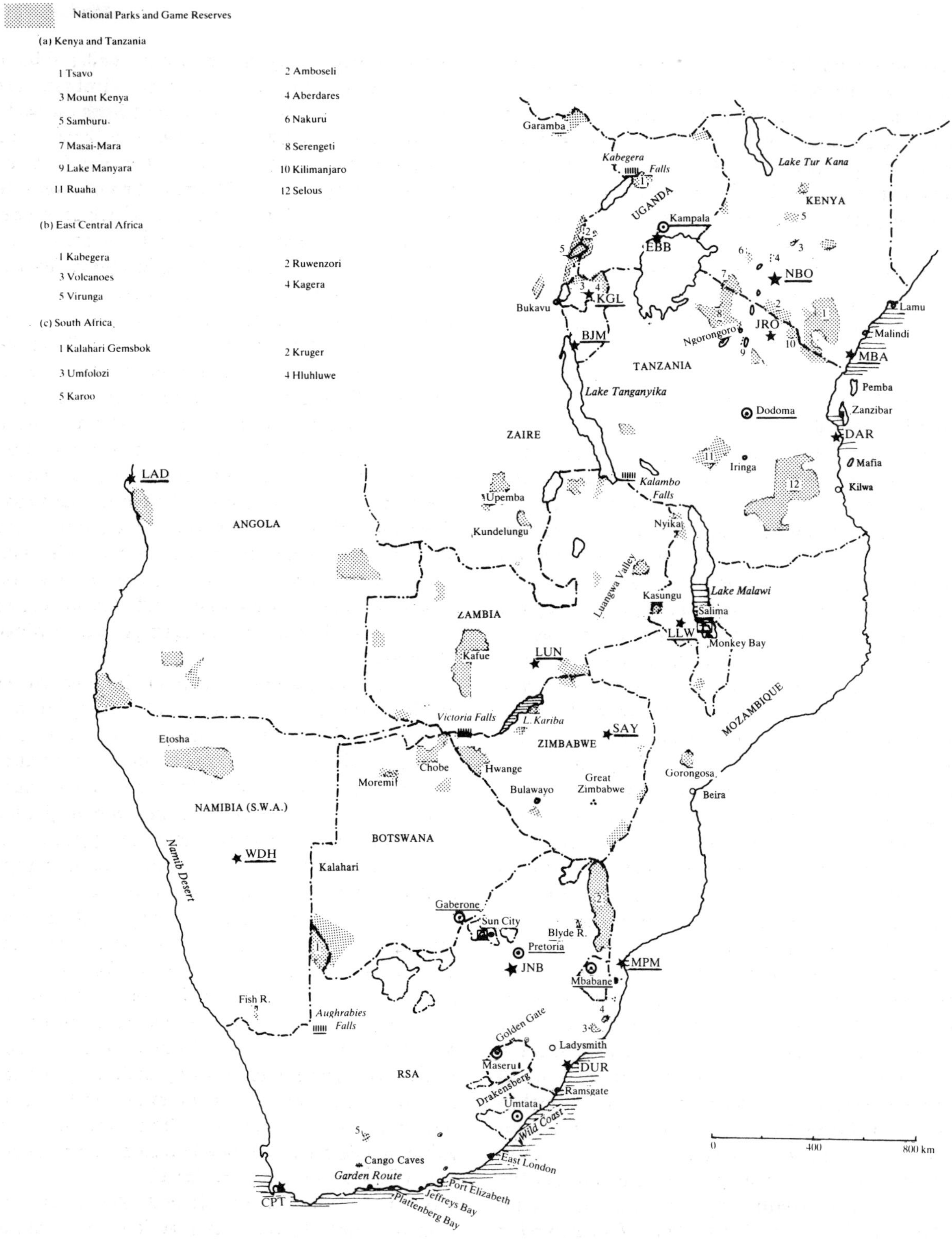

National Parks and Game Reserves

(a) Kenya and Tanzania

1 Tsavo	2 Amboseli
3 Mount Kenya	4 Aberdares
5 Samburu	6 Nakuru
7 Masai-Mara	8 Serengeti
9 Lake Manyara	10 Kilimanjaro
11 Ruaha	12 Selous

(b) East Central Africa

1 Kabegera	2 Ruwenzori
3 Volcanoes	4 Kagera
5 Virunga	

(c) South Africa

1 Kalahari Gemsbok	2 Kruger
3 Umfolozi	4 Hluhluwe
5 Karoo	

Garamba

Kabegera Falls

Lake Tur Kana

KENYA

UGANDA

Kampala

EBB

NBO

KGL

Bukavu

JRO

Lamu

BJM

Ngorongoro

Malindi

MBA

TANZANIA

Pemba

Zanzibar

Lake Tanganyika

Dodoma

DAR

ZAIRE

Mafia

Iringa

Kilwa

LAD

Upemba

Kalambo Falls

Kundelungu

Nyika

ANGOLA

Luangwa Valley

Kasungu

Lake Malawi

Salima

ZAMBIA

LLW

Monkey Bay

Kafue

LUN

Victoria Falls

L. Kariba

SAY

Etosha

ZIMBABWE

Chobe

Hwange

Gorongosa

MOZAMBIQUE

Moremif

Bulawayo

Great Zimbabwe

Beira

NAMIBIA (S.W.A.)

BOTSWANA

WDH

Kalahari

Namib Desert

Gaborone

Sun City

Blyde R.

Pretoria

MPM

JNB

Mbabane

Fish R.

Aughrabies Falls

Golden Gate

Ladysmith

Maseru

DUR

RSA

Drakensberg

Ramsgate

Umtata

Wild Coast

Cango Caves

East London

Garden Route

Port Elizabeth

Jeffreys Bay

Plattenberg Bay

CPT

0   400   800 km

Figure 15.2   *Major tourist resources in Southern and East Africa*

come to include budget-priced mini-bus tours of the most accessible national parks, based on Nairobi, or one of the coastal resorts. In the luxury price bracket tour operators offer camping expeditions with a courier, or a stay in one of the luxury game lodges established by the government in the national parks. These are designed to blend with the local environment, the most famous being 'Treetops' in the Aberdare mountains and Seronera in the Serengeti. Other options in East Africa include fishing expeditions to Lake Turkana; camel safaris in the remoter parts of northern Kenya; trekking and mountaineering on Kilimanjaro or Mount Kenya; or air and balloon safaris to the more inaccessible game reserves.

The main gateway to the wildlife reserves and major scenic attractions of East Africa is the modern city of Nairobi which is Kenya's capital and has good communications by air, road, and rail to most of the region, and good facilities for shopping and entertainment. Most foreign tourists spend some time in Nairobi, and with its Kenyatta conference centre business travel is increasing. Ironically, the parks of Northern *Tanzania* (i.e. Serengeti) can be reached more easily from Nairobi than from Dar-es-Salaam on the coast. This has caused the Tanzanian government to invest in a new airport at Kilimanjaro and hotel complexes in and near Arusha. The enormous game reserves of Southern Tanzania are remote and under-visited, with only limited accommodation facilities at Iringa. It remains to be seen whether the new road and rail links from Dar-es-Salaam to Lusaka in Zambia will lead to an increase in tourism to the area. *Uganda's* tourist attractions such as Kabagera Falls and the Ruwenzori National Park can be reached from the airport at Entebbe or from Kampala. The Ugandan capital is linked by ferry services across Lake Victoria and by road and rail links to Nairobi. The tourism industry in Uganda suffered severely from mismanagement and political unrest during the 1970s and early 1980s from which it has not yet recovered.

The East African coast is also attracting tourists for a more conventional 'sun, sea, and sand' holiday, with the added ingredient of an excursion to a game park in the interior. In fact, beach tourism is expanding in East Africa, whilst visits to the game reserves are declining. Tourists are mainly West Germans, Swiss, or Italians on package tours staying at one of the new resorts like Diani Beach, or centres such as Mombasa (with its expanded airport), or Malindi. From Lamu to Kilwa there are long stretches of white sands, beaches, and lagoons protected by a coral reef, providing ideal conditions for skin diving, underwater photography, and other watersports. The underwater wildlife of the reef is protected by marine national parks at Malindi and Watamu. Here visitors may view from glass-bottomed boats but spear fishing or shell collecting is prohibited. On the coast many of the ports, notably the island of Zanzibar, and Mombasa, are ancient Arab settlements and traditional crafts such as metalwork and dhow-building still flourish. The urban civilization of the coast contrasts sharply with the interior where many tribal groups maintain their semi-nomadic way of life. The markets of Nairobi, Mombasa, and Dar-es-Salaam sell tourist curios such as beadwork, wood-carvings, and animal trophies.

The administration of tourism in East Africa would lend itself to regional co-operation, but this was rendered effectively impossible by turmoil in Uganda and in 1977 Tanzania closed its borders and publicly distanced itself from Kenyan tourism. However, in 1985 the two countries were beginning to negotiate co-operative tourism agreements. Kenya, which had a large number of European settlers before independence, encouraged foreign investment in the hotel industry, but is now looking for local ownership of the tourist industry. The Kenyan Tourist Development Corporation is not only responsible for tourism but also oversees the wildlife in the country. Kenya sees tourism as an important source of foreign currency and encourages private enterprise, including foreign investors. Tanzania is less committed to the rapid development of tourism. The country has African-style socialism based on rural communities and many enterprises are largely state-run. The Tanzanian Ministry of Natural Resources and Tourism controls the Tanzanian Tourist Corporation and the Tanzanian Wildlife Corporation.

East Africa may be extended to include the countries of the Horn of Africa and the Sudan, where development has been adversely affected by drought and political strife. *Ethiopia* is of particular interest to cultural tourists as its heartland is an ancient Christian civilization separated from its Moslem neighbours by high mountain barriers. Due to the altitude the climate of the highlands compares favourably with the excessive heat and humidity of the Red Sea coastlands. Attractions include the game reserves of the Rift Valley, Lake Tana, and the monasteries of Axoum and Lalibela. Most of *Somalia* is semi-desert and tourism is not significant although the long coastline has potential. The tiny country of *Djibouti* is a major port of call. The *Sudan* suffers from divisions between the Arabic speaking north and the African tribal cultures of the south. Nile cruises and diving in the Red Sea offer scope for development.

Southern Africa

Most of the countries of Southern and Central Africa have also realized the importance of wildlife conservation, and there are for example large national parks and game reserves in Angola and Mozambique where tourism has been adversely affected by long-standing internal unrest.

The most highly developed tourism industry in the continent is found in the *Republic of South Africa* (RSA). In contrast to most of the 'black' African countries south of the Sahara, South Africa has a highly developed economy, which has been built upon the basis of its vast mineral resources, and it is now the most industrialized and urbanized society in Africa. Incomes are particularly high among white South Africans of mainly Dutch or British descent, who form 4.6 million of the total population of over 30 million. The provinces of Transvaal and Orange Free State are mainly Afrikaans (Dutch) speaking, whereas English is mostly used in Cape Province and Natal. In 1976 the area known as the Transkei became a quasi-independent state to be followed by other 'homelands' occupied by different Bantu tribal groups. Most black Africans however work outside the

homelands in mining, agriculture, or manufacturing in the big cities, where they live in separate neighbourhoods or 'townships', the largest being Soweto near Johannesburg with well over a million inhabitants.

Among the white minority an affluent lifestyle is expressed in the demand for recreation and outbound tourism. Around half a million trips abroad were generated each year in the early 1980s, of which 75 per cent were for holiday purposes. About two-thirds or more of South Africans travelling to Europe are from English-speaking homes, and many were returning to Europe to visit friends and relatives. Recently there have been indications that more non-whites – particularly Cape Coloureds and Asian – are travelling out of South Africa for business or pleasure. Europe is still the main destination but, with the availability of new fares and direct air routes there is interest in the Americas, Australia, and the Far East. The Seychelles and Mauritius are important beach holiday destinations.

Demand for domestic tourism is important in the RSA, far more so than inbound foreign tourism in terms of bednights. The foreign tourism industry is a relatively new development in the RSA, and since 1970 growth has been affected by political events. By 1980, 700,000 arrivals were recorded. Africa generates two-fifths of visitors – the majority from neighbouring Zimbabwe. By far the largest single contributor of visits from outside Africa is the UK, followed by West Germany, and the USA. A high proportion of British tourists visit relatives in the English-speaking areas. The Netherlands is a much less important market despite the fact that the majority of white South Africans, especially in the Transvaal and Orange Free State, are Afrikaaners, descendants of the original Dutch settlers.

South African tourism is not markedly seasonal as the climate allows tourism for most of the year. Only the timing of school holidays in the Christmas period produces a marked seasonal peak and places pressure upon accommodation, particularly on the Natal coast. The South African winter is the best time to see game in the eastern parks as the tracks are dry and the grass is short.

Although South Africa is situated a long way

from the main travel markets, it is served by several international shipping lines and inter-continental airlines. The gateway for the great majority of visitors by air is Johannesburg, while Cape Town, situated at the 'crossroads' of the world's seaways, is the main point of entry for visitors by sea. Internal communications are also very good. South African Airways operate most of the scheduled domestic services, with several flights a day linking the main cities. Another convenient way of seeing the country is by South African Railways. The luxury 'Blue Train' runs between Pretoria and Cape Town, a distance of 1600 kilometres, in twenty-five hours, passing through some magnificent scenery in its descent from the Karoo Plateau to the coast. There is also a nationwide system of metalled highways – rare in most parts of Africa – and a large number of tours by coach or mini-bus are readily available.

Tourism has been low on the list of government priorities but a national tourism policy is about to be produced and in 1983 the South African Tourism Board took over the functions of the South African Tourist Corporation and the Hotel Board. The new Tourism Board is a statutory body charged with the promotion of tourism and fostering the development and improvement of accommodation which has already achieved high standards of service.

Generally speaking, South Africa has a warm temperate climate which is almost ideal for Europeans and the country enjoys more sunshine than most Mediterranean resorts. With the exception of the western part of Cape Province, most of the rainfall occurs in the summer months (October to April). There are important differences in climate between the coastal areas and high interior plateaus of the Karoo and the Veldt, where temperatures frequently fall below 0°C at night during winter months. The Atlantic coast north of Table Bay is washed by the cold Benguela current which renders sea bathing uncomfortable and is a major cause of the aridity which characterizes much of Southern Africa. In contrast, the Indian Ocean coasts from False Bay eastwards are affected by the warm Mozambique current and experience high temperatures and ample rainfall throughout the year.

The herds of big game animals which roamed the Veld a century ago are now confined to South Africa's eleven national parks and many game reserves, most of which are quite small in area. One exception is Kruger National Park located in the bushveld along the Mozambique border, and covering an area the size of Wales. It is served by an extensive network of roads, and accommodation is mainly self-catering in groups of rondavels, African-style thatched huts, but equipped with modern conveniences. Other notable reserves, such as Hluhluwe and Umfolozi, are situated in Zululand, and in the Kalahari Desert, which, despite its aridity, supports a surprising variety of game.

The main holiday area for South Africans, especially those from the Veldt, is the coast of Natal, where conditions are ideal for swimming, sunbathing, and surfing throughout the year. Durban is the largest holiday resort, as well as being a busy cosmopolitan port. Inland from Durban the Drakensberg ranges are visited by large numbers of people from the coast during the hot, humid summers, and Pietermaritzburg, Estcourt, and Ladysmith are important centres for touring the mountains.

The Cape Peninsula and the hinterland of Cape Town are considered to be the most beautiful part of South Africa. Cape Town, situated on one of the few good harbours in Southern Africa, is the oldest European settlement, the second largest city in the RSA, and its legislative capital. The best-known landmark is the 900 metres high Table Mountain, while to the east along False Bay there are many fine sandy beaches. Inland lie the vineyards of the Hex River Valley and many old farmhouses in the distinctive 'Cape Dutch' style of architecture. Port Elizabeth and East London are also important centres for the eastern part of Cape Province. Along this part of the coast rugged forest-covered mountains alternate with fertile valleys ending in small sandy bays. The road linking Cape Town to Port Elizabeth is often called the 'Garden Route' because of the luxuriance of the vegetation.

On the central plateau the main centres are the cities of Johannesburg, Pretoria, and Bloemfontein. Johannesburg, with a population of one and a half million, is South Africa's largest and most prosperous city, owing its origin to the gold mines of the Witwaterstrand nearby. An important centre of communications it has become the financial capital of the Republic. Not far away to the north lies Pretoria, the administrative capital, and to the south is Bloemfontein, the judicial capital. Both cities are very different in character from the brashness and bustle of Johannesburg. In the black state of Bophutatswana near Johannesburg an important tourist industry has developed based on gambling and multi-racial entertainment (both illegal in the RSA) in Sun City, an African 'Las Vegas'.

The small countries of *Botswana*, *Lesotho*, and *Swaziland* are dependent on the tourist fortunes and political developments in the RSA. They obtain most of their visitors from the RSA, particularly weekenders for gambling, though Botswana also receives tourists from Zimbabwe. Lesotho and Swaziland attract foreigners who are visiting the RSA. But these three countries have more to offer tourists than gambling. Their resources include the national parks and game reserves of Botswana, the scenic beauty of Lesotho's mountains and waterfalls with the winter sports complex at Oxbow, and the valley of Heaven in Swaziland. Cultural attractions include the traditional ceremonies in Swaziland, the bushmen paintings in Lesotho and Botswana, and the historic pioneering centre at Fort Gaborone. Overland arrivals dominate, but direct air travel is possible to Botswana and Swaziland, though there are no international-standard airports. Lesotho is completely surrounded by the RSA and totally dependent on South Africa for communications.

Zimbabwe's independence was recognized internationally in 1980 after a period of political isolation and civil war. By 1983 inbound tourist arrivals stood at around a quarter of a million, but both these and domestic tourism are declining in the wake of continued unrest in Matabeleland, and the exodus of white settlers. The main source of visitors is Zambia, as the two countries have good relations and communications, whereas the number of South African visitors has fallen considerably. The Zimbabwe Tourist Development Corporation (ZTDC) was formed in 1984 with promotion and development powers and has taken over the running of some hotels to improve occupancy rates. The major tourist attractions are the Victoria Falls and Lake Kariba shared with neighbouring Zambia, and the Hwange National Park.

Neighbouring *Zambia* has a cooler climate than many parts of tropical Africa owing to the altitude (up to 1500 metres) of the plateau which forms most of the country. Zambia is rich in wildlife and is very conservation-minded. National parks make up 8 per cent of the land area, the most important being the Luangwa Valley. Since 1980 there has been a Ministry of Tourism and a master plan for the development of the industry has been drawn up. The most important tourist centres are Livingstone near Victoria Falls, and Lusaka, an international gateway and conference centre.

Neighbouring land-locked *Malawi* is also attempting to attract tourists on 'adventure holidays'. Resorts such as Salima and Monkey Bay on scenic Lake Malawi offer a range of water-sports. Most tourists arrive via Harare in Zimbabwe although there is an international airport at Lilongwe.

Angola and *Mozambique* differ from the other countries of Southern Africa as they are Portuguese-speaking and most of the limited inbound tourism comes from the Iberian Peninsula. Safaris are the main attraction and there are a number of important game reserves, notably Gorongosa in Mozambique. During the 1960s and early 1970s Mozambique was popular with South Africans and Rhodesians for beach tourism, with Maputo and Beira as important entertainment centres. Since independence tourism in both countries has been severely disrupted by civil war.

The islands of the Indian Ocean

East of Mozambique lie the volcanic Comoros Islands and *Madagascar*. The latter (officially the Malagasy Republic) has great tourism potential. The population of around ten million is of Asian, African, and Arab origins, while the French influence is still strong from colonial times. The scenery of this vast island ranges from tropical rain forest along the east coast to semi-desert in the south west, while the central highlands have a temperate climate. These provide a habitat for Madagascar's unique plants and animals which attract nature-lovers from all over the world. However the island is remote, expensive to get to, and once there surface transport is poor. The two major beach resorts – Nosy Be and Ile Saint Marie are accessible only by air transport. The Malagasy government has not given the tourism industry the support it needs and is opposed to the country's largest potential market – South Africa.

Immigrants from India form a large proportion of the population of Mauritius and the Seychelles. Culturally, the islanders therefore have much more in common with Asia and Europe (especially France – the one time colonial power) than with Africa, which is physically so much closer. The *Seychelles* are a geological curiosity, the main islands being of granite formation while the vegetation is luxuriant. The smaller outlying islands are coral atolls which are renowned for their birdlife. The construction of the international airport at Mahe in 1971 brought a formerly remote destination within reasonable flying time from the generating markets of Western Europe and South Africa. Whilst tourism investment is encouraged, only a few localities, mainly on Mahe, have been developed for tourism, the smaller islands remaining as nature reserves. Tourism has not made the economy of the islands less vulnerable to recession in Europe and the present socialist regime has a problem in reconciling its egalitarian principles with the need to cater for wealthy foreigners, and at the same time reduce its dependence on imported foodstuffs.

Mauritius is developing tourism as part of a programme of industrialization to reduce dependence on the sugar crop. Unlike the neighbouring French island of Réunion, Mauritius is accessible with direct air links to South Africa (its main source of tourists), Europe, India, and Australia. Scenically less attractive than the Seychelles or Reunion, its lifestyle is more sophisticated. Port Louis the capital offers gambling and is a cosmopolitan city. Curepipe in the interior highlands has a cooler climate and a French creole atmosphere.

West Africa

Most of West Africa has failed to develop important tourism industries, not only because it lacks modern infrastructure, but also because its wildlife and scenic resources are not as well known or as spectacular as those of East Africa. Yet it is just within reach of the inclusive holiday markets of North West Europe, and 'winter sunshine' resorts have been developed on the beaches of some of these countries. The Gambia for example, is around six hours flying time from much of northern Europe and it is in the same time zone. This means that its dry and sunny winter climate allows the Gambia to compete with the Canary Islands as a winter-sunshine destination for the British and Scandinavians, with the added ingredient of an 'encounter' with West Africa. Another large potential market for West Africa is the USA where perhaps 12 per cent of the population have their ethnic origins in the region. The French are attracted to the French-speaking countries, notably the Ivory Coast, while the Italians have 'discovered' Togo as a destination. Business travel is not particularly important except in a number of coastal cities such as Lome (Togo) which have developed conference facilities.

West African tourism gravitates to the coast where the climate is tropical, with high temperatures and humidity for most of the year, except during the dry season from December to March when the 'Harmattan' blows from the Sahara. There are great social and economic contrasts between the cities of the coast – where commercial agriculture is well developed – and the drought-prone Sahel region bordering on the Sahara Desert where traditional ways of life still prevail. The low incomes of the land-locked Sahel countries – Mali, Niger, and Burkina Faso – has handicapped any development of a tourism industry. Where tourist development has taken place, the extent of foreign ownership of hotels does mean that many of the economic benefits of tourism leak out of West Africa.

In 1976 the Economic Community of West African States (ECOWAS) was formed to promote economic co-operation between French- and

English-speaking member states. The French-speaking countries (Ivory Coast, Burkina Faso, Togo, and Benin) are joined by the Conseil de l'Entente which has a committee for the organization of tourist co-operation. The committee promotes uniformity and standardization in the tourist industry, particularly the harmonization of entry requirements between neighbouring countries in a bid to promote the mobility of tourists throughout the region.

In the early 1980s around 700,000 tourists visited West Africa annually. This is small by world standards – even the most popular countries such as Senegal and the Ivory Coast attracted only 200,000 visitors per year in the early 1980s, while in the Gambia arrivals were 50,000 per year.

Lagos, Dakar, and Abidjan are the focus of air routes into the region, many operated by Air Nigeria. Most tourists arrive by air as daily flights connect West Africa to the world airline network. The capital of Senegal, Dakar, is an important stop-over for flights from Europe to South America; and the winter-sunshine countries of the Ivory Coast, Sierra Leone, and the Gambia, are developing charter flights from Europe to counter the high scheduled fares to West Africa. Surface transport is geared to the past needs of agriculture and trade where routes led from the interior to the ports. This inhibits travel between the countries of West Africa, but does allow excursions to the interior. However these problems will be overcome with the completion of the Trans-Africa highway linking East and Central Africa to West Africa and the Trans-Sahara highway linking Algeria to Nigeria. Investment in infrastructure is taking place, particularly in hotels (as in the Ivory Coast where foreign investment is encouraged and state-owned travel and hotel companies are involved). In the Gambia a major World Bank tourism and infrastructure plan has been implemented by the government, involving hotel investment, provision of water, and sewerage, a hotel training school, and extensions to Yundum international airport.

West Africa's tourist attractions include the variety of tribal folklore, the colourful markets, and the handicrafts. The Atlantic coast has many fine beaches backed by lagoons in some areas which provide shelter from the heavy surf. Conventional hotels in the Gambia, holiday villages in the Ivory Coast and more traditional African-style accommodation in Senegal are available. Water-sports and activity holidays are being developed on the coast with safaris and discovery tours penetrating inland. The Gambia has shown that the region's history is an attraction, particularly to black Americans. The trading forts of the slave trade are also preserved in Goré (Senegal) and on the Gold Coast (Ghana).

Nigeria deserves special mention, not because it is as yet a holiday destination, but in view of the fact that it is the most populous nation in Africa with an area of over 900,000 square kilometres and ninety million inhabitants, and as an OPEC member country, one of the most developed. Tourism is the responsibility of the individual states but progress has been uneven. There are considerable contrasts between the north, which is predominantly Islamic, and the Christian south, dominated by the more business-minded Ibo and Yoruba ethnic groups. As a large market Nigeria attracts a high volume of business travel but there is a shortage of hotels and the infrastructure is inadequate. Some national parks have been designated but the main interest of the country lies in the great variety of tribal groups and their artistic achievements – Kano in the north and Ibadan in the south are particularly outstanding.

Central Africa

Between East and West Africa an extensive area of the continent remains almost undeveloped for tourism, mainly due to its inadequate transport and accommodation facilities. Much of this region consists of tropical rainforest occupying a broad belt along the Equator. Communications are generally difficult during the rainy season which corresponds to most of the year along the Equator. The largest country in the region is *Zaire*, which under Belgian rule had been a pioneer in African wildlife conservation. It occupies most of the basin of the Congo, the largest waterway network in Africa. River transport is used almost entirely for small-scale native commerce and many improvements will need to be made to both vessels and port facilities if these inland waterways are to be viable for tourism. The *Cameroons*, described as 'Africa in miniature', offers savannas rich in game, rainforest, the volcanic Mount Cameroon, and fine beaches along the Gulf of Guinea. Like most African states it is also made up of a bewildering variety of tribal groups but has the advantage that both French and English are widely spoken.

Summary

Africa is the second largest of the continents and is rich in both natural and cultural tourist resources. Aside from a sizable North African tourist industry serving the mass inclusive tour markets of Europe, Africa's tourist potential is largely unfulfilled. This can be attributed to a rudimentary transport network, the generally poor organizational framework, and the low level of industrial development of most African countries. Yet in such a vast continent generalizations are inappropriate; South Africa for example, has an advanced economy, a high standard of tourist organization and infrastructure, and also generates international tourists. Some African countries have identified tourism as an area for expansion to attract foreign currency and enhance their economic position. This is particularly the case in Kenya, most of Southern Africa, and some of the West African countries.

The tourist resources of North Africa are based on both winter and summer beach resorts with the added ingredient of a taste of Arab culture and excursions to the Sahara. East Africa's tourist resources primarily comprise the national parks and game reserves, but developments at the coast allow combined beach and safari tourism. South Africa's attractions include beaches and wildlife, as well as spectacular scenery and a warm temperate climate. In West Africa beach tourism is important but here, as in all African countries, holidaymakers can sample the colourful everyday life of African towns and cities.

SIXTEEN

The Levant and the Middle East

LEARNING OBJECTIVES

After reading this chapter, you should be able to:

1 *Describe the major physical features and climate of the countries of the Levant and the Middle East and understand their importance for tourism.*
2 *Recognize that, despite relative proximity to the tourist-generating markets of northern Europe, the region's tourism potential is largely unfulfilled.*
3 *Appreciate that inbound tourism to the region encompasses beach holidays, cultural tourism, and business travel.*
4 *Recognize the Middle East as an important generator of international tourism.*
5 *Identify the major features of tourist infrastructure in the region, particularly transportation and the location of accommodation.*
6 *Demonstrate a knowledge of the tourist regions, resorts, business centres, and tourist attractions of the region.*

Introduction

The countries of the Levant and the Middle East are close enough to the mass inclusive tour markets

of northern Europe to have developed a tourism industry, based on sun, sea, and sand. In fact this simply represents a logical extension of the Mediterranean littoral developments, facilitated by improved air transport technology. However, the response to this opportunity has been uneven. Cyprus was an early entrant into tourism in the 1950s but other countries with the potential to enter the market are only doing so on any scale in the 1980s – Turkey and the United Arab Emirates are notable examples here. Of course, countries such as Egypt or Israel as well as others in the Levant, based their tourism industry on the attractions of the Holy Land and relics of ancient civilizations and have long attracted cultural travellers, while more recently the oil-based prosperity of many Middle East states has attracted a large business travel market. There is also a large volume of intra-regional travel, particularly between the Arab countries.

Aside from the oil-based wealth of the Middle East, the countries in this region need tourism's foreign exchange earnings, the employment it brings, and the opportunity to even out regional imbalances. Both foreign investment and that of host governments has produced an extensive tourist infrastructure throughout the region. Accommodation is concentrated into the coastal developments and in the major cities. Transport has always been good as the region is a crossroads between Europe, Africa, and Asia. New developments include airports (such as Mugla Dalaman in Turkey) and in fact, although most tourists arrive by air, intra-regional movements, outside of the Arabian peninsula, are predominantly by road.

This infrastructure serves a very varied tourist product. The climate allows winter beach resorts, as well as skiing in the mountains. At the same time the region has the relics of successive civilizations from early man to the Egyptians and Romans, and also has the attractions of the Holy Land.

The countries around the Eastern shore of the Mediterranean are known as the Levant region, or the Near East, to distinguish them from the countries around the Persian Gulf, known as the Middle East. Some countries in both these regions are torn by war, terrorist activity, and extremist governments. In consequence tourism has suffered, despite the relative proximity of both the Levant and the Middle East to the tourist-generating markets of northern Europe.

The Levant

In this region agriculturally productive land is restricted to the Nile Valley which runs the length of Egypt from north to south (much of the rest of Egypt is desert), and the narrow coastal plain of Palestine and the Lebanon which has good rainfall. These areas link up with the alluvial plains of Mesopotamia to the east to form the so-called 'Fertile Crescent'. To the east of the coastal strip, mountain ranges cut off the rain-bearing winds and the valleys and plateaux pass rapidly into desert. The deep valley of the river Jordan and the Dead Sea lie below sea level and enjoy a subtropical climate. In the north of the region, the heartland of Turkey is a dry plateau with an extreme climate contrasting with the warm fertile coastlands adjoining the Aegean, Mediterranean, and Black Sea.

The Levant has developed trading links with other regions since the earliest times, and it has supported a variety of civilizations for at least 6000 years. As might be expected, the region is rich in archaeological sites, which range from the rock dwellings of Cappadocia in Turkey and the Greco-Roman temples at Baalbek, to the Crusader castles of the Middle Ages.

Traditionally some of these countries, notably Israel and Jordan, have attracted large numbers of Christian pilgrims, especially at Easter, to the holy places associated with the Bible (many of them are also sacred to the Moslems and the Jews). However, a growing number of holidaymakers now come purely for recreation and relaxation, and a number of resorts have developed to serve their needs.

Egypt

Egypt exemplifies tourism in the Levant. It is a meeting ground of east and west, has the twin resources of world famous archaeological and cultural sites, and beach resorts. Travellers from the West have visited Egypt's unique antiquities for over two thousand years but since the 1960s other Arab countries have also provided a source of tourists to Egypt. By the early 1980s Western and Arab tourists each accounted for over 40 per cent of Egypt's inbound tourism which stood at around one and a half million visits. Arabs tend to stay during the summer months when Egypt, or more accurately the Mediterranean coast around Alexandria, is cooler than the desert countries to the east,

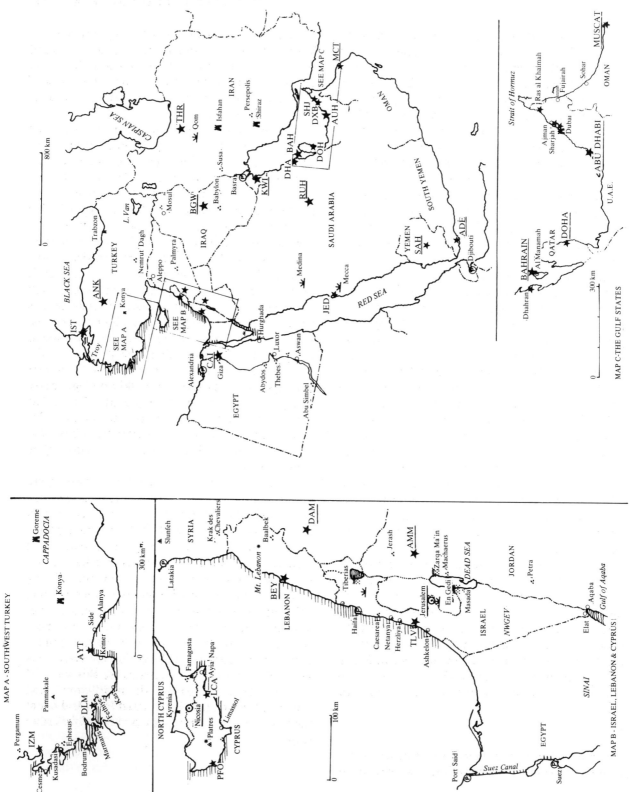

Figure 16.1 *Major tourist resources in the Levant and the Middle East*

while many Western sightseers arrive in the mild winters. Egypt is the largest, most populous (over forty-five million inhabitants), and culturally the most advanced Arab country but, unlike many of its neighbours, it is not self-sufficient in petroleum and suffers from severe problems of providing enough employment and housing for its people. The vast majority of the population are concentrated in the narrow ribbon of cultivated land along the Nile, as they were in Ancient times.

Although there are few charter services, most tourists arrive by air, into the international airport at Cairo. Most of Egypt's hotel rooms are found in Cairo, and in the sightseeing centres of Alexandria and Luxor. The government encourages investment in the accommodation stock by both Egyptian and foreign companies. This is part of an attempt by the government to boost Egyptian tourism as both a revenue earner and employer, and to this end, a Supreme Council of Tourism has been formed, presided over by the Prime Minister. In 1981 EGAPT (Egyptian General Authority for the Promotion of Tourism) was established with both promotion and development responsibilities. EGAPT is spearheading tourism's renaissance in Egypt. Tourists are being tempted away from the Nile Valley to the Red Sea and Mediterranean coastal resorts where a year-round season is possible and opportunities include excellent diving and other water sports. Egypt is also attempting to widen its tourist resource base by encouraging hotels with conference facilities, health tourism, and motoring holidays.

However, there are problems to overcome, not the least of which is Egypt's poor infrastructure (particularly water and power supply and an inadequate road system). Environmental considerations are also important, especially along the coast where there is concern for the ecology of the coral reefs. But perhaps the main problem is still the uncertain political atmosphere of the region which causes severe fluctuations in tourist arrivals.

Israel

The political climate is currently dominated by the Arab/Israeli conflict and Israel's tourist potential is severely affected. Israel is politically isolated in a largely Arab and Moslem region. It is a small country, even including the occupied territories on the West Bank of the Jordan, with a total area of almost 21,000 square kilometres and just over four million inhabitants.

In the early 1980s Israel received over one million visitors annually, the majority from European countries, an important market since the liberalization of charter flights in 1976. The USA is the single most important country providing tourists to Israel (around one-third of all arrivals). The Ministry of Tourism is developing new markets (Japan, the Far East, and the Iberian Peninsula) and works closely with the national carrier El Al.

Israel is an extremely varied country as it includes the Dead Sea, and some quite high mountains in the Galilee region. Seaside resorts have been developed along the Mediterranean coast at Herzliya and Netanya north of Tel Aviv, and at Ashkelon to the south. Eilat, Israel's outlet to the Red Sea, has become a popular centre for winter holidays, with facilities for skin-diving, water skiing, and underwater photography. (Jordan has developed a rival resort nearby at Aqaba.) The 'inland seas' – Galilee and the Dead Sea – have also been developed as health centres (as indeed they were in Roman times).

The main reasons for visiting Israel however, are still cultural. Visitors come not only to view the remains of past civilizations, but also to see a nation in the making, composed of Jewish immigrants from all over the world; Israel's achievements in making the arid Negev Desert productive are renowned, as is the experiment in communal living by the kibbutzim; the latter not only offer working holidays for young people of many nationalities but also many now provide accommodation for more conventional tourists. Jerusalem is the most important tourist centre and is becoming important as a venue for international conferences, although Tel Aviv on the coast remains the main commercial centre of the country. Haifa, attractively laid out at the foot of Mount Carmel, is a port of call for cruise ships.

Jordan

Jordan is a poor Arab country, with almost 100,000 square kilometres but only 3.2 million inhabitants, and tourism plays an important role in the economy. However, over-reliance in the past on the attractions of Jerusalem, Bethlehem, and Jericho meant that most of Jordan's major tourist attractions and hotel stock were lost when Israel occupied this area (the West Bank) in 1966. Since then, Jordan has had to redevelop tourism on the East Bank – albeit from a less promising resource base. Even so, in the early 1980s Jordan received around a million tourists annually, but the majority were Arabs with only a small number of European or American visitors. This is still partly because of Jordan's lack of tourist infrastructure and good hotels, though the authorities are continually improving this situation. By the mid 1980s, Jordan had over two and a half thousand hotel rooms and a network of rest houses in the popular tourist centres such as Petra, around the Dead Sea, in Amman – the capital, and at Aqaba.

Tourism in Jordan is administered by the Tourism Board which has the normal development and promotion responsibilities, but also oversees standards in the industry. The Board is supervising the promotion of domestic tourism, promoting the development of Aqaba as a major beach resort on the Gulf of Aqaba (Jordan only has a twenty-four kilometre coastline), and developing a health spa at Zarqa Ma'in.

Syria

Syria has a population in the region of ten million, and an area of over 185,000 square kilometres. It is a country of major tourist potential, yet political instability and poor infrastructure have depressed the development of tourism. Syria offers beach resorts on the Mediterranean north of Lattakia, as well as cooler mountain resorts at Kasab, archaeological sites (particularly in the Euphrates valley), and fortresses in the desert. Syria received almost a million visitors in the early 1980s, mainly arriving overland from neighbouring Arab countries but the international airport at Damascus is an important gateway. Hotels are geared to the business market and accommodation is concentrated in the major cities of Damascus, Aleppo, Lattakia, and Palmyra. However, accommodation and other facilities for holiday tourism are being developed, particularly on the coast and around Aleppo, Homs, and Palmyra. This is in a bid to reduce the number of transit visitors or day visitors from neighbouring countries. Yet, until peace is declared in the region, there is little scope for holiday tourism.

Lebanon

The Lebanon is a small mountainous country with a population of less than three million. By the 1960s it had become the entertainment centre for Arabs from more 'puritanical' countries where the tenets of Islam were more strictly applied; they also came to the mountains to escape the summer heat of their own countries, while Beirut was the chief entrepôt and financial capital for a large area of South West Asia. However, the development of tourism has received severe setbacks as a result of political unrest and uncertainty. Throughout the early 1980s Lebanon has been a virtual 'no go' area for tourists, and its beach resorts and inland skiing centres have survived on domestic tourism and Arab visitors. Few Western tourists, normally attracted to Lebanon's rich legacy of historic and archaeological sites, have been visiting it in recent years.

The three Arab countries of Jordan, Lebanon, and Syria have much in common from a tourism point of view and regional co-operation, certainly in terms of promotion, would be sensible. Although Syria and Jordan do co-operate on an economic basis, Lebanon's co-operation is unlikely, given the war and the government's minimal involvement in tourism.

Turkey

Turkey is over three-quarters of a million square kilometres in area, and has a population approaching fifty million. Of all the countries in the region, Turkey has the advantage of relative political stability and both a Black Sea and

Mediterranean coastline. Yet Turkey was not part of the boom in Mediterranean tourism which characterized the 1970s. This is because it was expensive to reach and poorly publicized. It is only in the 1980s that it is beginning to exploit its tourism potential, as it has identified tourism as a priority area and is encouraging foreign investment in the industry.

By 1980 tourist arrivals stood at around one and a half million. West Germany and the USA are the leading generators. Visitors to Turkey arrive in almost equal measure by air, land, and sea. Most air arrivals are into Istanbul, but the opening of the Mugla Dalaman airport in the tourist area of south west Turkey, will change this balance, and work has begun on Antalya airport. A further obstacle to the development of tourism is the poor standard of accommodation. Accommodation is concentrated in the Marmara region, and along the Mediterranean and Aegean coasts. The Ministry of Culture and Tourism is attempting to overcome these problems by zoning tourist development areas and encouraging investment in new accommodation complexes (capacity should reach 200,000 rooms by 1990), training manpower, and encouraging domestic tourism. Infrastructure, especially communications, is also being upgraded – a second Bosphorus bridge is planned and a new airport for Istanbul has been opened.

Turkey has much to offer the tourist. The Aegean and Mediterranean coasts are both the focus of major investment programmes, offering a traditional beach holiday but with the added ingredient of Turkey's oriental ambience and the wealth of archaeological sites such as Troy and Ephesus. Istanbul, astride the Bosphorus, which divides Europe and Asia, is the cosmopolitan former capital of the Byzantine and Ottoman Empires with many historic monuments and a vibrant nightlife. The Black Sea coast and most of the Anatolian Plateau remain undeveloped.

Cyprus

Cyprus is the third largest of the Mediterranean islands (over 9000 square kilometres), but its location in the eastern Mediterranean has meant that tourism has not only been affected by the dispute between Turkey and Greece over the island itself, but also it is unavoidably drawn into the political situation of the nearby Middle East. The island's tourist arrivals have therefore fluctuated after a period of growth in the 1960s and early 1970s. After the Turkish invasion and occupation of the Northern part of the island in 1974 there was a drastic decline in numbers. However, by the early 1980s there had been a major investment in tourist facilities in Southern Cyprus and arrivals topped half a million. Most tourists come by air via the gateways of Larnaca and Paphos.

Northern Cyprus was the hub of tourism before the invasion but few Western tour operators are prepared to deal with a government which is not recognized internationally. Before 1974, Famagusta and Kyrenia were the major resorts of the island but are moribund today for this reason.

Cyprus has a varied resource base for tourism including an 800 kilometre coastline with a number of beach resorts. In the southern zone the main coastal developments are at Paphos, Limassol (also an important business travel centre), Larnaca, and Ayia Napa. Inland the pine-clad mountains reach 2000 metres and allow skiing around Troodos. Culturally too, Cyprus has a great deal to offer in the way of classical Greek and Byzantine art treasures. Tourism is important to southern Cyprus, employing around 17,000 people. For this reason and to reduce the impact of tourism on the island, the government has adopted a policy of attracting middle and high income tourists and has departed from the mass tourism philosophy of other Mediterranean countries. This policy is implemented by the Cyprus Tourism Organization who are attempting to distribute tourists more evenly throughout the country and are encouraging winter tourism in order to utilize spare accommodation capacity.

The Middle East

For the present purposes the Middle East covers the countries of the Arabian peninsula, Iraq, and Iran. The Middle East is dominated by the Arabian peninsula, between the Red Sea and the Persian Gulf, stretching some 2000 kilometres southwards from Syria and Iraq. Mostly the peninsula is characterized by dry, hot desert landscapes though the western edge is mountainous and in the east is the smaller Hajar range. With an area of over two million square kilometres – more than half the size of Europe – Saudi Arabia dominates the peninsula and the remaining Arab states cluster along the coasts. There is little in the way of good agricultural land, and most of the region is uniformly arid. Saudi Arabia also dominates in population terms, contributing ten million to the peninsula's twenty-five million inhabitants, but a significant percentage of the population are expatriate workers. To the north east lie Iran and Iraq. Iran is a large country of 1.6 million square kilometres with well over forty million people, dominated by the central plateau which rises to over one thousand metres and is framed by mountain ranges. Iraq is only a third the size of Iran in population and a quarter in area but comprises the fertile plains of the Tigris and the Euphrates.

The rapid development of the vast oil reserves of the countries around the Persian Gulf has led to a tremendous growth in demand for all kinds of goods and services among a population which a generation ago were largely nomads and peasant farmers. Indeed the whole region has become an important generator of international travel. Saudi Arabia is now a major generator of international travel and Kuwait has the world's highest foreign travel expenditure per head in the world. The major outbound flows are to the UK and France though Egypt and Cyprus are also significant destinations. Outbound travel is concentrated between June and September when the summer heat is intense.

Spending by residents of the region abroad is estimated to be almost twice that of inbound foreign visitors. Visitors come to the Middle East mainly for business reasons. Before the 1980s there was little in the Middle East to attract inbound holiday tourism and the Islamic religion distrusts the influence of outsiders on Arab society. However, a small number of sophisticated, culturally aware European tourists are beginning to be attracted to the United Arab Emirates – particularly Dubai and Sharjah – in the winter months, and both business travellers and expatriate workers take advantage of their stay to explore the region. These groups now benefit from the slight decline in business travel (after the boom in the 1970s) as the airports and luxury hotels on the Gulf tend to be underused.

Most travel both within and to the region and further afield is by air, with a comprehensive network of flights serving the lengthy inter-city distances on the peninsula. The region has always been a communications link between the Mediterranean and the Orient, and Bahrain is important as a stop-over for inter-continental flights between Europe and the Far East. It is also becoming an entrepôt and banking centre for the region.

The peninsula's attractions include the coasts of the Persian Gulf and the Red Sea with a number of good beaches and opportunities for water-sports. There are small hill resorts, mineral springs, and archaeological sites in the mountains, which also have the attraction of a cooler climate. The Arab culture itself is an attraction to Western visitors.

Saudi Arabia is important in the Islamic world as it contains the holy cities of Mecca and Medina. The haj, or annual pilgrimage, is performed by over three-quarters of a million Moslems coming from outside Arabia but these are concentrated into a period of a few weeks. The Saudi Government has spent millions of dollars from its oil revenues on highway construction and the expansion of the terminal facilities at Jedda Airport, as the majority of pilgrims come by air rather than use the slow and perhaps dangerous land and sea routes. *Oman* and *North Yemen* have considerable tourist potential due to their scenic variety and cultural heritage, notably in the mountains, along the Batinah coast, and at Sana – the Yemeni capital. In *South Yemen* Aden is a major port of call but the present socialist regime has not encouraged tourism.

Before the revolution *Iran* – ancient Persia – attracted a significant volume of tourism though, with the current severe Islamic fundamentalist regime, few foreign tourists visit the country at present. However, Iran has enormous tourist potential with a long Persian Gulf coastline as well as a northern coast on the Caspian Sea. Inland the Moslem cities of the central plateau traditionally attracted many tourists, particularly Isfahan, Shiraz, and notably Teheran in its spectacular mountain setting.

Iraq has less to offer the tourist. It has a socialist regime and a moderately healthy economy based on its petroleum industry. Its main tourist resources are focused on the ancient civilizations of Mesopotamia – for example the site of Babylon. The cities of Baghdad, Basra and Mosul attract business travellers.

Summary

The countries around the eastern shore of the Mediterranean are known as the Levant to distinguish them from those around the Persian Gulf known as the Middle East. In both these regions tourist development is hampered by war, terrorist activity, and extremist governments. However, the countries of the Levant and the Middle East are close enough to the tourist-generating markets of northern Europe to have developed a sizable tourism industry. Only Cyprus and Turkey have developed beach tourism on any scale, while the countries of Egypt and the Holy Land have developed cultural tourism. The Middle Eastern countries receive a considerable volume of business tourism and the Middle East is now also a major generator of outbound international tourism.

Investment in much of the region has produced an extensive tourist infrastructure with accommodation concentrated both at the coast and in the major cities. Transportation to and within most of the region is good as it lies at the crossroads between Europe, Africa, and the Orient, and new airports have been provided to meet the increased demand for international travel. The region's tourist attractions are varied and range from the beach resorts for both winter and summer tourism, winter sports in the mountains, cultural attractions, and the facilities for business travel offered by the Gulf states.

SEVENTEEN

Asia

LEARNING OBJECTIVES

After reading this chapter, you should be able to:

1 Describe the major physical features and climates of the region and understand their importance for tourism.
2 Recognize that the economies of the countries in the region show many contrasts ranging from advanced Western economies to some of the poorest countries in the world.
3 Appreciate that domestic tourism and recreation are of growing importance in the more prosperous countries of Asia.
4 Recognize that, with the exception of Japan, outbound tourism is limited.
5 Show that inbound tourism is being encouraged by many countries as a source of income, foreign currency, and jobs.
6 Understand that the region is remote from the major tourist-generating areas of the world (with the exception of Japan) and further suffers from comparatively poor infrastructure.
7 Recognize that the tourist appeal of Asia lies in the exotic cultures, languages, and people, as well as in the familiar resources

of beach tourism.
8 Demonstrate a knowledge of the tourist regions, resorts, business centres, and tourist attractions of the region.

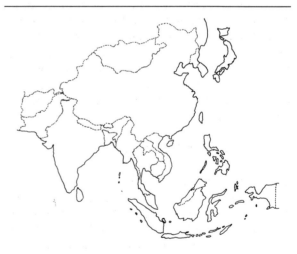

Introduction

The countries of the Indian Subcontinent, Southeast Asia, and the Far East are of great interest to Europeans and North Americans. This is because the traditional way of life of the people is so different with colourful and exotic costumes, foods, and buildings. Religion plays a great part in the everyday life of many of these countries, and the most magnificent buildings and treasures are generally found in temples and shrines rather than in secular buildings. The climates are generally warm, though the Monsoon does disrupt the tourist season, and the landscapes are picturesque, often the result of centuries of patient hand labour.

The governments of most of the Asian countries have begun to realize the importance of tourism, and many have joined co-operative organizations for promoting travel (the Pacific Area Travel Association and the East Asia Travel Association are important here). From the viewpoint of the Western tourist living costs are generally low (Japan is one of the few exceptions) and hotel service is more personalized than in the West, although frequently the provision of infrastructure outside the main tourist areas is inadequate.

The most important countries for inbound tourism are Singapore, Hong Kong, Malaysia, and Thailand, but China's renewal of contacts with the West may alter the situation drastically. With the exception of Japan, the Asian countries themselves generate few tourists, and those who do travel abroad tend to do so within the region. With the rapidly developing economies of Southeast Asia however, demand for tourism is growing – particularly in the business sector. It is convenient to consider Asia in three parts: the Indian Subcontinent; Southeast Asia; and the Far East.

The Indian Subcontinent

The Indian Subcontinent, separated from the rest of Asia by high mountain barriers to the north, consists of the Republic of India, Nepal, Bhutan, Pakistan, Bangladesh, and Afghanistan. With the exception of Afghanistan, almost the whole of the region was under British rule or influence for a century or more. With the ending of the British 'raj' in 1947 the predominantly Moslem areas of the north west and east Bengal were separated from the remainder of India to form Pakistan. Subsequently, in 1971, the eastern portion of Pakistan in turn broke away to become Bangladesh. English is still widely used in official communications because of the many native languages and dialects. In much of the Subcontinent tourism is of limited signi-

ficance, especially in Bangladesh because of the dire economic problems, and in Afghanistan war has severely disrupted the limited amount of overland traffic proceeding over the Khyber Pass into Pakistan and India.

Physically, the subcontinent can be divided into three main regions. The Himalayan mountains and their foothills extend from Bhutan to Afghanistan and rise to over 6000 metres. Because of their altitude the mountains have a much cooler climate than the rest of the subcontinent, but during the Monsoon rainfall in the mountains is often excessive with Cherrapunji in Assam holding the world's highest rainfall record (over 1000 cm). The second region consists of the plains of Northern India through which flow the great rivers Indus and Ganges. The plains contain most of the historic cities of India and the main tourist centres. The climate can be excessively dry, although generally warm in winter, and scorching hot from April to June before the arrival of the Monsoon. The initial relief provided by the onset of the rains is followed by months of sweltering weather with high temperatures and humidity. The third region – Peninsular, or Southern, India consists of a great plateau of volcanic rocks known as the Deccan. It is separated from the narrow coastal plains by the mountains of the Western and Eastern Ghats. Scenically this is a very attractive area, with a climate which is hot and humid throughout the year.

The rapidly growing population of *India* is a largely rural one, which exceeded 700 million in the early 1980s. Over a third live in the North Western States and many millions live in the large cities of Bombay, Calcutta, Delhi, and Madras. Well over half of the population are below subsistence level, but a sizable middle class generates a substantial demand for domestic travel. Often this takes the form of pilgrimages. Foreign travel is less significant, partly due to exchange controls.

By the early 1980s, India was receiving over a million foreign visitors, but there were annual fluctuations caused by political upheavals and national emergencies. However, given India's huge tourism potential there is scope for further growth in arrivals. The main generating markets are India's Southeast Asian neighbours, Western

Europe, North America, the Middle East, and Japan. Many Americans are particularly attracted by the 'other worldliness' of India, as exemplified by its ashrams, or centres of religious life. Many UK arrivals are, in fact, either travellers resident in Asia or East Africa, or returning Indian immigrants who make scant use of tourist facilities. Visitors to India have one of the longest stays in the world, at around one month. This is because ethnic Indians stay for long periods with friends and relatives, but other foreign visitors also often stay for three or four weeks. The most popular season to visit India is October to December when the weather is at its best, but there is a steady flow of business travellers throughout the year. Given a limited amount of foreign travel among the Indian population, tourism earnings are a useful supplement to the Indian balance of trade, and tourist expenditure benefits the Indian domestic economy by directly sustaining one and a half million jobs in a labour intensive industry.

Most foreign visitors arrive by air to the three major international airports at Delhi, Bombay, and Calcutta. Growth in air traffic has led to expansion of airport facilities at Bombay and Delhi and with liberalization of aviation policy further expansion is expected with tourist charters direct to resorts. Indian Airways operate the internal flights, so essential in a country the size of India, and Air India handle international flights. There has been a growth in the number of tourists who arrive overland, despite political unrest in the Middle East. Internal long-distance communications are good with a comprehensive railway network, operating quickly and cheaply between major cities. The system still has many steam trains and is a tourist attraction in itself. Tourists can cover the country by rail in relative luxury using special tickets. There are also over one million kilometres of passable roads.

The seasonal concentration of visits (over one-third) into the final quarter of the year does create occupancy problems for Indian accommodation. A major construction programme has boosted the number of hotel rooms, though there is still a shortage in middle-price ranges. The top-class hotels are concentrated in Delhi, Calcutta, and Agra, but also include converted palaces, formerly occupied by India's princes or rajahs. Many tourist and 'dak' bungalows and private guest houses are available. Camping facilities are being developed along the overland routes and lodges are available in the wildlife areas.

In 1967 India set up the Ministry of Civil Aviation and Tourism under a Cabinet Minister and began to include tourism investment in its five-year plans. Two years earlier the India Tourism Development Corporation (ITDC) was formed to provide infrastructure. It now owns and runs hotels, resorts, restaurants, and transport businesses. As well as supporting many tourist developments through the ITDC, the government also provides financial incentives to domestic and foreign companies to develop tourism. However, in a country with many problems, tourist development has to take a low priority, especially when the authorities realise that the great majority of their population will not be able to afford to use the facilities.

India's three and a quarter million square kilometres offer a unique tourist blend of ancient cities and monuments, spectacular scenery, wildlife reserves, beaches, and mountain resorts. There are four main regions. Firstly, the North India region is rich in history with ancient cities full of architectural and cultural attractions. Delhi is visited by most tourists as it is a major gateway and the beginning of one of the 'classical tourist circuits' (Delhi – Agra (for the Taj Mahal) – Jaipur (the pink city) – Udaipur – Bombay); it is also an important business travel city with a purpose-built conference centre. In the far north there is some winter sports development in Kashmir at Gulmarg. There are also several 'hill stations', or mountain resorts in the foothills of the Himalayas, set up by the British rulers in the nineteenth century, where they could escape the heat of the plains. These resorts are now largely the preserve of the Indian middle class but retain their English character; the most important are Simla and Darjeeling.

The second major gateway is Bombay in Western India, an important business centre close to the newly developed beach resorts along the lagoons of the Malabar coast. Of these Goa is a major tourist

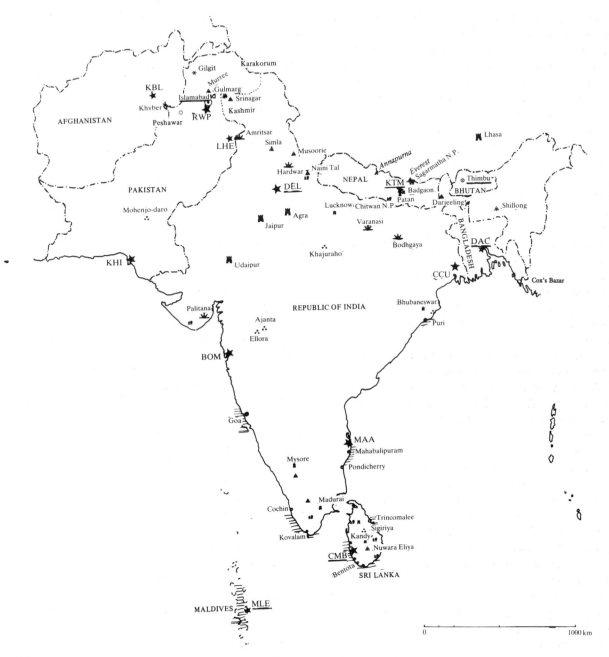

Figure 17.1 *Major tourist resources in the Indian Subcontinent*

centre with a Portuguese heritage. The East India region is centred on Calcutta, the one-time capital of the Raj, an overdeveloped metropolis with few attractions. Within easy reach are the beach resorts on the Bay of Bengal and the religious centres of Orissa. Madras is the gateway to South India, where tours of the multi-storey temples at Mahabapurilam and Madurai begin. Despite this wealth of tourist possibilities the majority of foreign visitors do not stray from the 'golden triangle' of Agra,

Delhi, and Jaipur, or the shopping and beach circuit of Bombay and Goa.

Pakistan has been less successful than India in developing its tourist potential. In part this is due to Islamic fundamentalism and border restrictions. The northern part of the country can offer winter sports at Gilgit and the spectacular scenery of Karakorum Highway (the world's highest road). Karachi is the main gateway and along with Rawalpindi attracts business travellers. Lahore and Peshawar have much greater appeal to cultural tourists.

The Himalayan Kingdom of *Nepal* remained closed to visitors until the late 1950s. It contains eight of the world's highest mountain peaks, including Everest and Annapurna. Although the numbers of foreign visitors are relatively small, trekkers and mountain climbers have made a major impact, notably around Everest. Here a national park has been designated to protect forest resources, enlisting the help of local Sherpa villagers. In the subtropical foothills lies the Tiger Tops wildlife reserve. Cultural attractions also abound, especially at Bhadgaon and Patan near Katmandu.

The tropical islands of the Indian Ocean are long-haul destinations attracting in particular Europeans seeking winter sunshine. *Sri Lanka*, with its good air communications and nearness to India, began to develop tourism with the establishment of the Ceylon Tourist Board in 1966. It not only has some of the finest beaches in the world, but also abundant wildlife and a wealth of cultural attractions, especially at Kandy, the ancient mountain capital, and in the art treasures of Anuradhapura and Sigiriya. The Ceylon Tourist Board has developed hotels of international standard to supplement the network of rest houses established under British colonial rule. The main holiday region extends from Colombo, the capital and international gateway, through the resort of Hendaba on its lagoon, to Bentota on the south coast. There has been some development on the dry east coast around the port of Trincomalee. The main problems are deficient infrastructure and social tensions between the Sinhalese and the Tamil minority.

To the south west of Sri Lanka, lie the hundreds of tiny coral islands that make up the *Maldives*. Some forty resort hotels have been built in the traditional style, within boating distance of the harbour and airport at Male, the capital. West Germans in particular are attracted by the superb underwater wildlife and unspoiled lifestyle of the islanders.

Southeast Asia

This part of Asia, extending from Burma to the Philippines, has a culture which is a blend of that of India to the west and China to the north. The whole area, with the exception of Thailand, was under colonial rule until after the Second World War; the British ruled Singapore, Malaysia, Brunei, and Burma; the French – Indo-China; the Dutch – Indonesia, and the Spanish occupied the Philippines for three centuries until 1898 when they handed over to the USA. In recent years much of the region has suffered political upheaval. Tourism has been severely restricted in Vietnam, Laos, and Cambodia (Kampuchea) since the Communist take-over of the 1970s and Burma, potentially one of the richest Asian countries, has given tourism low priority under its socialist regime. Nevertheless, Burma and Indo-China have considerable tourism potential, as Pagan, Mandalay and Angkor Wat rank among the world's greatest historical monuments.

A number of countries in the region have joined together to form ASEAN (Association of Southeast Asian Nations), which promotes co-operation in all spheres of economic activity. Indonesia, the Philippines, Singapore, Thailand, and Malaysia are members, and although they compete for visitors, they each see the advantages of joint promotion aimed at the main tourist-generating markets. Economically, there are wide contrasts in the region. Tiny Singapore's per capita income approaches that of some European countries, while its giant neighbour Indonesia is one of the least developed nations in the world and one of the most populous.

All the ASEAN countries are in the tropics and experience warm to hot weather throughout the year, with frequent but brief torrential downpours.

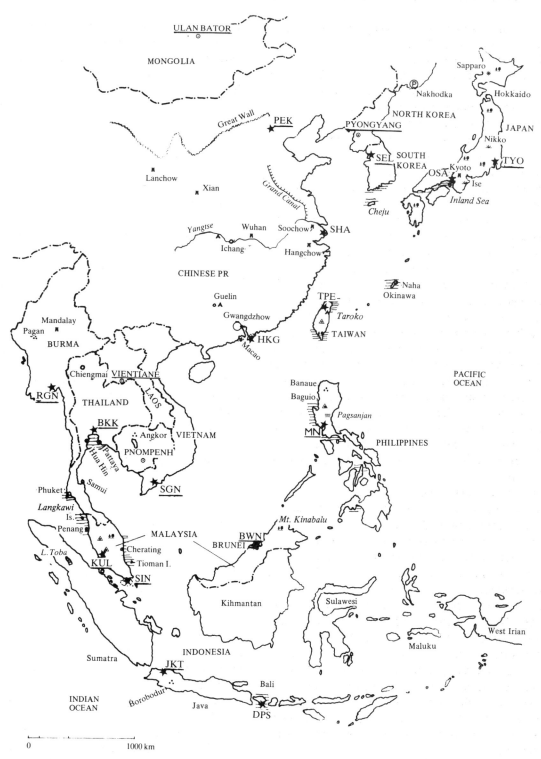

Figure 17.2 *Major tourist resources in East Asia*

The northern parts of Thailand and the Philippines have a clearly defined cool season. Mountain resorts are important for domestic tourism as they provide relief from the heat, though their development is hampered by poor road access. More important in vying for the international market are the beach resort developments on the palm-fringed coasts of the region. These are either based on established towns or cities (as at Penang); or they have been planned on a comprehensive scale (as at Langkawi). This development reflects the fact that tourism is booming in the region, particularly travel between the ASEAN countries. However, some countries such as the Philippines and Thailand, tax their residents heavily if they travel abroad. The main inbound markets are Japan, Australia, Western Europe, and the USA.

Singapore is often regarded as the gateway to Southeast Asia. Its cosmopolitan lifestyle and efficient administration offers Westerners a painless glimpse of 'instant Asia'. This small island republic (only 580 square kilometres), due to its geographical location between two oceans, has become one of the largest seaports in the world, and it is also a major focus of air routes. The national carrier is Singapore Airlines, who work closely with the Singapore Tourist Promotion Board. A convention bureau has also been established to promote Singapore's World Trade Centre and facilities such as the new Raffles City Convention centre. Singapore attracted three million tourists anually in the early 1980s, even though its tourist attractions are all man-made. These include zoos, wildlife parks, and the all-important shopping centres.

Singapore is a good base for visiting *Malaysia*. This country is a federation of several culturally distinct entities; Sabah and Sarawak on the island of Kalimantan (Borneo) are separated from the Malaya peninsula by 1000 kilometres of sea. West Malaysia in turn is divided into many sultanates which preserve their traditional pageantry, although the capital Kuala Lumpur lacks historical interest. Over two million foreign visitors annually came to peninsular Malaysia in the early 1980s, the vast majority from other ASEAN countries. The rail link with Thailand is now much less important than the air services operated by the Malaysian Airline System (MAS), with Kuala Lumpur the major hub. Tourism promotion and development is handled by the entrepreneurial Malaysian Tourist Development Corporation.

Peninsular or West Malaysia is by far the most popular region particularly the free port of Penang, with its beaches and bazaars, the old Portuguese city of Malacca, and latterly resort development on the Langkawi islands. The beaches along the east coast of the peninsula deserve to be better known internationally. Inland is the Genting Highlands complex with its hotels, casino, and funicular railway, as well as the Batu caves and jungle-covered mountainous Taman Negara National Park. Turning to East Malaysia, Sabah and Sarawak are much less developed but are attracting the more adventurous holidaymaker who is interested in the lifestyle of the Dyak tribes and the forested mountains of the interior. Neighbouring *Brunei* derives most of its considerable wealth from oil rather than tourism.

To the south of Malaysia lie the islands of *Indonesia*, extending over a distance of almost 5000 kilometres from Sumatra in the west to Timor and New Guinea in the east. Indonesia is one of the largest countries in the world with well over one hundred and fifty million inhabitants. Much of the economic development has taken place on densely populated Java where mountain land has been brought under cultivation by an elaborate system of terracing. In contrast Irian Jaya (Western New Guinea) is virtually undeveloped. Indonesia has begun to realize its great tourism potential, especially with the Australian market nearby, and it has restructured its Directorate General of Tourism in a drive to attract conventions, exhibitions, and incentive travel. The main international gateway is Jakarta and air transport (the national carrier is Garuda) holds together this vast and fragmented nation. Indonesia contains a great variety of scenery, much of it volcanic, and it is rich in cultural and historic monuments. On Java, the temple of Borobudur is the largest Buddhist edifice in the world. Bali, linked by air to Jakarta, is the most important holiday island with its surfing beaches, temples, dances and festivals, and easy-going lifestyle. Sumatra offers interesting lake and mountain scenery and the folklore of tribes such as the Batak. The outlying islands, such as Sulawesi (Celebes), Kalimantan (Borneo), and Maluku (Moluccas) see relatively few tourists; Sulawesi is particularly interesting as it contains the Toraja people as well as being a botanist's paradise.

The *Philippines* is another populous island nation with more than fifty million inhabitants. Like Indonesia it is made up of many ethnic groups but here Roman Catholicism and the English language provide a unifying factor and Western influences are strong, particularly in Manila. In the early 1980s around a million foreign tourists visited the islands annually, mainly from Japan and the USA. As in Thailand there has been concern over the dubious morality of some of this tourism. Tourism promotion is the responsibility of the Ministry of Tourism, while tourism development is handled by the Philippines Tourism Authority. Most of the investment has been in the Metro-Manila conurbation and in the development of fifteen beach resorts of international standard. Manila is now an international conference venue. As in Indonesia, air transport is vital with good international and domestic connections. However, road transport and the inter-island ferries can be slow and uncomfortable. The Philippines are mostly of volcanic origin and on Luzon there is attractive mountain and coastal scenery within easy reach of Manila, although the famous rice terraces of Banaue are less accessible.

Of all the countries in Southeast Asia, *Thailand* (Siam) has probably done most to encourage visits from Europe, North America, Japan, and Australia. With more than two million visitors annually in the early 1980s, tourism is the largest foreign currency earner after rice and rubber. The majority (75 per cent) of tourists arrive by air. Bangkok is served by over forty scheduled international airlines and it has good western-style hotels, restaurants, and night clubs. Yet despite acute traffic congestion and pollution, it still retains its charms as the 'Venice of the East' – so called because of the numerous canals with their floating markets. There are numerous royal palaces and Buddhist temples, aspects of folklore such as Thai

dancing and boxing, the traditional silk industry, and uninhibited nightlife. A few hours drive from Bangkok lies fashionable Pattaya Beach, Thailand's most lively and developed resort. In the south of Thailand another beach resort is the island of Phuket which has been developed on a virgin site on a massive scale. In the mountainous northern part of the country the main centre is Chiengmai which can be reached by air, road, or rail from the capital. Air transport has opened up much of Thailand for tourism, particularly now that new international airports have opened away from Bangkok. This can only assist the Tourism Authority of Thailand's desire to spread the load of tourism away from Bangkok and Pattaya.

The Far East

The lands around the East China Sea and the Sea of Japan include some of the world's largest modern cities, as well as some of its oldest civilizations. Japan and South Korea have become important destinations for the business traveller and the culturally-inclined tourist. However, China has now emerged as a potentially formidable competitor in this field. In contrast Mongolia is still largely a nomadic society, where a visit to a traditional yurt features on the traveller's itinerary.

Japan is the leading industrial nation of Asia with an economy based on overseas trade. Located on the eastern fringe of the continent it consists of four main islands – Honshu, Hokkaido, Kyushu, and Shikoku. The Japanese archipelago offers considerable contrasts in climate and scenery. The west coast of Honshu, the largest island has a continental climate which is affected in winter by blasts of cold air from Siberia, whereas the east coast is influenced by the warm Kuro Siwo current. Hokkaido in the north has a severe climate which resembles that of Eastern Canada while Okinawa, 2000 kilometres to the south, enjoys subtropical warmth.

Japan's total area is only 370,000 square kilometres but with 120 million inhabitants population density is high, and exacerbated by the fact that over 80 per cent of the country is mountainous and geologically unstable. Over three-quarters of the population live on Honshu, with 15 per cent of them living in the major cities of Tokyo and Yokohama, Osaka, and Nagoya. Japan is the most prosperous country in Eastern Asia with incomes approaching those of the USA and Western Europe, and it is the largest generator of tourists in the region.

The concept of an annual holiday is only slowly being accepted in Japan which is still largely a work-oriented society. Japanese employees are entitled to about two weeks paid holiday but government employees have four weeks. Despite attempts to reduce working hours, many still work a six-day week and long hours often through choice. Holidays are frequently sponsored by industrial corporations for their employees and resemble outings. Japanese tourists are gregarious by nature and accept a degree of regimentation in their holiday activities. The domestic holiday market accounted for almost 150 million trips in the early 1980s, with holidays and recreation accounting for 90 per cent of trips, and business or VFR the remainder. The traditional shrines and hot spring resorts continue to be very popular with family groups, although the Western influence is evident in the rapid growth of skiing, golf, and water-sports. Outbound travel has shown phenomenal growth since 1964 when restrictions were lifted. Over four million Japanese travelled abroad in the early 1980s, again the majority for pleasure but a significant minority on business. Over half go to destinations in Asia – many to Taiwan, South Korea, and Hong Kong, around a third go to the USA (particularly to honeymoon in Hawaii or Guam), and the remainder go to Europe or Australasia. However, with limited holiday entitlement, the Japanese overseas only stay on average, eight days, yet their spending leaves the travel account consistently in debt.

Inbound travel stands at around one-third of the volume of outbound travel. This is due to Japan's relative isolation from the traditional generating markets of Western Europe and the USA, making a trip to Japan expensive. However, despite the fact that many of Japan's nearer neighbours are relatively undeveloped, inbound tourism has grown steadily since 1975, in part due to a growth in visits from Japan's increasingly affluent neighbours of Taiwan, South Korea, and Hong Kong. Southeast Asia accounts for half of all visitors to Japan with a further quarter from the USA.

For domestic travel, road and rail is most commonly used. There is an extensive network of railways (20,000 kilometres) including the famous 'bullet train' between Tokyo and Osaka. A comprehensive road network and many ferries between the islands are also available. Most foreign visitors arrive by air, the majority through Tokyo, but other airports are growing in importance, particularly Osaka and Okinawa (which handles visitors from Taiwan). The busiest air routes are from Southeast Asia, Hawaii, and the USA. Japan Airlines fly about one-third of the passenger capacity and are actively involved in the tourism industry in Japan.

Visitors can stay in Western-style hotels or in 'ryokan' – Japanese-style inns where traditional food, clothing and furniture of tatami matting are customary. Japan's hotel rooms serve both the international and domestic market (where medium-priced hotels are popular and are growing in smaller towns, as well as in the major cities). Ryokan are increasingly sought after by foreign tourists. In the domestic market subsidized family travel villages and lodges are popular. Government aid is available for construction and extension of accommodation.

Responsibility for tourism lies with the Department of Tourism, part of the Ministry of Transport. It supervises the Japan National Tourist Organization (JNTO) which promotes tourism and projects a 'fair and realistic image of Japan' to increase international understanding of the country, particularly amongst the world's business community.

Japan's tourism resources are a unique mixture of the traditional and the modern, successfully adopting western industrialization without sacrificing cultural identity. Despite severe pollution problems, much has been done to conserve the landscape, including the designation of twenty-seven national parks in the most scenic areas (such as the Japan Alps, the Fujiyama district near Tokyo with Mount Fuji and the lakes, and around the Inland Sea). The national parks cover 5 per cent of the total area and there are also over 300 other reserves and designated landscapes, including the ancient cities. In such a densely populated country, tourism has been driven to the forests, mountains, and coasts where competition for land use is less intense. Even so, pressures on the coast have led to conservation measures and the designation of marine parks.

The most important centres for foreign visitors are the cities – notably Tokyo, Osaka, Nagasaki, and Kyoto – the ancient capital. All these cities are within reach of Japan's scenic and cultural resources such as the religious centres of Nikko, Ise, and Nara. The most scenic region is probably the Inland Sea between western Honshu and Shikoku, studded with picturesque islands and numerous Buddhist temples. Less well known is Hokkaido, which is now linked to Honshu by the fifty-four kilometre Seikan tunnel. Heavy snowfalls encourage skiing and in 1972 Sapporo was the venue for the Winter Olympics.

As in Japan, the populations of South Korea and Taiwan (which regards itself as the legitimate Republic of China) are increasingly urbanized, and thriving economies based on electronics and ship-building, allied to a recent lifting of travel restrictions, have created a boom in foreign travel, as well as a significant domestic tourism industry. In the early 1980s South Korea and Taiwan contributed a million foreign tourists, mainly travelling between the two countries, to Japan, or to Hong Kong. Around a third of all travel is for business purposes. Inbound tourism has also assisted in the economic transformation of these two countries as both are within easy reach of Hong Kong and Japan.

Taiwan offers spectacular scenery at the Taroko Gorge, and some of the highest cliffs in the world on the east coast, as well as preserving much of the traditional Chinese art and culture. *South Korea* with its much colder continental climate can offer winter sports in the mountains of the interior. Although there are attractive beaches in the south of the country, the main attraction of South Korea lies in its cultural heritage. The choice of Seoul as the venue for the 1988 Olympic Games should do

much to boost South Korea as a destination, once the problem of lack of accommodation has been resolved. The Olympics may also benefit Communist *North Korea* which has previously closed its doors to foreign tourists.

Tourism in the *People's Republic of China* (PRC) is in its infancy, although few countries have such potential: great scenic variety in a landmass the size of the USA; the world's oldest civilization; and the fact that it contains almost a quarter of the world's population. After the 1949 Communist revolution the country was virtually closed to Western visitors. In 1978 after the collapse of the 'Cultural Revolution' the so-called 'Bamboo Curtain' was lifted and inbound tourism was henceforth encouraged. This was part of the campaign to make the Chinese more receptive to Western ideas and technology and also to generate foreign exchange needed to modernize the economy. By 1981, one and a half million foreign tourists were recorded, many entering the PRC through Hong Kong or Macau.

Needless to say this phenomenal growth in tourism has not been without growing pains. Pricing, service standards, and a lack of trained personnel remain a problem, as does the adjustment of a socialist, centrally planned economy to one trying to accommodate enterprise and market forces. Tourist infrastructure is rapidly being provided – by 1983 accommodation stood at around 100,000 beds with care being taken to preserve traditional building styles in accommodation. At the same time well over one hundred towns and regions have been opened up for tourism, transportation modernized and airports expanded. The central government organization for tourism is the General Administration of Travel and Tourism which has a virtual monopoly of the development and management of tourism in the PRC, though some devolution to the provinces is evident. Outbound tourism is still not encouraged, except for the purpose of business or study, however, the Chinese do travel extensively within their own country, despite the low earning power of the average worker.

Most travel in China is by rail or air, as the road network is rudimentary. In such a vast country there are considerable contrasts in climate, scenery and lifestyles – including cuisine – between North and South China, and also between the sparsely populated western provinces such as Tibet, where the people differ fundamentally in culture from the 'Han' Chinese. North China with its cold dry winters and rather barren landscapes of windblown loess deposits is the historic core of the country, centred on Beijing (formerly Peking). The Chinese capital contains the former Imperial City and provides easy access by a fifty kilometre rail link to the Great Wall and Xian, with its ancient tombs. The scenery of Sichuan and South China is much more luxuriant, the climate is warm and humid and large areas of forest still remain in the mountains. The gorges of the Yangtze River near Ichang, and the karst mountains around Gueilin are particularly impressive. Also featured on most itineraries are Soochow and Hangchow, renowned as cultural centres among the Chinese. The great ports of Shanghai and Gwangdzhou (Canton), which handled considerable trade with the West in the past, are important centres for business travel. The western provinces are now accessible via Beijing to groups of more adventurous foreign tourists; hotels have been opened in Lhasa with its former monasteries and palace of the Dalai Lama, and along the 'Silk Road', the overland trade route which linked China to the outside world centuries ago.

In the past, foreigners have been able to sample traditional Chinese culture more easily by visiting the British Crown Colony of *Hong Kong*. Hong Kong developed in the nineteenth century as a naval base on one of the finest harbours in Asia. It consists of several islands at the mouth of the Pearl river and the peninsula of Kowloon and the New Territories, which are linked by ferries, tunnels, and highways. It has become a great industrial centre due to the influx of millions of refugees from the PRC, its freewheeling private enterprise economy, and its geographical location at the focus of air and shipping routes. With a population of more than five million and only 1000 square kilometres, the tiny colony has one of the highest population densities in the world. Rising education and living standards make Hong Kong an important source of

tourists to the rest of the Asian and Pacific region, but with some three million foreign visitors tourism makes a significant contribution to the economy. The main markets are Southeast Asia, Japan, and the USA. After 1997 Hong Kong will be reunited with China and it is uncertain what effect this will have on the tourism industry. Inbound tourism has been aided by the availability of charter flights into Kai Tak airport, and a well developed business travel market. Tourism is promoted by the Hong Kong Tourist Association who have remedied an acute accommodation shortage. The primary tourist attractions are the inexpensive shopping, floating restaurants, and colourful nightlife. Except on the outlying islands beaches are crowded and little space is available for recreation. The small Portuguese colony of *Macau* 120 kilometres to the west can be reached by hydrofoil. Here the attractions are gambling and the Portuguese ambience of cobbled streets and leafy boulevards which offer a peaceful contrast to hectic Hong Kong.

Summary

Asia contains some of the most populous countries in the world, as well as countries at varying stages of economic development. The region is remote from the major tourist-generating areas of the world (with the exception of Japan) but many countries are developing an inbound tourism industry as a source of income, foreign currency, and jobs. The entry of China into the tourism market may change the situation considerably. Domestic tourism and recreation are becoming important in the more prosperous countries, and outbound tourism is also growing, particularly from the established market of Japan. Business travel is important throughout the region.

Apart from the better established tourism industries of say, Japan or Thailand, infrastructure is of a comparatively low standard, though many countries are remedying this state of affairs, mainly by improvements in airport facilities and the development of self-contained resort complexes.

The attractions of Asia are rooted in the exotic cultures and landscapes. Of particular note are the classic tourist excursion circuits in India; the beauty and gentle way of life of the Indian Ocean islands; the cities, culture, and landscapes of Japan and the Far East; shopping in Singapore and Hong Kong; and the 'sleeping giant' of tourism in the region – China – with so much to offer the tourist.

EIGHTEEN

Australasia

LEARNING OBJECTIVES

After reading this chapter, you should be able to:

1 Describe the major physical regions and climate of Australasia and understand their importance for tourism.
2 Understand that Australia and New Zealand are part of the developed Western world while the Pacific Islands are mainly developing Third World countries.
3 Understand the social and economic background of the region and its influence on tourism and travel patterns.
4 Recognize that due to the distance from tourist-generating regions, domestic tourism dominates in much of the region.
5 Appreciate the impact of tourism on the region.
6 Demonstrate a knowledge of the tourist regions, resorts, business centres, and tourist attractions of the region.

Introduction

Australia, New Zealand, and the islands of the Pacific east of Indonesia and the Philippines, form a separate geographical entity called Australasia. An alternative name 'Oceania' is also appropriate as the constituent islands are insignificant by comparison with the vastness of the surrounding ocean, the only landmass of considerable extent being the 'island continent' of Australia. The total population is small compared to that of neighbouring Southeast Asia – well under thirty million – and there is generally less pressure on resources. Much of Australasia is economically and politically part of the developed Western world. However, except for Australia and New Zealand, the region consists mainly of island 'mini-states' with small populations and limited economic resources. Most of these have become politically independent only since the 1960s and some of the smaller islands are still governed by France, Britain, or the USA.

The Pacific Area Travel Association (PATA) represents all the countries in the region and believes that Australasia will attract considerable growth in international tourism by the end of the century, by virtue of its favourable climate, unspoiled scenery, and political stability. The market potential is certainly present. Several countries bordering the Pacific are currently experiencing rapid economic growth, with the most impressive developments taking place in Japan and in California. Since 1970 Australia and New Zealand have developed close trading links with the USA and their Asian neighbours – especially Japan.

This pattern of trade is bound to result in an increased volume of air traffic across the Pacific; indeed the sheer size of the ocean (12,000 kilometres at its widest) means that air transport plays a vital role in the economy of the region and the peoples of Australasia are very aviation minded.

Australia

For more than a century Australia, and New Zealand, have been the destinations for large numbers of emigrants, chiefly from the British Isles. Until recently Australia was not important as a holiday destination, the great majority of visitors being business or VFR travellers. This situation is now changing, partly as a result of the promotional efforts of both the Australian Tourist Commission and the Australian state governments, and more competitive air fares. In the mid 1980s the 'island continent' received for the first time more than one million visitors and tourism receipts currently account for 5 per cent of all exports of goods and services.

In area Australia is as large as the continental USA (without Alaska) or Europe (excluding Rus-

sia). Not surprisingly the country has a Federal system of government, not unlike that of Canada, in which the six states and the Northern Territory enjoy much freedom to manage their own affairs, including the development and regulation of tourism. The Commonwealth of Australia has great tourism potential with a coastline over 36,000 kilometres in length including some of the world's finest beaches. Over a third of Australia is desert, consisting mainly of expanses of gravel or sand dunes with a sparse covering of scrub vegetation. The monotony of this landscape is occasionally relieved by inselbergs, isolated hills rising abruptly from the surrounding plains. The most famous example is Ayers Rock, nine kilometres in circumference and over 300 metres high. Much of the remainder of the 'outback' is semi-arid country where rivers are usually just a succession of pools or 'billabongs'. In some areas tourists can prospect for gold or gemstones, while four-wheel-drive vehicle safaris allow the more adventurous to visit remoter areas away from the all-weather roads. High mountains are confined to the eastern part of the country, elsewhere the land consists of vast plateaux and lowland basins. The most interesting natural resources of Australia are the plants – mainly drought resistant eucalyptus or 'gums', and the animals – marsupial species which are only native to the island continent. To protect this heritage a large number of national parks have been designated.

Most of Australia, with the exception of Tasmania, lies within tropical or sub-tropical latitudes, so that winter cold is rarely a problem. The desert interior has an extreme climate; in winter pleasantly warm days are followed by nights with temperatures dropping below 0°C. The northernmost region of Australia around Darwin experiences a tropical monsoon type of climate with a rainy season between December and May, accompanied by high temperatures and humidity. The great majority of Australians live in the south eastern part of the country and enjoy a warm temperate climate, which in general is ideal for outdoor recreation. However, summer temperatures frequently exceed 40°C due to winds from the desert interior, which bring the risk of bush fires to the city. Snow is almost unknown except in Tasmania, and in the Australian Alps where it provides good skiing conditions from June to September. Perhaps the best climate is around Perth where summers are dry but not excessively warm due to a constant sea breeze.

The population of Australia passed fifteen million in the early 1980s and is concentrated into a few large cities – Sydney and Melbourne each with around three million inhabitants account for 40 per cent of the population. Other major centres include Brisbane (1,100,000 inhabitants), Adelaide (900,000), and Perth (700,000). Canberra (200,000) is a relatively small city, though it is the Federal capital. The urban character of Australia's population has an important influence on the patterns of tourism which have developed.

A developed and diversified economy means that Australians enjoy a high standard of living. The ownership of motor vehicles approaches North American levels and the effects are seen in suburban sprawl around the major cities. Participation in outdoor activities is high by European standards. The most popular participant sports are tennis, swimming, sailing, and surfing. Sports facilities are excellent and spectator sports include football, cricket, and horseracing. Gambling is also popular, with casinos in Tasmania and Northern Territory producing considerable revenue.

Australians take each year, on average, at least two pleasure trips involving a stay away from home, and 50 per cent of these are classed as main holidays. The majority of holidays are in December and January, mostly to beach resorts in the south east. During the winter months there is a smaller but much more concentrated migration to the semi-tropical beaches of Queensland and large numbers also head for the ski slopes of the Australian Alps, while others seek the unspoiled desert scenery around Alice Springs.

Australia is the largest generator of tourism in the Southern Hemisphere. Expenditure on overseas travel, excluding fares, was 50 per cent more than that received from foreign visitors. The majority (70 per cent) of Australian tourists abroad are residents of the two most prosperous states, New South Wales and Victoria, which between them contain 60 per cent of the population. Despite the high costs involved, large numbers of Australians visit Europe on holidays extending over two months or more, during which several countries may be visited. They include a high proportion of young people combining a European tour with work experience, some travelling overland from Singapore via India and the Middle East. Australians are equally attracted to the Pacific Islands for winter sunshine and to New Zealand where the skiing conditions are acknowledged as superior.

The tourism industry in Australia caters in the main for the large domestic demand, and until recently little attention was paid to the needs of foreign visitors. Change has come about partly as a result of the influx of large numbers of emigrants from southern and eastern Europe, and to a lesser extent from Asia. These 'New Australians' have greatly improved standards in the hotel and catering industry as well as expanding the range of entertainments on offer in their adopted cities.

Only a small percentage of foreign visitors to Australia come on inclusive tours, while over half of those from Britain are in the VFR category. A growing number of tourists come from Japan and the USA. The Japanese are mainly attracted to the resorts of the North Queensland coast while the Americans feel an affinity with the pioneering spirit of Australia and are most likely to take a touring holiday.

The great majority of foreign visitors to Australia arrive in Sydney or Melbourne and few travel beyond the south eastern part of the country to take advantage of the 'See Australia' fares offered by the major domestic airlines. Providing adequate transport in such a vast, sparsely populated country is a problem. The journey across the continent from Perth to Sydney (3300 kilometres) involves a two hour time change, a five hour flight, or a journey by train or bus lasting three days. The Australian rail system is not a viable alternative to flying as the network is incomplete and interrupted by changes of gauge at state boundaries. An exception is the 'Indian Pacific' express which allows direct travel from Sydney to Perth.

Sydney has a better climate, a more spectacular setting, and a more varied nightlife than its rival Melbourne. This capital of New South Wales has developed around one of the world's finest harbours and the beaches of the Pacific are within easy reach of hydrofoil or ferry. Attractions include the famous suspension bridge across the harbour and the controversial Opera House. The best known of Sydney's beaches is Bondi, with its superb conditions for surfing; but since the strong tidal surges can be dangerous many families prefer the more sheltered beaches of Port Jackson. Within easy reach of the city are the gorges of the Hawkesbury river, the Hunter Valley vineyards, and the forested ridges, caves, and waterfalls around Katoomba in the Blue Mountains.

From Sydney a scenic coastal route leads northwards into Queensland. The area fifty kilometres south of Brisbane, known as the 'Gold Coast' is the most popular holiday area for Australians. Except for the mountains rising a short distance inland, the semi-tropical climate, fine beaches, and amusement parks produce an environment similar to Florida. There is a good deal of badly planned, commercialized development outside Surfer's Paradise. Australia's unique tourists attraction, the Great Barrier Reef, begins 350 kilometres north of Brisbane and extends 2000 kilometres to Cape York. Here opportunities for scuba diving are unequalled elsewhere. Between the reef and the coast lies an enormous sheltered lagoon which is dotted with hundreds of islands. Some of the islands have been developed as exclusive holiday resorts with marinas, golf courses, and other sports facilities, while others cater more for campers. Pollution and over-fishing are problems on the more popular islands with consequent danger to the reef ecosystem; to remedy this some areas have been designated as nature reserves. The ports of the Queensland coast, notably Cairns and Townsville, are the starting point of excursions to the reef and off-shore islands. Sugar plantations and the forests of the Atherton Tableland provide the main interest away from the coastal resorts.

Melbourne is more conveniently placed than Sydney for touring the Australian Alps, the picturesque Victoria coast, and the Murray river – Australia's only navigable waterway. Melbourne rivals Sydney as the commercial capital of the country, with a less flamboyant lifestyle than Sydney. Melbourne has an equally wide range of cultural and sporting attractions and is almost as cosmopolitan as Sydney with large Italian and Greek communities.

The small island state of Tasmania lies 400 kilometres to the south of Melbourne, across the Bass Strait. With its mild oceanic climate and perpetually green countryside, Tasmania contrasts with the rest of the country. The small resorts along the north coast (such as Stanley) are particularly attractive for senior citizens escaping the summer heat on the mainland. Inland there is mountain and lake scenery in the Lake St Clair-Cradle Mountain National Park. The south west of the island receives the heaviest rainfall in Australia and is covered by barely explored rain forest.

Adelaide and Perth, despite their importance as port cities and state capitals, are not as well placed as Sydney and Melbourne to attract foreign visitors. Adelaide, South Australia's 'festival city' is close to the vineyards of the Barossa Valley and the scenic Flinders Mountains. Perth has surfing beaches fronting the Indian Ocean and is a good base for exploring the West Australian outback.

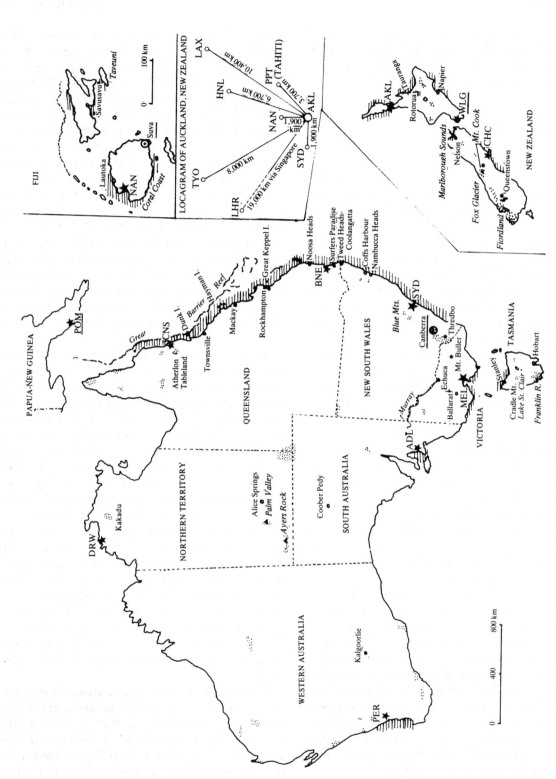

Figure 18.1 *Major tourist resources in Australia, New Zealand, and Fiji*

Darwin is the largest city of the 'Top End', Australia's tropical northlands with their game-rich grasslands and reserves on which the Australian aborigines continue their traditional lifestyle.

New Zealand

Australia and New Zealand are often associated in people's minds, but the Tasman Sea separating them is 1900 kilometres wide, and scenically they are very different. Except for the Maori minority the New Zealanders are predominantly of British origin. The New Zealand Government was one of the first to recognize the importance of tourism, setting up an official tourist organization in 1901. Tourism currently accounts for 5 per cent of the country's foreign exchange earnings and over 400,000 foreign visitors arrive each year, compared to only 100,000 before 1970. This growth has been achieved by successful promotion and development of the nation's resources, and in spite of the remoteness of this small island-nation from the world's major trade routes and centres of population.

Most of New Zealand's 270,000 square kilometres is hilly or mountainous and the country's greatest tourist asset is the beauty and variety of its scenery, within a small land area. The two large islands that make up the bulk of New Zealand offer quite different environments. Much of North Island consists of a volcanic plateau, while South Island is dominated by a range of high fold mountains, the Southern Alps, which contain glaciers, snowfields, and a fjord coastline.

The climate of New Zealand favours the more active types of outdoor recreation, with its equable temperatures and pollution-free atmosphere. The islands enjoy an average of 2000 sunshine hours annually and the range of latitude occupied by the islands means that Auckland has a sub-tropical climate while at Invercargill 1600 kilometres further south the temperatures more closely resemble those experienced in the western islands of Scotland. The mountains of both North and South Island are high enough to receive heavy snow falls, the skiing season lasting from July to October.

Two-thirds of New Zealand's three million people are concentrated in North Island, and they are town dwellers in the main. Major cities are Auckland (750,000 inhabitants), Wellington (350,000), Christchurch (320,000), and Dunedin (110,000). The standard of living of New Zealanders is high with the state providing many social services. The economy is however precariously dependent on the export of primary products, such as meat and wool, while most consumer goods have to be imported. Nevertheless motor vehicle ownership approaches Australian levels. Despite the distances that must be covered and the high cost of air fares, New Zealanders have a high propensity to travel abroad, with tourism expenditure per capita being more than twice that of the Australians, but with much the same preferences regarding destinations. About half of all overseas visits are to Australia, with the encouragement of cheap air fares.

A much greater number of New Zealanders take annual summer holidays in their own country, mostly during the six weeks from mid-December to the end of January. Since this coincides with the peak period of arrival for foreign visitors there is considerable pressure on the available hotel accommodation in most resort areas. Motels are the type of accommodation most favoured by holiday-makers, although caravanning, camping, and youth hostelling are also popular and many families also own or share a second home at the coast.

Most tourist enterprises in New Zealand are small concerns catering mainly for domestic demand. However, foreign visitors are often attracted to remote and sparsely populated areas where it would be uneconomic for the private sector to develop resort facilities of international standard. The government has therefore intervened by financing the Tourist Hotel Corporation, which operates a chain of quality hotels in scenic locations.

The majority of inbound tourists are Australians, though the North American market is growing in importance, especially for hunting and fishing holidays. The Japanese market also has considerable potential, especially for skiing holidays when the Northern Hemisphere season has ended. British visitors fall predominantly in the VFR category, and stay on average over six weeks.

New Zealand's transport system is well developed. The mountainous topography of the country has encouraged the widespread use of domestic air services connecting the cities and resort areas. Specially-equipped light aircraft bring the Southern Alps within easy reach of tourists, while hiking trails and scenic mountain highways are used by the more adventurous. Other surface transport includes New Zealand Railways' express service between the major cities from Auckland to Invercargill, the vital ferry across Cook Strait between Wellington and Picton, and the network of bus services to most parts of the country. Internationally, Auckland and Wellington have become important gateways to the South Pacific while Christchurch is used for expeditions, charter flights, and summer cruises to the Ross Sea in Antarctica.

Auckland is the centre for touring the subtropical north of the country, including the Bay of Islands – noted for its big game fishing, and the Bay of Plenty – with its surfing beaches. More unusual attractions however, are to be seen in the volcanic plateau occupying the centre of North Island, particularly in the Tongariro National Park. To the north of Lake Taupo hot springs have made Rotorua one of the world's most important spas. Wellington is less conveniently placed for touring North Island as it is hemmed in by mountains, but it is the gateway to South Island by air and sea. Other attractions include the rapids of the Wanganui and Mount Egmont, and the traditional culture of the Maori people.

On South Island the Mount Cook National Park contains New Zealand's highest mountain, and the Tasman Glacier, one of the largest in the Southern Hemisphere outside Antarctica. On the western slopes of the Southern Alps glaciers flow spectacularly amid dense evergreen rain forests in the Westland National Park. Dunedin is the nearest large centre to the lakes and mountains of Southland and Otago, where Queenstown on Lake Wakatipu is New Zealand's most important winter sports centre. Te Anau is the gateway to Fiordland, a barely explored wilderness which is the nation's largest national park.

The Pacific Islands

The Pacific Islands' image of warm seas, coral beaches, lush scenery, and hospitable easy-going islanders has a powerful appeal to would-be escapists from the industrialized societies of the West. So far the great distances separating the islands from the tourist-generating countries has prevented the development of mass tourism based on sun, sand, and sea. The exceptions are Hawaii (later described as an outlying state of the USA in Chapter 19) and to a lesser extent, Fiji. In contrast to Australia and New Zealand, there is little demand for tourism from their own people. The islands are divided into three culturally distinct regions – Polynesia to the east, Micronesia to the northwest, and Melanesia in the southwest Pacific.

The Pacific Islands have a tropical humid climate, characterized by abundant rainfall and strong solar radiation, with air and sea temperatures averaging well above 20°C throughout the year. Sea breezes mitigate the heat and humidity, especially in Polynesia, but tropical storms are frequent during the rainy season and can cause widespread damage. The larger islands are generally of volcanic origin, mountainous and covered with luxuriant vegetation, with fringing coral reefs along the coast. The smaller islands are mostly coral atolls, low-lying and consisting of little more than a narrow strip of sand, almost enclosing what may be an extensive lagoon.

Inter-island distances are great and make it difficult to visit more than a few countries in one itinerary, whilst the absence of interline agreements between the airlines of the region adds to the cost of travel. Tourism is becoming increasingly important, with most governments turning to overseas capital for the development of facilities. Hotel accommodation is generally of a high standard, designed in sympathy with the environment and local building traditions. The main problem is a lack of infrastructure, especially poor roads, and declining shipping services between the islands.

Apart from the islands of Guam and Saipan, which are strategically important to the USA, little tourism development has taken place in *Micronesia*. Most of the region consists of a wide scattering of tiny atolls, so that the visitor is very dependent on inter-island air services. The main tourist attraction is scuba diving.

Melanesia on the other hand, consists of larger, mountainous, and densely forested islands. Papua-New Guinea's tourist potential is so far barely developed. In area it is the second largest country in the Pacific after Australia, with highlands rising to 4000 metres, and is inhabited by over 400 different tribes, some of whom are now included on the tourist circuit. New Caledonia offers more sophisticated facilities and an attractive coastline, protected by a barrier reef. Its capital Noumea has a strong French ambience. Some development has also occurred in the neighbouring volcanic islands of Vanuatu.

Polynesia contains the most attractive islands from the viewpoint of climate, scenery and cultural traditions. The many island groups are separated by much greater expanses of ocean than is the case in the South West Pacific. Tourism has made most progress on those Polynesian islands which act as staging points on the trans-Pacific air and shipping routes. This is particularly true of Fiji, and to a lesser extent of Tahiti and Samoa. Rarotonga, in the Cook Islands, and Tonga are frequently visited by cruise ships, but attract few long-stay holidaymakers due to their lack of facilities.

No Pacific destinations have captured the imagination of artists and writers more than Tahiti, Moorea, and Bora-Bora which form part of the territory of French Polynesia. The scenery of jagged mountain peaks, lush vegetation, and sheltered lagoons is exceptionally beautiful. French culture has made a considerable impact on the islanders and the economy is largely dependent on imports and subsidies from France. The Tahiti Tourist Development Office has been successful in attracting large numbers of Americans and there has been some revival of traditional Polynesian handicrafts and dances.

As an ex-British colony Fiji has a different appeal. The country consists of over one hundred inhabited islands. Most of the population live on the large volcanic island of Vita Levu, which contains the major port of Suva (catering for cruise ships), the international airport at Nadi, and resort development along the drier west coast. The Coral Coast to the south offers fine beaches and offshore atolls which are ideal for water-sports. Entertainment facilities cater mainly for Australians and New Zealanders. Fiji's culture, including fire walking and war dances, is of secondary importance to the beaches and duty-free shopping. In the islands of Samoa the development of tourism reflects differences in national styles; American Samoa is commercialized, like Hawaii, whereas Western Samoa is unspoiled and traditional.

Much of the spending by tourists in the Pacific Islands fails to benefit the economy as it does not stay in the islands. Most of the hotels are owned by foreign companies, and considerable imports of food and beverages have to be made to meet the requirements of tourists. Governments see in tourism almost the only chance of raising living standards and reducing their dependence on world markets for the sale of cash crops. Tourism has helped to revive the folklore of the islanders and provided new markets for their traditional handicrafts. However, unless the development of tourism is carefully planned, further damage is likely to be inflicted on the traditional cultures of the islands, and the fragile marine environment which is their primary tourism resource.

Summary

Australasia consists of relatively small islands separated by wide expanses of ocean. Isolation from the rest of the world is now being overcome by the development of air transport, but distance from the major tourist-generating countries of the world has prevented the region from becoming a major holiday destination.

Australia and New Zealand clearly belong to the affluent West, while the Pacific islands have more in common with developing countries of the Third World. The tourism industries of Australia and New Zealand have primarily developed to satisfy demand from their own populations, and foreign tourism is not nearly as significant or as vital to the economy as it is to the smaller, poorer islands of the Pacific.

Australasia is primarily a destination area for those travelling for recreational rather than cultural reasons. The climates are generally favourable, and there is less population pressure on available resources than is the case elsewhere. Environments such as the Australian Outback, the Great Barrier Reef, the Southern Alps of New Zealand, and the atolls of the South Pacific offer a range of opportunities for adventure holidays. Another factor favouring the development of tourism is the political stability of the region which creates good conditions for investment.

NINETEEN

North America

LEARNING OBJECTIVES

After reading this chapter, you should be able to:

1 Describe the major physical regions of North America and understand their importance for tourism.
2 Appreciate the scale and character of domestic tourism, especially in the United States.
3 Understand the importance of the United States and Canada as tourist-generating areas.
4 Appreciate the significance of the conservation movement and the importance of the national park system and other protected areas to tourism.
5 Recognize the importance of communications in the development of the tourism industry.
6 Demonstrate a knowledge of the tourist regions, resorts, business centres, and tourist attractions of North America.

Introduction

Both the United States and Canada have a wealth of natural resources in a vast physical setting and the

outlook of the people is both informal and competitive. Both are nations of immigrants who have blended to form a distinct North American culture with much in common sharing not only the English language and the democratic structures of government inherited from Britain, but also similar attitudes toward business enterprise and leisure activities.

From the visitor's point of view the size of the continent is important – extending as it does over six time zones – but so is the rich variety of geography and life. The western part of North America is dominated by high mountain chains, including the spectacular scenery of the Rockies and the Sierra Nevada. Near the eastern seaboard rise the forested Appalachians, much lower in altitude than the Rockies. Between these two mountain systems lie vast interior plains, drained by great rivers such as the Mississippi and its tributaries in the south, and the St Lawrence, Athabasca, and Mackenzie in the north.

The climate of North America is largely determined by relief and tends to be more extreme than similar latitudes in Western Europe, with warmer summers and colder winters. In winter south-moving Arctic air can bring freezing temperatures to Louisiana and Northern Florida. Yet in summer, most of the continent is open to warm moist airstreams, originating in the Gulf of Mexico, so that humidity tends to be high in the eastern half of the United States. Along the western seaboard high mountain ranges intercept moisture-bearing winds from the Pacific Ocean, and bring heavy rainfall to a narrow coastal zone which also experiences much milder temperatures. Most of the western United States however, has a dry climate, due to its situation in the 'rain-shadow' of the mountain barriers. The most important climatic divide, with far reaching social and economic implications, is between the 'Snowbelt' consisting of Canada and the northern states of the USA, and the 'Sunbelt' stretching from the Carolinas to California, which increasingly attracts industry and residents.

North Americans are very conservation-minded. Unique areas have been designated as national parks where the land is owned and managed by the government with the dual objectives of conservation and outdoor recreation and all incompatible types of development are prohibited. However, some services are allocated to the private sector as concessions and have caused concern in some of the more popular parks.

North America has many man-made attractions including its achievements in science and technology, and the arts. Although both Canada and the United States are 'young nations' compared to European countries, there are many historic buildings associated with famous people or important events, which have been carefully restored or reconstructed. The presentation of North American history plays an important part in many of the 'theme parks' such as Disneyland and Disneyworld.

In the early 1980s the United States population passed 230 million, almost ten times Canada's twenty-five million. Over 75 per cent of North Americans live in urban areas. There are now thirty-five metropolitan areas with populations exceeding one million in the United States, and another three in Canada. As population centres they generate much holiday travel and as commercial centres a considerable amount of business travel. Relatively few North American cities are tourist attractions in themselves as the pattern of high-rise central business districts, commercial strip development, and low density suburbs is standard throughout.

The United States

The United States of America is not only one of the world's leading generators of international tourism, but it is also a major destination with the world's largest hotel industry. This caters mainly for domestic demand, and it is only recently that the Federal government has made serious efforts to attract more foreign visitors. By the early 1980s over twenty million international tourists visited the United States annually. Each year Canadians represent about a half of the total (in addition to many more day visitors) and the second most important source is Mexico – both the only two countries with a common land frontier with the USA. The third place is taken by Japan, which has shown a consistent growth for a number of years. Visitors from Europe fluctuate with the strength of the dollar and level of air fares; the UK having been by far the most important European generator.

The approach of the United States towards tourism is influenced firstly by the belief in free enterprise with the minimum of government interference, and secondly by the division of responsibilities between the Federal government in Washington and the State governments. In 1981 the National Tourism Policy Act created the

United States Travel and Tourism Administration (USTTA) to co-ordinate the policies of the Federal government regarding tourism and to promote the country more vigorously abroad. All fifty states have some kind of official body concerned with tourism, but these vary considerably in their effectiveness.

For many years Americans have spent considerably more on travel abroad than the United States has been receiving from foreign tourists; 1980 and 1981 were the only years since the Second World War with a surplus on the US international travel account. The United States is, after West Germany, the second largest generator of international tourism in the world, and much of this is long-haul travel. Although much larger numbers visit neighbouring Canada, between eight and ten million Americans travelled overseas in the early 1980s, and three to four million of them visit Europe. However, the market for foreign travel is relatively small, compared to domestic tourism, and accounts for less than 10 per cent of total tourist expenditure by Americans.

There are signs that American society is becoming less work-oriented and there is a growing demand for participation in recreational activities such as sailing, backpacking, and skiing, and for the purchase of second homes, camper-caravans, and off-the-road recreational vehicles. Americans enjoy less annual leave than West Europeans but more than 70 per cent of households take a vacation away from home. Vacations are mainly taken in the months of July and August and the beaches are almost deserted before Memorial Day in late May and after Labor Day in early September.

As far as domestic tourism is concerned the most popular vacation areas are Florida, the beaches of Long Island and New Jersey, California, and the lakes of Michigan. Americans seeking unspoiled scenic beauty and physical challenge go to the national parks, especially Yellowstone and Yosemite. Much greater numbers visit the state parks, which are generally more accessible to the cities of the Eastern Seaboard and Middle West, whereas most of the national parks are located in the sparsely populated Western states. The United States Forest Service also provides recreational facilities, and has designated some areas as 'wilderness' or 'primitive' ares where all development is prohibited for the benefit of backpackers and canoeists, rather than the motorized tourists who mainly visit the national parks.

Since the United States has the highest car ownership in the world it is not surprising that over 80 per cent of vacation trips are taken by car. There are excellent highways, including the interstate network linking the major cities. Most medium-sized cities have an airport and air fares are much cheaper than those paid for equivalent distances in Europe. The de-regulation of the civil aviation industry since 1978 enabled many of the smaller airlines to begin operating overseas services. Carriers generally took the opportunity to offer highly competitive fares not only to their gateway cities but also to the onward destinations on their networks. Public transport by road and rail compares unfavourably with the situation in most other developed countries. The major bus companies – Greyhound and Continental Trailways – do provide an extensive network of intercity services, and inclusive tours and bargain fares for foreign tourists. Passenger train services declined dramatically after the 1950s and would have disappeared altogether, had not the Federal government set up AMTRAK, a public corporation which operates trains over the networks of a dozen private railway companies. However, apart from the densely populated 'corridor' between Washington and Boston (which carries 50 per cent of the traffic) train services are few and infrequent. Overall travelling in the USA is easy. An extensive network of motels provides inexpensive accommodation and camping sites are available for family holidays. City centre hotels derive much of their revenue from conventions, while resort hotels in holiday areas provide a range of sports facilities.

The North East

The North Eastern states facing Europe constitute the most densely populated, and one of the most visited, parts of the country for here are the four major gateway cities of Boston, New York, Philadelphia, and Washington. The urbanized belt –

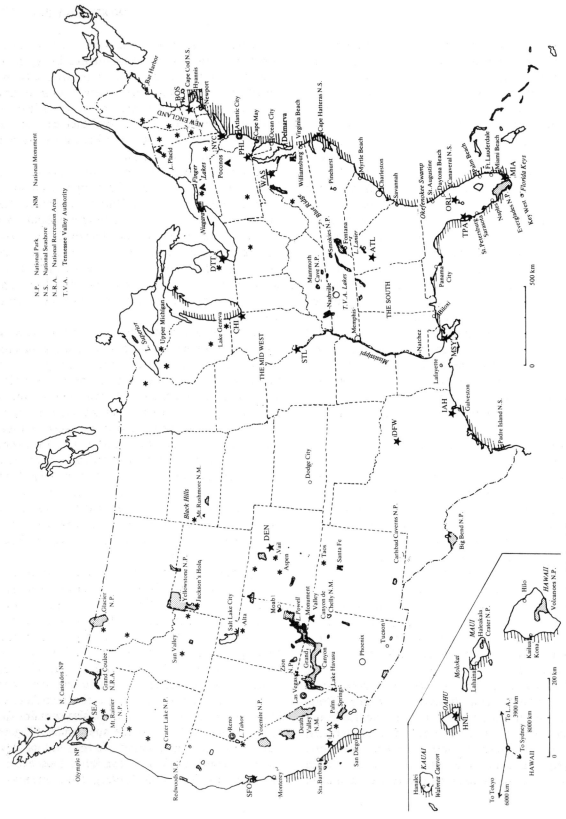

Figure 19.1 *Major tourist resources in the United States*

'Megalopolis' – extending from Boston to Washington contains over thirty-five million inhabitants and has excellent transport facilities in the form of road, rail, and shuttle air services. In contrast, there are large areas of forested wilderness in the mountains of the Northern Appalachians.

New England is the most interesting region of the North East from an historical standpoint. For the most part it is rugged and infertile and winters are cold with heavy snowfall. Three centuries ago this region was occupied by English settlers whose Puritan heritage is still evident in the picturesque villages of clapboard houses. Many of their farms have since been abandoned, to be used today as weekend or summer retreats by city dwellers.

Northern New England is noted for its winter sports centred on the Green Mountains of Vermont, and the White Mountains of New Hampshire. In summer the rocky, deeply indented coastline of Maine attracts many sailing enthusiasts, while anglers, hunters, and canoeists visit the rivers of the forested interior. During the autumn, the brilliant colours of the woodlands of Vermont are one of the state's biggest tourist attractions.

Massachusetts, Rhode Island, and Connecticut are less rural, with industry and commerce playing a much greater part in the economy. The coastline is low-lying with many fine beaches. This is especially true of the Cape Cod peninsula, where a number of summer resorts, such as Hyannisport cater for wealthy second home owners. There are many fine harbours and historic seaports, such as the old whaling centres of Nantucket, New Bedford, Salem, and Mystic. Newport, Rhode Island, is one of the world's most famous yachting centres. Boston remains an important seaport and major cultural centre. The city has preserved many historic buildings associated with the War of Independence.

The Middle Atlantic states comprise New York, New Jersey, Pennsylvania, Maryland, Delaware, and the Virginias. Of the many cities in the region, New York is the one which attracts the majority of tourists and business travellers. Although it is not the national or even a state capital, it is the country's primary city in almost every other respect. It is the largest city of North America, with fifteen million people living in its metropolitan area. It is a major commercial city and finance centre while Kennedy Airport is the leading gateway to the United States for foreign visitors. It has more hotel rooms than any other city, and is one of the world's leading conference venues and an international meeting place.

New York owes its dominance to its role as a port city, with the advantage of having a deep water harbour and access via the Hudson Valley into the interior of North America. The city is built on a number of islands and peninsulas which are linked by numerous bridges, tunnels, and ferries. The nucleus is Manhattan Island, one of the world's most densely populated urban areas and perhaps the most cosmopolitan with its numerous ethnic communities.

'Midtown' Manhattan to the south of Central Park contains the majority of tourist attractions for the foreign visitor. These include the skyscrapers, the Broadway Theatre district, the shops lining Fifth Avenue, and the best hotels. 'Downtown' – the oldest part of New York at the southern tip of the island – includes the Stock Exchange, 'Chinatown', and the artistic quarter of Greenwich Village. Located fifteen to thirty kilometres from Manhattan are the three airports serving New York, namely Newark, La Guardia, and J. F. Kennedy. The last two are situated on Long Island, which has a number of fine beaches within easy driving distance of the city, such as Jones Beach and Fire Island.

'Upstate' New York, outside the metropolitan area, also has a wealth of tourist attractions. The Catskill Mountains to the north west are favoured for summer homes and for skiing in winter. The Adirondacks in the north east are much less developed, with the exception of Lake Placid, venue of the 1980 Winter Olympics. The Hudson Valley, with its vineyards, historic mansions, and wooded scenery has been called 'the Rhineland of North America'. New York State also contains the scenic Finger Lakes and the spectacular Niagara Falls on the Canadian border. To the south of New York a series of offshore barrier islands extend along the coastline of New Jersey. Here, the major resort of Atlantic City was rescued from decline by legalizing gambling in 1978, and the casinos of Atlantic City now receive almost as many visitors as those of Las Vegas. The resort's most famous feature, however, is the boardwalk (promenade) along the beach.

Philadelphia, the third largest city in the United States, is a business rather than tourist centre. However, it does contain Independence Hall, and other reminders of the early history of the United States. In rural Pennsylvania, the Poconos and Allegheny mountains provide facilities for hunting, fishing, and skiing.

Washington was founded in 1802 as the capital of the newly formed United States. It was planned on spacious lines, with wide avenues and attractive parks. The most important feature is the Mall extending from the Washington Monument to the Capitol housing the American Congress; grouped nearby are other important public buildings such as the White House, Smithsonian Museums, and National Gallery of Art. The Federal government and international agencies generate a considerable volume of business travel. Washington lacks the entertainment facilities of New York but attracts American tourists for patriotic and cultural reasons. With the growing importance of Dulles International and Baltimore as gateway airports the number of foreign tourists should also increase. Washington is conveniently placed for visiting the scenic Blue Ridge Mountains and Shenandoah Valley of Virginia to the west, the beaches of the Delmarva Peninsula, and the battlefields of the American Civil War such as Gettysburg. To the south of Washington there are many reminders of the colonial period in Virginia, including Williamsburg, George Washington's home at Mount Vernon, and the first English settlement at Jamestown.

The South

The states south of the Mason-Dixon line have a separate cultural identity which before the Civil War was based on plantation agriculture and is nowadays expressed in folk music and a lifestyle which is more traditional than elsewhere in the USA. Cities like Atlanta, Birmingham, and Char-

lotte represent the dynamic 'New South' of industrial development in contrast to the pockets of rural poverty that may still be found in states like Mississippi and in the Southern Appalachians.

The heritage of the past, often highly romanticized, is an important part of the region's appeal as shown in the seaports of Charleston and Savannah which have preserved many of their eighteenth century buildings. The coastline of the Carolinas and Georgia features many barrier islands with beaches warmed by the Gulf Stream. Some of these have developed as exclusive resorts, while others have been preserved as state parks or wildlife refuges. The hilly, well-wooded Piedmont in the interior also provides many recreational facilities. Pinehurst in North Carolina is a premier golf resort and Lake Lanier in Georgia is one of many reservoirs created by the US Corps of Engineers providing an ideal environment for water sports.

Atlanta is the major conference venue of the south east with its modern hotels and excellent communications. Its airport is second only to Chicago in terms of domestic traffic and is an international gateway of growing importance. Two of the largest airlines of the United States – Delta and Eastern – use Atlanta for their services.

North of Georgia and west of North Carolina rise the Southern Appalachians, a series of forest-covered ranges where the Smoky Mountains National Park is suffering from severe visitor pressure. The many dams built by the Tennessee Valley Authority for power generation have created a number of lakes, which are popular for water sports and fishing.

To the west of the Appalachians lie the fertile Nashville Basin and Bluegrass country of Kentucky. Nashville is the 'capital' of the 'country and western' music industry. Kentucky is noted for its equestrian sports and also for Mammoth Cave, a remarkable natural attraction.

The 'Deep South' comprises the states of Louisiana, Mississippi, and Alabama. The region is characterized by meandering slow-moving rivers and swampy bayous. The Mississippi is still an important waterway, although the sternwheeler steamboats now only survive as tourist attractions. Louisiana in particular has a rich French Creole and Cajun culture. New Orleans is widely regarded as the birthplace of jazz and is noted for its annual Mardi-Gras carnival. New Orleans is the United States' second largest port and ranks among the five most popular cities visited by foreign as well as American tourists. Tourists are particularly attracted by the picturesque old French quarter. However, the tourism industry is also firmly based on conventions and sports events. Other tourist centres include Natchez famed for its 'antebellum' plantation houses, and the beach resorts of Gulfport and Biloxi on the Gulf of Mexico.

Florida

The high percentage of retired northerners and the scale of its tourism industry sets Florida apart from the rest of the south. Since 1960 southern Florida has received a massive influx of Cubans, who have made Miami to a great extent a Spanish-speaking city and effectively the financial centre of Latin America. Florida is among the world's leading holiday destinations, attracting forty million visitors each year, and its annual income from tourism is well in excess of Spain's receipts from foreign visitors. 80 per cent of Florida's visitors are North Americans, mainly from the states east of the Mississippi, and from Canada. Of the overseas visitors, 40 per cent come from Latin American countries; while almost half originate from Europe. The reasons for Florida's success can be attributed to its sub-tropical climate, long coastline of white sandy beaches, and to a major investment by private enterprise in sports facilities and amusements.

Florida originated as a winter resort for wealthy Americans in the 1890s. By 1920 Palm Beach and Miami Beach were developed on barrier islands off the Atlantic coast. Since the 1950s Florida has broadened its appeal to become a summer destination within the reach of the majority of Americans. However, the southern third of the state has retained its image as a winter haven for northerners and Canadians and this is reflected in lower hotel rates during the summer months. Most of Florida is low-lying and there are large areas of wetland which provide a refuge for wildlife, notably the Okefenokee swamp on the Georgia border, and the Everglades National Park in the extreme south.

In the south east a string of holiday resorts have developed, the most important being exclusive Palm Beach, Fort Lauderdale (known as the 'Venice of Florida' with its marina facilities), and Miami Beach – with its convention centre and concentration of high-rise accommodation. Miami itself is the largest city in Florida with two million residents. Miami Airport is the major gateway to the Caribbean and South America, and the Port of Miami a major departure centre for cruises. South of Miami the Florida Keys provide ideal opportunities for scuba diving.

The development of tourism on such a large scale has created problems. Many resort hotels have been built so close to the sea that the beaches have become badly eroded, and a great deal of the best recreational land has been bought up as sites for private homes. The ever increasing demand for water by the population of Greater Miami has endangered the unique wetland environment of the Everglades.

The south west of Florida along the Gulf of Mexico is much less developed, with the exception of the Tampa Bay area. The most important resorts are St Petersburg – America's major retirement centre, Sarasota, and Clearwater; while further south Naples and Fort Myers provide less expensive self-catering accommodation. The northern Gulf coast is popular only during the summer months.

Central Florida is probably the fastest growing area of the state, due largely to the establishment of the Disneyworld theme park in 1971, followed by EPCOT in 1982. By 1985 Disneyworld had received 200 million visitors, a world record for any single tourist attraction. The main impact has been on the nearby city of Orlando which has opened a major new international airport to deal with the influx of visitors. Other attractions include the surfing beaches along the Atlantic coast, the main resort being Daytona Beach; and the NASA space research centre at Cape Canaveral.

The Mid West

The area south of the Great Lakes is one of the world's most productive agricultural areas. From the air the landscape from Iowa to Ohio appears like a huge chessboard, with fields, roads and settlements laid out on a grid pattern. Further north in Wisconsin, Minnesota, and Michigan the scenery is much more diverse, with innumerable lakes, and large areas of forest. The Great Lakes themselves are major attractions; there are fine beaches along the southern shores of Michigan and Huron, while Lake Superior is lined by spectacular cliffs. The State of Michigan has a well-established tourist industry based on these resources. The numerous resorts cater mainly for the demand from the regions' cities; important examples being Lake Geneva thirty kilometres from Chicago, and Kensington which serves Detroit. In winter large areas of northern Wisconsin and Minnesota are set aside for snowmobile trails, while Upper Michigan provides facilities for skiing.

Some of the cities of the Mid West are important cultural as well as business centres. Detroit is the world's leading city for motor vehicle manufacture. At nearby Dearborn Henry Ford revolutionized transport and tourism with his Model T, and founded Greenfield Village as an open-air museum of American history. Chicago is the transportation centre of the USA and its second largest industrial city. O'Hare Airport is the world's busiest, the city is a major rail terminal, and despite its distance from the sea it is also a port (thanks to the St Lawrence Seaway). Chicago is famed for its avant-garde architecture, museums and art galleries, while the city's recreational facilities include twenty-four kilometres of public beaches, yacht marinas, and parks along the shore of Lake Michigan. As a commercial centre it has excellent facilities for conventions and trade fairs. St Louis, Cincinatti, Indianapolis, Milwaukee, and the twin cities of Minneapolis-St Paul each have a particular appeal for visitors.

The West

West of the 100th meridian the climate becomes too dry for most types of agriculture and cities are widely scattered. The Great Plains are relatively featureless with the exception of the granitic Black Hills of South Dakota rising abruptly from the surrounding prairies. In several states lying west of the Rocky Mountains, tourism provides more jobs than any other industry, due in large measure to magnificent scenery and the 'frontier image' – this region contains most of the national parks and Indian reservations.

The northern part of the region – called the 'Mountain West' by the USTTA consists largely of a number of enclosed basins separated by high forested mountain ranges. Good 'powder' snow for skiing is to be found in the Rocky Mountains of Colorado, where resorts such as Aspen have developed, easily accessible from the gateway city of Denver. In some areas there is evidence of former volcanic activity, notably in Yellowstone National Park with its geysers, bubbling mud pools, and hot springs. In the late nineteenth century, ores resulting from these earth movements supported thriving mining communities, and their locations are now restored as tourist attractions.

The tourism industry of Nevada is a special case in that it is based essentially on gambling (illegal in most other states). Las Vegas, which attracts twelve million staying visitors annually to its neon-lit 'strip' of casinos, claims to be the 'world's entertainment capital'. It is easily reached from Los Angeles, whereas its rival, Reno, is more accessible from San Francisco. In contrast, Salt Lake City, Utah, is the headquarters of the Mormon Church and entertainment is more inhibited.

The south western states of Arizona and New Mexico have a particularly rich heritage derived from Spain and the culture of the Pueblos and other Indian tribes. Indian handicrafts are much in demand and tourist accommodation is available on some reservations. Santa Fe, Tucson, and Phoenix are the major tourist centres. There are also many rodeos and 'dude ranches' where the tourist can sample, albeit with modern conveniences, the cowboy lifestyle. Dams on the Colorado River have created an important resource for water-based recreation. The best known tourist attraction of the South West continues to be the desert and mountain scenery of the Colorado Plateau, including the world famous Grand Canyon in Arizona, and the lesser known Zion and Bryce Canyon National Parks in Utah.

Texas has a booming economy which has generated a considerable volume of business travel to Dallas and Houston. Galveston is a major beach resort while San Antonio is an important cultural centre.

California and the Far West

Since the gold rush of 1849 Americans have regarded California as a land of opportunity. It is now the wealthiest state with a population that is extraordinarily mobile even by American standards. California is renowned for its warm, sunny climate, and it is also remarkable for the variety of its scenery. This includes for example the vineyards of the Napa Valley, citrus orchards, spectacular forests, Mount Whitney, and Death Valley. All this has made California the primary vacation destination for American families, and one of the most popular states with foreign tourists. However, tourism is less important to the Californian economy than the 'high tech' engineering industries and agriculture, unlike in Florida where it is the main revenue earner.

There are important differences between the climate of the Pacific coast, which is influenced by the cold offshore Californian current, and the Central Valley east of the Coast Ranges where summer temperatures frequently exceed 40°C. Northern California has a generally colder and more humid climate than the south, where conditions are ideal for outdoor recreation.

The Los Angeles metropolitan area sprawls over 2000 square kilometres and is held together by the most extensive freeway network in the United States. The city's tourism industry was boosted by the 1984 Olympic Games. On its Pacific shore Los Angeles offers the magnificent beaches of Santa Monica and Malibu, and the large yacht harbour at Marina del Rey. There are many theme parks in the Los Angeles area, the most important being Disneyland.

San Francisco is very different from Los Angeles. It is relatively compact, with a good public transport system, and is widely regarded as being the most scenic and 'European' of all North American cities. It is a major seaport situated on the natural harbour provided by San Francisco Bay and the Golden Gate. Much of the waterfront is now devoted to tourism and entertainment. Other important attractions include Chinatown and the 'cable cars'. San Francisco is situated within a few hours' drive of the ski resorts around Lake Tahoe and the scenic Sierra Nevada mountains. These include the popular Yosemite National Park, with its spectacular waterfalls and sheer granite cliffs, and the Sequoia National Park where the world's largest trees are protected. To the north of San Francisco a coastal highway provides access to the redwood forests.

Some of the world's finest surfing beaches and coastal scenery are to be found between San Francisco and Los Angeles, the most important resorts being Monterrey and Santa Barbara. Not far from the Mexican border lies the port and naval city of San Diego, which has excellent beaches at La Jolla with facilities for sailing and sport fishing. Even the desert interior of California has been affected by tourism due to its closeness to Los Angeles, and in some areas trail bikes and dune buggies have made a severe impact on the environment. The most important inland resort of Southern California is exclusive Palm Springs.

The other Far Western states, Oregon and Washington have been less affected by tourism, and in fact the conservation-conscious government of Oregon has severely limited development along its coastline. The main tourist attractions include several national parks, the most popular being Crater Lake and Mount Rainier, both of volcanic formation.

Alaska and Hawaii are included by the USTTA in the Far West, although both are physically detached from the other forty-eight states of the USA. The volcanic islands which comprise the State of Hawaii lie 3900 kilometres south west of San Francisco in the North Pacific and form part of Polynesia. Alaska adjoins northern Canada and is separated from Soviet Siberia only by the narrow Bering Strait.

Hawaii

The Hawaiian Islands attracted almost four million annual visitors during the early 1980s, 60 per cent of whom came from 'mainland' USA. They have become one of the world's major holiday destinations as a result of cheap air fares and competitive tour pricing aimed at the American mass market. As a result tourists from New York and Mid-Western cities are more numerous than Californians. Other important markets are Japan and Canada, while visitors from Europe are deterred by distance and cost. Hawaii's appeal is due to the beautiful mountain scenery, lush vegetation and waterfalls, the surfing beaches, and a tropical climate which is ideal for outdoor recreation throughout the year. Although native Hawaiians are greatly outnumbered by those of Asian or white American origin the romanticized Polynesian life-style of the islanders is promoted as part of the tourist image. This is expressed in the lei or garland of welcome, the Luau banquets and hula dancing, while outrigger canoes are a reminder of seafaring traditions.

Oahu is the most important island of the group, containing 80 per cent of the population, 60 per cent of the tourist accommodation, the naval base of Pearl Harbor, and the state capital Honolulu, which is the gateway to the islands. Honolulu is a major city which has become increasingly important as a business centre for trade between North America and East Asia, and as a cultural centre for Polynesia. Honolulu's world-famous Waikiki Beach, containing scores of high-rise hotels, extends for three kilometres to the cliffs of Diamond Head. The best surfing beaches lie along the north coast of Oahu.

Since the 1960s the State government has become increasingly concerned at the undesirable impact of mass tourism on Oahu and has encouraged projects on the other major islands which are generally of a higher standard than Waikiki. On Maui for example most of the development consists of condominia which have attracted large numbers of wealthy Americans from the mainland. Maui contains the impressive Haleakala Crater National Park and the former whaling port of Lahaina. Kauai is particularly renowned for its lush scenery, exemplified by the fern grotto at Wailua, the Waimea Canyon and the beaches of Hanalei. The 'Big Island' of Hawaii offers great scenic and climatic variety due to the high volcanic peaks of Mauna Loa and Mauna Kea. Hilo on the windward side of the island receives heavy rainfall whereas the west coast between Kona and Kohala is dry. Frequent volcanic eruptions have created a strange landscape of firepits, craters, and lava caves in the south east of Hawaii. The rugged island of Molokai, and Lanai with its pineapple plantations, have been little affected by tourism.

Alaska

Alaska is physically separated from other parts of the United States by some of Canada's most difficult mountain terrain. Air transport is essential in this vast, sparsely populated state and Alaska's main external links are by air – its major city Anchorage is situated on the trans-polar route from Europe to Japan. Alternatively it can be reached by coastal shipping services from Seattle, or by a long journey overland along the Alaskan Highway from Edmonton in Canada.

The south east of Alaska has probably the greatest tourism potential as it is a region of spectacular scenery, including fjords and some of the largest glaciers in the Northern Hemisphere. These can be visited on summer cruises out of Long Beach, San Francisco, and Seattle. The Denali National Park containing North America's highest mountain attracts over 300,000 visitors annually.

Canada

The severe climate and rugged terrain of much of this vast country explains why 85 per cent of Canadians live within 200 kilometres of the United States border. In economic and cultural terms Canada is overshadowed by its powerful neighbour to the south. Canadian separateness is demonstrated by its political institutions and by the popularity of historic sites associated with the former British and French presence. However, Canada's quest for a national identity is made difficult by the existence of two official languages representing two different cultural traditions. The

French settled in the St Lawrence Valley long before the British and other Europeans arrived in Canada, and they are still mainly concentrated in the province of Quebec where there is a strong separatist movement.

Domestic and international tourism together account for 5 per cent of Canada's GNP and provide over one million jobs. As early as 1929 tourism was a major earner of foreign exchange and in 1934 the Canadian Travel Bureau was established under the Department of Commerce to carry out promotion abroad. However, it is only since the late 1960s that the Federal government has become more directly involved through the Canadian Government Office of Tourism (CGOT), in partnership with the governments of the ten provinces.

In the early 1980s between 80 and 90 per cent of international tourists were Americans and less than 10 per cent came from Europe. Americans also account for the bulk of a large volume of excursionists whose numbers fluctuate according to differences in prices on either side of the border and the strength of the respective currencies. The great majority of American tourists arrive by car and are attracted mainly by the recreational facilities of the Canadian countryside. Most overseas visitors arrive by air at Toronto or Montreal and almost a half of these, especially the British, come primarily to stay with friends and relatives in the cities.

Canada's main tourist resource lies in its mountains, forests, and lakes. The sparseness of the population means that infrastructure for international tourism is largely absent from 90 per cent of Canada. The severity of the winter season is another major constraint, although Canadians themselves participate in a wide range of snow-based activities. Many ski resorts have developed to meet domestic demand within easy reach of all the major cities. Summer offers a complete contrast as temperatures are warm enough to be suitable for a wide range of outdoor activities. Boating and canoeing are especially popular on the many lakes and rivers of the Canadian Shield, following the tradition of the French Canadian voyageurs or fur traders. Transport and equipment for fishing and hunting trips is provided by specialist outfitters to even the most remote areas.

The Canadian winter partly explains why Canadians have a high propensity to travel abroad, which results in a considerable deficit on the country's international travel account. Many retired people spend several months in Florida or on Hawaii, and this exodus may increase in the future with the general ageing of the population. Most of the expenditure on foreign travel, especially to Europe, is generated by the more prosperous and urbanized provinces, particularly Ontario.

In such a vast country transport is a major problem and road vehicles have to be 'winterized' to cope with low temperatures much of the year. Two trans-continental railways were instrumental in opening up Canada for settlement at the beginning of the century. The Canadian National Railroad (CNR) extends from Halifax to Prince Rupert, while its more famous rival, the Canadian Pacific Railroad (CPR) links St John in New Brunswick to Vancouver in the West. The 6400 kilometre journey is a popular way of seeing the country. In 1972 CNR and CPR combined their passenger services under the banner of VIA Rail, an independent Crown corporation which is subsidized by the Federal Government. The great majority of recreational trips are undertaken by private car. Most of the major cities are linked by the Trans-Canada Highway from St Johns in Newfoundland to Vancouver. In northern Canada and Labrador aircraft provide the only practical method of transport.

Ontario

Ontario is by far the most visited province, due to its excellent road connections with New York to the south and Michigan to the west. It contains a third of the country's hotel capacity while Quebec accounts for another quarter. Toronto is Canada's most cosmopolitan city, as well as being the most important gateway for overseas visitors. In Ontario Place along the waterfront Toronto has a major recreational resource, while the Muskoka Lakes to the north are popular for weekend visits.

Most of the population of Ontario is concentrated in the fertile Lake Peninsula in the extreme south. Toronto and Ottawa (the Federal capital)

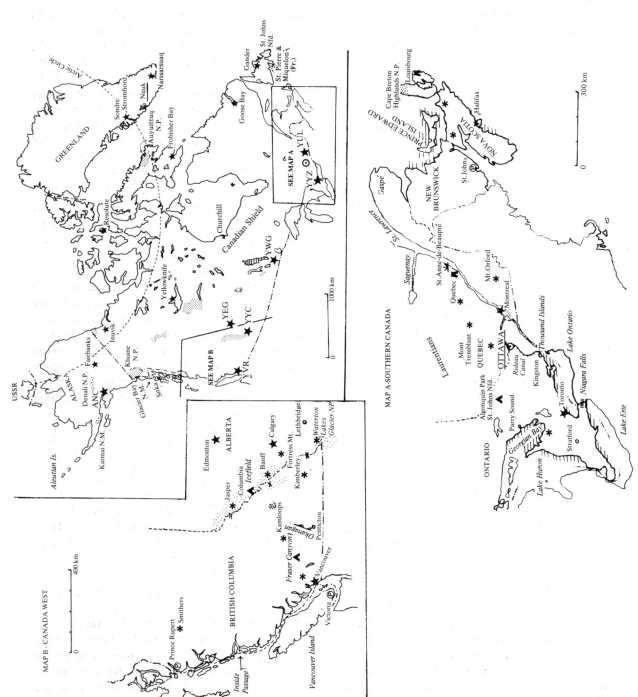

Figure 19.2 *Major tourist resources in Canada and its northern neighbours*

are within easy reach of the southern edge of the Canadian Shield, which includes the scenic Algonquin Park. One popular form of accommodation is the tourist cabin with facilities for 'adventure holidays'.

Quebec

Quebec Province is culturally distinct from other parts of Canada. Apart from a narrow strip along the St Lawrence River it is mostly sparsely populated. The most scenic areas are the fjord-like estuary of the Saguenay, the mountainous Gaspe Peninsula with its fishing villages, and the Laurentian Mountains. The influence of eighteenth century France is particularly evident in the city of Quebec with its walled upper town, Winter Carnival, horse-drawn caleches, and pilgrimages to the nearby shrine of St Ann de Beaupré. Montreal also has a strong French ambience but it is very much larger than Quebec, with a population of over two million. It is a major port and financial centre with a range of cultural attractions and sophisticated entertainment. The 1967 World Fair and the 1976 Olympic Games did much to improve the city's transport and recreational facilities. Montreal is within easy reach of the major ski resort of Mont Tremblant in the Laurentians.

The Maritime Provinces

The Maritime Provinces along the Atlantic seaboard are relatively poor and traditional. This is particularly true of Newfoundland, where hundreds of small fishing villages cling to the rugged, deeply indented coastline. Gander and Goose Bay in Labrador have some importance as airports. Prince Edward Island's tourism industry is based on its fine sandy beaches. New Brunswick's forests and rivers attract fishermen and canoeists, while Nova Scotia offers attractive coastal scenery. Tourist centres include Halifax, Canada's major port on the Atlantic, and the former French fortress of Louisbourg on Cape Breton Island. The small islands of *St Pierre* and *Miquelon* remain part of France and attract many day visitors from Newfoundland.

The West

West of Lake Superior the scenery is low-key until the foothills of the Rockies are reached at Calgary. Winnipeg is the major cultural centre of the wheat-growing Prairies. Winters compare with those of Siberia but during the hot summers Lake Winnipeg is popular for sailing. In contrast Alberta is largely cattle country and rodeos are popular. Together with British Columbia this province offers some of the most spectacular and varied scenery to be found in the North American continent. The Rocky Mountains are crossed by only three major overland routes. Edmonton has for long been regarded as the gateway to the Canadian North; Calgary is another fast-growing city and, close to the ski-fields of the Rockies, it is the venue for the 1988 Winter Olympics.

Within the Rockies are situated seven of Canada's national parks, which are administered on similar lines to those of the United States, by the Federal Bureau of Land Management and Indian Affairs. Banff National Park is the most popular area, attracting over seven million visitors annually. The town of Banff was developed by the CPR as a spa due to its hot springs; it is now a major all-year resort, with a skiing season lasting from November to May.

The Pacific coast of British Columbia is rugged and deeply indented, with spectacular fjords. The main tourist centre is Vancouver, Canada's third largest city and a major seaport. It has a scenic location at the mouth of the Fraser River, with fine beaches and excellent facilities for sailing. The provincial capital, Victoria on Vancouver Island, with its mild winters and sunny summers, is also a major holiday resort and retirement area with a strong English ambience.

The interior of British Columbia beyond the Coast Range comprises high mountain ranges, broad plateaux, and deep canyon-like valleys. The climate is much drier, with cold winters but very warm summers. This is particularly true of the sheltered Okanagan Valley with its lake resorts such as Penticton and Kelowna where sailing and water skiing are popular. On the Fraser River visitors can experience whitewater rafting, or pan for gold near former mining towns. Excellent winter sports facilities are available in the Selkirk mountains at Kimberley, and at Kamloops, heart of the cattle ranching country.

The North

Only about 65,000 people, mainly Indians and Inuit (Eskimos) live in the half of Canada which lies north of the sixtieth parallel, where the severe climate and permafrost restrict development. In the more accessible Yukon Territory the former gold mining towns of Whitehorse and Dawson have become tourist centres. The North West Territories are for expeditioners rather than tourists. Limited facilities are available at supply centres like Yellowknife, Inuvik on the Mackenzie Delta, and at Frobisher on Baffin Island, which contains the Auyittuq National Park. Even though there are few tourists, they can still make a serious impact on the fragile tundra ecosystem. Increasing numbers of Inuit are obtaining an income from guiding or outfitting expeditions, or from the sale of handicrafts made from soapstone.

Greenland

Geographically part of North America with a sparse, mainly Inuit population, the huge Arctic island of Greenland is a self-governing Danish territory. It is more closely linked to Denmark and Iceland by air and shipping routes than to northern Canada, and it has some of the chracteristics of a Third World country, such as a rapidly growing population and economic dependence on the export of a few primary products. Prospects for tourism are limited by the extreme unreliability of the weather, even in summer, and the expense of transportation which is mainly by helicopter services. Nevertheless Greenland is visited for dog-sled expeditions; by excursionists from Iceland; and by summer cruises to view the fjords and glaciers of the west coast.

Summary

North America is a vast continent of scenic and climatic contrasts. With the exception of northern Canada and Greenland it is highly developed economically. Urban areas, lifestyles, transport, and tourist facilities are broadly similar throughout both the United States and Canada, and there is a considerable volume of travel between the two countries. The main problem for the overseas visitor is the great distances involved, but this has been largely overcome by excellent highways and an extensive network of air services. Tourist facilities have been developed mainly to serve the enormous domestic market, and it is only in recent years that the federal governments of the United States and Canada have become directly involved in encouraging inbound tourism.

Canadians and Americans spend heavily on travel abroad, resulting in a large deficit on the international travel account. Overseas visitors to the United States and Canada are attracted mainly to the cities, for broadly cultural reasons and there is a large VFR market, especially from Britain. However, Florida is regarded mainly as a beach destination. Both the United States and Canada have realized the importance of conservation and their state-controlled national parks and forest reserves are probably the world's finest. The private sector of tourism is very much larger and is responsible for all profit-making enterprises; sports facilities and theme parks are particularly important.

TWENTY

Latin America and the Caribbean

After reading this chapter, you should be able to:

1 Describe the major physical features and climate of the region and understand their importance for tourism.
2 Appreciate the significance of tourism to the economies of the Caribbean islands.
3 Appreciate the cultural heritage of Mexico and the South America countries, and its appeal to tourists.
4 Assess the potential of South American countries as long-haul destinations.
5 Recognize the importance of adequate infrastructure and political stability in encouraging tourist development.
6 Recognize the importance of the Panama Canal as a shipping route and the isthmus of Panama as the link between North and South America.
7 Appreciate the value of air and road communications in the development of South American tourism.
8 Demonstrate a knowledge of the tourist regions, resorts, business centres, and tourist attractions of the region.

Introduction

'Latin America' is a cultural entity consisting of all the countries of the Western Hemisphere south of the USA/Mexico border. The mainland was colonized by Europeans from the Iberian Peninsula from the sixteenth century onwards and they imposed their language, religion, and culture on the native

'Indians'. As a result two-thirds of Latin America is made up of sixteen Spanish-speaking republics, while Portuguese-speaking Brazil accounts for most of the remainder. The great majority of the Caribbean islands and the Guianas were later colonized by the British, the French, or the Dutch. Virtually the whole area can be regarded as part of the Third World, with a level of economic development well below that of North America, but above that of most African and South Asian countries. Most Latin American countries are largely dependent on the export of minerals or cash crops. There are usually great disparities within each country between the major cities, which resemble those of Europe or the USA, and the remoter rural areas where pre-industrial life-styles persist. Rural poverty has resulted in a massive exodus away from the countryside to the major cities, which are often surrounded by 'shanty towns' such as the favelas on the hillsides of Rio de Janeiro.

The Caribbean islands

The Caribbean islands extend from Florida to the northern coast of South America and contain some of the world's most attractive and popular resort areas. The Caribbean Sea, sheltered by the islands from the trade winds blowing in from the Atlantic, has been called the 'American Mediterranean', but it is warmer and less polluted than its Old World counterpart, with a greener shoreline and finer beaches. The Caribbean islands have a population of more than thirty million and are a mosaic of different races, cultures, and religions. There are four main languages but English is widely spoken, and this, together with proximity to the USA has been a factor encouraging the development of tourism. The region is highly fragmented politically, consisting of some thirty island states of which two-thirds are members of the British Commonwealth, and of CARICOM, the Caribbean Economic Community. Most of the remaining territories retain close links with France, the Netherlands, and the USA, while Spanish-speaking Cuba and the Dominican Republic have more in common with the Latin American mainland.

Most of the islands are over-populated in relation to their resources, which are not abundant. Tourism is encouraged by governments who perceive that beaches, sunshine, and scenery are more marketable than the export of sugar, bananas, and spices. Tourism creates' jobs in a region where unemployment is high, where emigration has been curtailed, and where manufacturing industry is not viable. Tourism is now the largest industry in the Caribbean; in the early 1980s it was estimated that more than 80,000 were employed in the accommodation sector alone, with a further 80,000 directly or indirectly dependent on tourism for a livelihood. However, its importance varies from country to country; for example, visitor expenditure accounts for 80 per cent of the GNP of the Bahamas but only 5 per cent in the case of Dominica, one of the least developed islands.

The tourism industry of most Caribbean countries is largely dependent on the North American market, which supplies two-thirds of all staying visitors and over 90 per cent of cruise passengers. Most national currencies are tied to the United States dollar and accommodation in the islands is designed and priced accordingly. Since 1981 the United States dollar has been consistently strong on world markets relative to European currencies, so that the cost of a Caribbean holiday has tended to deter visitors from for example, Britain or West Germany.

A major problem faced by the tourist organizations is the promotion of individual national identities. Tour operators tend to regard the Caribbean islands as an interchangeable holiday product consisting essentially of beaches and stereotyped entertainment, whereas each country differs considerably in scenery, cultural background, and sophistication from its neighbours. Sports facilities are more highly developed than in most tropical destinations. The natural environment is ideal for windsurfing, water-skiing, parasailing, and diving. The many harbours are well equipped for yachting and game fishing, while golf and tennis are offered by most resort hotels. As mentioned in Chapter 5, the short distances between the islands make the Caribbean the most favoured location for cruising holidays.

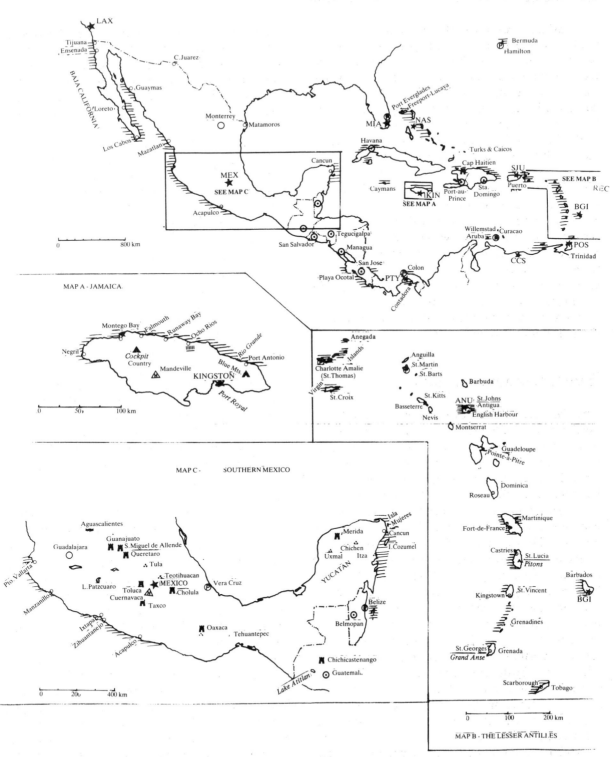

Figure 20.1 *Major tourist resources in Mexico, Central America, and the Caribbean Islands*

Since most islands lack the finance to promote themselves effectively overseas, the Caribbean Tourism Association (CTA) carries out joint promotion in Europe and North America for all the islands, with the exception of Cuba. In addition a number of small ex-British colonies in the Windward and Leeward Islands have joined together in the Organization of East Caribbean States (OECS) to pool their resources.

The Caribbean islands have demonstrated that tourism may be a mixed blessing. Much of the income from tourism is 'leaked' from the local economy through the importation of food and furnishings, much of which cannot be produced locally. Also profits are repatriated by foreign-owned travel companies and hotels, without really benefiting the local community. The alienation of some of the best beaches for resort development, and the conspicuously affluent life-style displayed by the predominantly white tourists in their resort enclaves has caused resentment in some of the more developed islands.

Although the climate of the Caribbean is tropical it is generally healthy. The North East Trade Winds moderate the rather high temperatures and humidity and bring heavy rainfall to windward coasts; locations on the same island in the lee of the prevailing wind can be remarkably dry, with desert-like vegetation. The best time for visiting the islands is from December to April when conditions are pleasantly warm, sunny, and relatively dry. This constitutes the 'high season' for winter sun-seekers mainly from North America. Summer temperatures are only a little higher, but there is a greater probability of rain; hotel prices are however considerably lower and this attracts a younger, less affluent visitor, including many from Europe.

While climatic conditions are fairly uniform, there are considerable differences in scenery between the various islands, and this partly explains why some have been more successful than others in attracting tourists. The largest islands, such as Trinidad and the Greater Antilles could be described as 'continents in miniature' in their relief and variety of landscapes. The smaller islands are either of limestone formation and low-lying, or of volcanic origin and mountainous. The 'low islands' such as the Bahamas and the Leewards have the best beaches of coral sand. The 'high islands' or Windward Islands which form a chain of the lesser Antilles from Saba to Grenada offer the more spectacular scenery, but have fewer beaches, and a wetter climate.

An island's success also depends on its ability to attract foreign investment, and its accessibility by air and shipping services. There are many small regional airlines in the Caribbean but only a few 'gateway' airports providing services to the smaller islands. Dominica for example is still undeveloped because its airport and harbour facilities are inadequate; there are no direct flights to either the USA or Europe, and the road system is poor on account of the dense vegetation and rugged terrain. On the other hand Barbados has a well-established reputation, with very good external and internal communications.

The Bahamas and Bermuda

Of all the Caribbean countries the Bahamas has achieved the greatest success in attracting tourists, due largely to the proximity of the islands to the USA. Nassau the capital is only 300 kilometres from Miami, the starting point for most cruises. Most of the hotels, casinos, shops, and sports facilities, especially for sailing, golf, and tennis are concentrated on the islands of New Providence around Nassau and Grand Bahama at the purpose-built resort of Freeport-Lucaya. The remaining 'Out' islands are for the most part undeveloped but are receiving increasing attention, along with the Turks and Caicos to the south. Abaco is renowned for its traditional boat-building industry, Eleuthera for game fishing, while the exceptionally clear waters around Andros are ideal for scuba diving.

Tourism is equally dominant in the economy of Bermuda. Although these coral islands are situated in the same latitude as Georgia, they are included with the Bahamas 2000 kilometres to the south west for their cultural similarities. Bermuda was originally developed as a winter resort for wealthy Americans from New York and Boston. However, the winters are now considered too cool for beach tourism and most visitors arrive during the summer months. The islands are still quite exclusive, offering excellent facilities for sailing, golf, and tennis.

Jamaica and the Cayman Islands

The largest of the English-speaking islands, Jamaica, has a well-established tourism industry with frequent air and shipping services to and from the capital, Kingston, and Montego Bay, the most important holiday resort on the north coast. During the 1970s it experienced a decline as a result of internal political strife and harrassment of white tourists. Outside Kingston, which is a major business centre for the Caribbean, most of the hotel accommodation is found along the north coast. Here the fine beaches are backed by forest-clad mountains, the most famous 'beauty spots' being Dunns River Falls near Ocho Rios and the Rio Grande near Port Antonio. There are excellent sports facilities, particularly in Montego Bay and Negril in the north west. The latter has been developed to cater for the younger more active type of tourist, whereas Port Antonio is more 'old fashioned'. Historical attractions include the 'great houses' built by the wealthy sugar planters in the days of slavery, and the old pirate stronghold of Port Royal at the mouth of Kingston harbour. Karst landscapes of the 'Cockpit Country' in the interior are relatively untouched by tourism.

The Cayman islands to the west of Jamaica specialize in diving holidays but offshore banking provides the main income for the British colony.

Barbados

Barbados is the easternmost of the Caribbean islands; and although one of the smallest it is highly developed and politically stable. Known as the 'Garden of the West Indies' the character of the island is largely the outcome of over three centuries of continuous British occupation. This partly explains its popularity with the British tourist, with an average of 60,000 arriving during the early 1980s, three times as many as for its main

competitors – Jamaica and the Bahamas. Sport, particularly cricket, is a major attraction and the island boasts some superb beaches along the west coast near the capital Bridgetown; the east coast is exposed to the Atlantic rollers and therefore much less developed.

The Windward and Leeward Islands

The smaller islands of the Commonwealth Caribbean vary in the extent of tourist development from Anguilla which is completely unsophisticated to Antigua which is a major holiday destination. Antigua has the advantage of an international airport with direct flights to and from London, the USA and Canada, and inter-island services to the other Leeward Islands. Antigua is noted for its many beaches, the two main centres being the capital St John – a major port of call for cruise ships, and English Harbour – an attractive yachting centre. Saint Lucia is the most highly developed of the Windward Islands, and to many visitors it represents the ideal holiday destination – fine beaches of coral sand as at Marigot Bay, and a mountainous interior, exemplified by the Pitons of volcanic origin rising sheer from the coast. The trend in the USA toward one-week Caribbean cruises has adversely affected Saint Lucia's income from shore excursions as the island is remote from Miami. Saint Vincent, the Grenadines, and Grenada, with their excellent deep water harbours are mainly popular with yachtsmen. Grenada also offers excellent beaches; on Saint Vincent they are mainly of black volcanic sand, as is the case with Montserrat, Saint Kitts, and Dominica.

Trinidad and Tobago

A large island whose population is divided between ethnic groups of African and Asian origins, Trinidad's economy is based mainly on petroleum, and tourism is of secondary importance. Nevertheless, Trinidad is famed for its steel bands, calypso singers, and limbo dancers culminating in the spectacular Carnival. Tourism figures more prominently in the smaller island of Tobago, with its mountainous scenery and superb beaches. The life-style here is much less frenetic than in Port of Spain, which is one of the main gateways to the Caribbean.

The French West Indies and Netherlands Antilles

Because of their status as overseas departments of France with the advantage of frequent flights to and from Paris, the islands of Martinique and Guadeloupe cater mainly for French visitors, although Club Mediterranee villages are increasingly popular with North Americans. Martinique is noted for the spectacular volcanic scenery of Mont Pelee and the folklore of its Creole population.

The Dutch islands of Curacao and Aruba, with their duty-free shopping and casinos attract large numbers of South American tourists, mainly from nearby Venezuela. Saint Martin much further north is an important port of call for cruise ships from Miami for similar reasons.

Puerto Rico and the Virgin Islands

As a result of their status as overseas territories of the USA, Puerto Rico and the islands of Saint Thomas, Saint John, and Saint Croix have the advantages of free access to sources of investment in the USA and frequent air and shipping services to and from the United States mainland. San Juan, the capital of Puerto Rico, preserves many reminders of its past as a Spanish colony while nearby there are beach resorts for American tourists. Saint Thomas is the most developed of the Virgin Islands and is a major port of call for cruise ships, offering duty-free shopping and sports facilities. The British Virgin Islands to the east are much less visited; however they are virtually dependent on the USA market and the American dollar is the local currency, although they retain much of their British character.

Cuba and Hispaniola

The tourism industries of Cuba, Haiti and the Dominican Republic, have been greatly affected by political factors. Cuba has many natural advan-

tages, not least its nearness to Florida and until the late 1950s it was the leading holiday destination of the Caribbean. The gambling and nightlife of the capital Havana attracted large numbers of visitors from the USA, which also largely controlled the country's economy. The Communist takeover resulted in an economic blockade of Cuba by the United States government which is still in effect, and the tourism industry suffered a drastic decline. Social tourism on East European lines has been encouraged by the Castro regime, and the remaining hotels are largely used by business travellers from Soviet bloc countries or youth groups. Since the late 1970s there has been some revival of inbound tourism from Western countries, notably from Canada and also Spain – which has retained close links with its former colony.

The Dominican Republic has been more successful in building up its tourism industry although it remains virtually an unknown country outside the USA and Spain. It can offer some of the oldest colonial architecture in the Americas, notably in the capital Santo Domingo. There are a number of purpose-built resorts based on the superb beaches along the north coast. The Dominican Republic has always had bad relations with its neighbour Haiti, the poorest country in the Western Hemisphere. Nevertheless, Haiti has a long history of independence so that racial tensions are largely absent and the visitor finds a unique blend of African and French Creole folklore. The most important tourist centres are the capital Port au Prince and Cap Haitien, with its spectacular citadel.

Mexico

Although physically part of the continent of North America, Mexico is one of the leading Latin American countries. Its heartland is a high plateau – the Meseta Central – with a relatively cool climate, separated by the mountainous barriers of the Sierra Madre from the tropical coastlands. With a rapidly growing population expected to reach eighty-five million by 1990, Mexico is the world's most populous Spanish-speaking nation. The Federal government exercises control throughout the country through the Mexican Revolutionary Party (PRI) which combines socialist and free enterprise policies. Mexico is one of the world's leading travel destinations. Between 1970 and 1980 income from tourism more than quadrupled, and now accounts for 10 per cent of the country's foreign exchange earnings. Over four million foreign tourists stay in Mexico annually, in addition to the much greater number of excursionists from the USA who briefly visit the border towns. The tourism industry is dependent on the United States market; less than 10 per cent of visitors originate from other countries. Mexico's appeal to North Americans is partly due to its beaches and winter sunshine, but more importantly the cultural contrast which the country offers. Although the majority of Mexicans are of mixed Spanish and Indian origin, the Indian heritage remains important, as shown by cuisine, folklore, and handicrafts.

There are abundant remains of pre-Columbian civilizations and these have been preserved by the government. Roman Catholicism also made a vital contribution as shown in the numerous fiestas, pilgrimages, and baroque churches.

While traditional Mexico provides the tourist image, modern Mexico is now a leading industrial nation, with large reserves of petroleum and other minerals. A substantial middle class generate a considerable demand for both domestic and international tourism. The latter is mainly directed towards the USA, where there are large Mexican immigrant communities. Until the economic crisis of the early 1980s Mexico seemed set to become one of the leading generators of international tourism. The majority of Mexicans do not have sufficient disposable income to take holiday trips even within their own country. There is however, some development of social tourism in holiday villages for industrial workers.

In an attempt to improve the economic situation the Mexican government has given tourism a prominent role in the current National Development Plan. Foreign developers are encouraged to participate in large hotel projects which will provide many new jobs, especially in the less developed parts of the country.

There is a strong Ministry of Tourism (SETUR) which is responsible for formulating policy. The federal government also take a direct role in tourist development through FONATUR, a funding agency. FONATUR not only provides finance to private developers and state governments but also plans and builds new resorts, namely Ixtapa near the fishing village of Zihuantanejo on the Pacific coast, and Cancun on the Caribbean coast of Yucatan, which now attracts over half-a-million tourists annually.

With the exception of an antiquated and rudimentary rail network Mexico is fairly well served by its transport services. The major cities are linked by modern highways to the USA but east-west communications are less adequate. Water supplies and sanitation are defective in many areas and these need to be improved if Mexico is to derive long term benefit from having staged international events such as the Olympic Games (1968) and the World Cup (1986).

Although most of Mexico's two million square kilometres fall within the tropics, the variations in altitude result in striking differences in climate over quite short distances. Mexicans refer to three altitudinal 'life' zones each offering a different habitat for plant and animal life. (A similar situation can be found throughout Central America and in the Andes.) First there is the tierra caliente or tropical zone up to 1000 metres; second is the tierra templada or sub-tropical zones between 1000 and 2000 metres where warm climate crops such as avocados and coffee are cultivated; and third is the tierra fria or cold zone above 2000 metres where nights are chilly, especially during the dry season although daytime temperatures are generally warm throughout the year.

Tourism in Mexico is fairly well distributed throughout the country, and each region has its own range of attractions. Some of the largest towns, including the capital, are located in the tierra fria, whereas most of the health resorts favoured by better-off Mexicans are situated in the mountain valleys of the tierra templada. The climate of the coastlands of the Gulf of Mexico and the low-lying isthmus of Tehuantepec is excessively warm and humid for most of the year. Conditions along the Pacific coast where there is a long dry season are generally more attractive for tourism.

The most visited tourist places are the towns along the USA border, particularly Tijuana. Spending by US visitors in the border towns accounts for over half of Mexico's receipts from tourism; such visitors are however cost-conscious and numbers vary according to the strength of the US dollar against the peso. Tijuana, Ciudad Juarez, and Matamoros have experienced mushroom growth and are rather over-commercialized entertainment centres, appealing mainly to young Americans.

The area richest in cultural and scenic attractions is the southern part of the Meseta Central which is easily accessible from Mexico City. The phenomenal growth of the capital from one million inhabitants in 1940 to seventeen million by the mid 1980s has been accompanied by severe congestion and pollution. The capital offers such varied attractions as the modern University with striking murals, the cathedral built on the site of an Aztec temple, the National Museum of Anthropology, and the floating gardens of Xochimilco. To the north of Mexico City are the impressive pre-Columbian sites of Teotihuacan and Tula. Dating from the Spanish colonial period are the former silver mining towns of Guanajuato, Taxco, and San Miguel Allende, and the cathedral cities of Cholula, Queretaro, and Puebla. Further west is Guadalajara, Mexico's second largest city, and the beautiful land of the Tarascan Indians around Lake Patzcuaro. In the south Oaxaca is another major Indian centre.

A number of holiday resorts which are popular with North Americans have developed along Mexico's long Pacific coastline. The most important centre on the 'Mexican Riviera' is Acapulco, along with former fishing ports like San Blas, Puerto Vallarta, Mazatlan, and Manzanillo. Developments consist mainly of luxury hotels and condominia. This region is now rivalling Florida as a retirement haven for North Americans due to its relative cheapness. Baja or Lower California to the north west is largely desert, but the beaches and excellent game fishing attract large numbers of Californians thanks to an excellent highway running the length

of the peninsula. Ensenada and La Paz have become major tourist centres, while the Mexican government is developing purpose-built resorts at Loreto and Los Cabos.

The Gulf coast of Mexico is much less popular as a holiday area although it contains the historic sea port of Vera Cruz. Further east is the Yucatan Peninsula with remains of the Maya culture, notably at Chichen Itza and Uxmal. These 'lost cities', dominated usually by pyramid-shaped temples have become major tourist attractions. The coastline consists of extensive beaches of white sand with coral reefs and islands offshore, providing an ideal environment for water-sports. As the region is somewhat isolated from the rest of Mexico the federal government has invested considerably in improving the infrastructure and developing facilities, notably at Cancun. This part of Mexico can easily be included in a Caribbean cruise itinerary and also has the advantage of greater proximity by air to Miami and the cities of the eastern USA.

Central America

Central America is a mountainous neck of land linking the continents of North and South America. It mainly comprises six small Spanish-speaking republics with a combined population of twenty-two million – English-speaking Belize is similar culturally and touristically to the Commonwealth Caribbean islands as shown by its membership of CARICOM and the CTA. The other countries have combined to form the Central American Common Market but economic integration and joint tourism promotion are unlikely to succeed in view of long standing political differences. Few air services link the region to Europe, and the great majority of tourists are from the USA, some travelling overland from Mexico City via the Pan-American highway as far as Panama, but most flying from Miami and other North American gateways.

Central America has considerable potential for tourism. There are great scenic and cultural contrasts between the Pacific and Caribbean coastlands, and the central highlands which traditionally have contained most of the population. *Costa Rica* with its stable government has been able to capitalize on these assets both in the capital San Jose and in beach resorts such as Playa Ocotal. In contrast, *Nicaragua* with similar natural resources has not developed a viable tourism industry due to the unfavourable political situation affecting that country. There are spectacular volcanoes throughout Central America and spas have developed around some of the numerous hot springs. The temples of pre-Columbian Indian civilizations can be seen, notably at Copan in Honduras and Zacaleu in Guatemala.

Central America is rich in folklore; this is particularly true of *Guatemala* which has a large Indian population retaining many of the traditions of their Mayan ancestors. Some of the Indian market towns such as Chichicastenango have attracted large numbers of mainly North American tourists and have become somewhat commercialized. Guatemala is also visited for the beauty of its lake and mountain scenery.

Panama has achieved the greatest success in developing a broadly based tourism industry. A vast volume of shipping uses the Panama Canal, while many airlines are served by the airport at Tocumen. The modern city of Panama and the free port of Colon are major centres of international commerce and as a feat of engineering the Canal is a major tourist attraction in itself. In complete contrast the jungles of Darien to the east still provide a barrier to the Pan-American highway linking North and South America; so that Panama has not yet realized its potential as the 'crossroads' of the Western Hemisphere.

Off the Atlantic coast the San Blas islands are noted for game fishing, while to the south of Panama City the Pearl Islands offer some of the finest beaches in the Americas. The most important of these, Contadora, has been developed as a luxury resort and conference centre.

South America

South America receives less than one per cent of the world's international tourist arrivals. The high cost of air fares and the lack of charter flights partly explains why South America remains a destination for the wealthy or adventurous traveller. There is also a shortage of suitable hotels for the inclusive tour market. Long term planning and investment in the tourism industry have been discouraged by political instability and inflation which have given the continent unfavourable publicity.

Climatic conditions, dense vegetation, and rugged terrain have been a great obstacle to road and railway construction in many areas. Water transport is still widely used wherever there are navigable rivers, such as the Amazon and its tributaries, but the shipping services are usually slow and uncomfortable. Transport infrastructure is gradually improving with the expansion of the Pan-American highway network, and the development of internal air services.

A number of countries in South America are undergoing rapid industrialization, with a resulting increase in business travel from Europe and the USA. As regards the holiday market, national tourist offices in South American countries generally are underfunded, so that overseas promotion has been left to specialist tour operators and airlines in the generating countries. So far Brazil has achieved a much greater degree of success as a long-haul destination than any of the nine Spanish-speaking republics. However five of these – the Grupo Andino (Andean Pact countries), consisting of Bolivia, Peru, Ecuador, Colombia, and Venezuela have agreed to facilitate transport between member states and carry out joint tourism promotion.

Northern South America

The northern countries of South America can be included as part of the Caribbean region; in fact two – Venezuela and Surinam – belong to the Caribbean Tourist Association (CTA) while Guyana is a member of Caricom. Colombia and Venezuela share an extensive coastline on the Caribbean and the cities of Cartagena and Caracas feature prominently on some cruise intineraries. Guyana, Surinam, and French Guiana have cultural similarities with the West Indian islands and retain close links with Britain, the Netherlands,

Figure 20.2 *Major tourist resources in South America*

and France. The folklore of the coast of Colombia, Venezuela, and the Guianas is African rather than American Indian in origin.

Colombia is the leading destination in northern South America. Mainly known for its coffee exports, Colombia has achieved considerable industrial development and contains a number of major cities such as Bogota, the capital, Medellin, and Cali. Tourism in the early 1980s accounted for around 2 per cent of the GDP and 13 per cent of the country's foreign exchange earnings. Tourist development is the responsibility of the Corporacion Nacional de Turismo (CNT) which has built a network of Paradors along the main tourist routes. Most visitors arrive overland from neighbouring Ecuador and Venezuela, attracted by shopping bargains. Promotion is mainly aimed at the United States market, although increasing numbers of tourists are coming from West Germany and France. The Andes make east to west surface communications extremely difficult and the national airline Avianca was among the first to pioneer domestic air services in Latin America. Another constraint on tourist development is the prevalence of crime, partly stemming from Colombia's role in the international drugs trade.

Colombia's Pacific coastline has an extremely humid climate and is relatively inaccessible. The Caribbean coastline is much more attractive with a long dry season. Tropical beaches are backed by the snow-capped mountains of the Sierra Nevada de Santa Marta. The most important tourist centres are the beach resort of Santa Marta and the historic seaport of Cartagena once the key fortress of the 'Spanish Main'. In the interior of Colombia the main tourist attractions are cities such as Popayan, located in beautiful mountain valleys, which still retain much of their Spanish colonial heritage.

In the early 1980s *Venezuela* received over 200,000 tourist arrivals annually, of whom almost half came from Europe. However, this is largely because the capital Caracas has become one of the leading gateways to South America. As a member of OPEC the country had the highest per capita income of any Latin American country and middle class Venezuelans travelled abroad in large numbers leaving a substantial deficit on the travel account.

For inbound travellers, prices are high, and apart from the services provided by the national airline, Viasa, transport facilities are inadequate. Caracas is a modern business centre near some of the best beaches in the Caribbean, on the island of Margarita and at Puerto la Cruz. Merida boasts the world's highest cableway to the summit of Pico de Espejo, Venezuela's highest mountain. In the sparsely populated south Angel Falls, the world's highest waterfall, can be reached by light aircraft.

Guyana and *Surinam* have much to offer wildlife enthusiasts, but tourism is of little importance. *French Guiana* is mainly famous for its former role as the penal colony of Devil's Island. Now an overseas department of France it benefits from frequent air services from Paris to Cayenne.

The Andean republics

South of Colombia the Andes become two major ranges separated by a series of intermontane basins or high plateaux. Mountain peaks provide a challenge for climbers from all over the world. The spectacular scenery of the Callejon de Huaylas valley in Northern Peru and Lake Titicaca – the world's highest inland waterway – also attract increasing numbers of trekkers from Europe and North America. Ecuador, Peru, and Bolivia also offer a great deal of cultural interest. The capitals – Quito, Lima, and La Paz – are rich in art treasures dating from the colonial period. Intricate cultivation terraces on the steep mountain sides as well as the massive remains of fortresses and temples bear witness to the achievements of the Incas who ruled this part of South America prior to the Spanish conquest. Archaeology has revealed mysterious features (such as the Nazca Lines) from much earlier civilizations.

Basically the region consists of three main divisions – the Pacific coastal lowlands, the Sierra or Andean mountain region, and the forested lowlands to the east of the Andes – which form part of the vast Amazon Basin. The majority of the tourist attractions are to be found in the Sierra, within which there is a great variety of climate and landscape due to differences in altitude. Conditions are particularly severe on the high Bolivian Plateau, or Altiplano, where the traveller has to endure tropical sun by day and sub-zero temperatures by night, as well as the risk of mountain sickness due to the rarified air. In contrast the enclosed valleys of the Sierra, especially in Ecuador, have an ideal climate which can justly be described as 'perpetual spring'.

Of the three Andean republics tourism is most developed in *Peru*, whose capital Lima is a major gateway to South America. Tourists from Western Europe accounted for over 40 per cent of all arrivals in the early 1980s, double those from the United States. Peru appeals both to the luxury tour market, which has proved resilient to the effects of recession, and to the young traveller on a budget, who is not deterred by the very basic nature of the low-cost accommodation available. Nevertheless Peru's earnings from tourism only account for 1 per cent of GNP. Furthermore wealthy Peruvians spend almost as much on travel abroad. The Peruvian government is involved in developing tourism through agencies such as Enturperu which runs a chain of state owned turistas (tourist hotels) and Copesco which is concerned with restoring historical sites.

Lima is the starting point for tours of the Sierra. These typically include the colonial city of Arequipa situated at the foot of the volcanic cone of El Misti, and the Inca remains around Cuzco, notably the 'lost city' of Machu Picchu. The concentration of tourists here is causing concern, and the Peruvian government would like to develop alternative attractions, such as Cajamarca with its thermal springs in the north of the country. However, a major handicap is the inadequate road transport which tends to be very slow due to the difficult terrain, while alternative air services are expensive. Spectacular narrow gauge railways, tourist attractions in themselves penetrate into the Andes. Although Peru has a long coastline tourism is little developed due to the cold Humboldt current flowing offshore which brings high humidity to this rainless coast.

Bolivia's development as a tourist destination has been held back by its landlocked location. *Ecuador* possesses more natural advantages as a long-haul destination by virtue of its Pacific beaches, volcanic mountain scenery, and picturesque Indian markets, all to be found within a relatively compact area, but so far, little has been done to develop and promote these assets effectively. The Galapagos Islands are a famous nature reserve, visited by cruises from Guayaquil 1000 kilometres away on the mainland of Ecuador.

Brazil

Unlike most Latin American countries Brazil has a well-defined tourism image based mainly on the beaches and the Carnival of Rio de Janeiro. Brazil is one of the world's largest countries, only slightly smaller than the USA in area. The great majority of its 130 million people are concentrated along the eastern seaboard. Like the USA Brazil is a 'melting pot' of immigrants from Europe, Africa, and Asia.

Brazil's market potential for tourism is increasing with the rapid development of the economy. Most of the country's industrial wealth is concentrated in the Sao Paulo – Rio de Janeiro – Belo Horizonte triangle. There is a considerable demand for tourism from Brazil's growing middle class but since the early 1980s the government has required bonds to be deposited by Brazilians travelling abroad and this has acted as a deterrent. Camping is enjoying a boom in popularity, but Brazilians are mainly interested in beach holidays and rarely venture for pleasure inland beyond Ouro Preto – an historic city 300 kilometres north of Rio de Janeiro. Under the country's labour laws, employees are guaranteed a forty-eight hour week and annual paid holiday of twenty days, but many are excluded from becoming tourists by low incomes, especially in the rural areas. However, recreational and catering facilities are provided by the government for city workers, while the beaches are freely available to rich and poor alike. The development of tourism is supervised by a Federal government agency, Embratur (Empresa Brasileira de Turismo), which reports to the Ministry of Industry and Commerce. Special incentives apply to the regional development areas in the North East and Amazonia which are the responsibility of two other Federal agencies – Sudene and Sudam respectively.

Despite these efforts tourism accounts for less than one per cent of GNP and 5 per cent of export earnings. However the number of visitors from Europe and the USA has increased much faster than those from other Latin American countries. The months of January and February see the greatest tourist activity, coinciding with the carnival season, although they can be too warm and humid for comfort. One-third of all visitors from Europe and the USA come primarily for business reasons.

The vast size of Brazil results in major problems for overland transport, especially during the rainy season from December to May. The Amazon and its tributaries constitute 20,000 kilometres of navigable waterway, but these are situated far from the major populated areas and port facilities are inadequate. The national transport strategy is to construct a number of major highways through the rain forest to improve access to the Amazon and eventually link up with the road system of neighbouring countries. Brazil's internal air network is excellent with nine international airports and hundreds of airfields allowing access to even the most remote areas. Services are provided by the national airline Varig and its subsidiaries.

Brazil has five tourist regions. Of these, Amazonia holds a fascination for foreign visitors as an ecological resource threatened with destruction. Most tourists arrive by air at Manaos and Belem. Both cities have fine buildings dating from the rubber boom of the 1890s, while Manaos has the additional attraction of duty-free shopping. Santarem at the confluence of the Amazon and the Tapajoz is another important tourist centre. River excursions to view the wildlife are available by 'floatel' and motor canoe, but visits to Indian villages are discouraged by FUNAI, the Indian Protection Agency.

The North East is Brazil's poorest region, where drought is a problem. The cattlemen of the backcountry and the fishermen of Recife are major elements in the local folklore. Embratur have developed beach resorts such as Itaparica. Among the cities, Salvador is the most attractive with its colonial architecture and spectacular carnival.

In the South of Brazil the major tourist attraction is the Iguassu Falls, (three times as large as Niagara) on the border with neighbouring Paraguay and Argentina. The South is the only part of the country to enjoy a temperate climate with occasional frosts during the winter.

The undeveloped heartland of Brazil, the Centre-West, benefited from the construction of Brasilia in the 1960s as the new Federal capital. Most of the region consists of savanna grassland, with extensive swamps along the Paraguayan border. The government sponsored National Environment Agency has designated national parks in this area to protect wildlife, but as in other parts of Brazil these have been opposed by ranchers and developers.

The South East of Brazil receives the most foreign tourists. Rio de Janeiro is the leading gateway to the country and is one of the world's great cities, with a magnificent natural setting on Guanabara Bay between the mountains of Corcovado and Sugar Loaf. Rio's most famous attractions are the beaches of Copacabana, Ipanema, and Gavea. The coastline between Rio and Santos backed by the lush mountain scenery of the Serra do Mar has been designated for major resort development. Inland, Sao Paulo, one of the world's largest cities, is a major business centre with shuttle air services to and from Rio.

Temperate South America

Chile, Argentina, Uruguay, and Paraguay occupy the southern third of the continent, tapering towards Antarctica. Distance from the generating countries has been a severe constaint on the development of international tourism. With the exception of Paraguay, a largely Indian country which is one of the poorest in the Western Hemisphere, there is a relatively high level of economic development and educational attainment. Argentina and Uruguay have attracted many immigrants from Europe; here the Indian influence is insignificant in contrast to most of Latin America. Tourism industries are well established in Chile, Argentina, and Uruguay, and there is a substantial middle class providing a large domestic market.

Chile and Argentina are separated by the Southern Andes. The only important route across this mountain barrier is the Uspallata Pass, with its famous statue of 'Christ of the Andes'. The Southern Andes are famed for their lake, forest, and glacier scenery, and a number of national parks have been established. The more accessible locations have been developed for winter sports, notably at Portillo in Chile and at San Carlos de Bariloche in the Argentine Lake District. These resorts attract many skiers from the USA during their summer.

Argentina has a population of twenty-six million of whom a third live in the capital Buenos Aires. The almost featureless pampas grasslands form the heartland of the country's 2.8 million square kilometres, but more interesting for tourism are the Andean foothills to the west with many historic towns.

Since the Peron era of the 1940s social tourism has been important in the form of subsidized rail travel and holiday villages organized by the trade unions. Wealthier Argentinians travel abroad to other South American countries, especially to neighbouring Uruguay, where the beaches and entertainment facilities of Punta del Este are the main attraction. Spending on outbound tourism is severely curbed by the low value of the Argentinian peso on international markets. Conversely the weakness of the currency has made Argentina an attractive proposition for foreign visitors, especially North Americans.

The gaucho (cattleman) of the pampas and the barbecue have become national institutions. In contrast, Buenos Aires is one of the world's great cosmopolitan cities. From the capital an extensive rail network provides access to many parts of the country. The most favoured resort areas are the hilly country around Cordoba which provides relief from the hot humid summers of Buenos Aires, the beaches of Mar del Plata, and the foothills of the Andes around Lake Nahuel Huapi.

Few tourists, other than wildlife enthusiasts, venture south of the Rio Negro into Patagonia, which is largely a windswept semi-desert. The birds and sea mammals of the South Atlantic should entice tourists to the *Falkland Islands*, whose scenery and climate are not unlike those of the Scottish Hebrides. The opening in 1985 of a modern airport at Port Stanley has made the islands more accessible to Europe.

Most of *Chile*'s fifteen million people are concentrated in the fertile Central Valley which has a climate not unlike that of California, and where the attractive countryside contains many vineyards. Santiago at the foot of the snowcapped Andes is one of the most attractive Latin American capitals, while the chief seaport Valparaiso compares in its situation with San Francisco. The popular beach resort of Vina del Mar is situated nearby. Northern Chile is arid but Southern Chile suffers from an excess of rainfall, and the rather bleak cloudy climate is a major constraint on the development of tourism. The magnificent fjord scenery is however accessible by coastal shipping services which link Central Chile to the free port of Punta Arenas on the Magellan Straits.

Summary

Latin America is a cultural entity consisting of three distinct geographical regions. Of these the Caribbean is the most important from the viewpoint of inbound tourism. The English language is widespread throughout the islands while the Iberian culture and languages are dominant on the mainland of Central and South America. Broadly speaking, the Caribbean islands cater mainly for 'recreational' tourism whereas Mexico, Central America, and South America appeal more to 'cultural' tourists.

The USA dominates the market for Caribbean travel although the Bahamas, Jamaica, and Barbados have achieved wider appeal as holiday destinations due to their accessibility by air and shipping services. On the Latin American mainland Mexico is clearly the most important destination, again due to its proximity to the USA. Despite having spectacular scenery Central and South America have been much less successful. This is partly due to political instability and the inadequacy of the infrastructure. Countries such as Peru and Brazil should benefit from the growing popularity of long-haul holidays. Business travel is also likely to increase to those countries which are achieving rapid economic development such as Brazil and Colombia.

Although incomes are generally low throughout Latin America domestic tourism is significant and there is a considerable demand for outbound tourism to Europe and the USA from a growing middle class.

Suggested further reading

Chapter 1

There are a number of recent texts which give an overview of tourism as a system. These include Mathieson and Wall's (1982) Chapters 1 and 2 where a conceptualization of tourism is outlined and tourism is placed in the context of leisure and recreation, and Chapter 1 in Ashworth (1984) which gives a clear account of the place of tourism in the leisure continuum. More general considerations of the scope and nature of tourism are found in Burkart and Medlik (1981), Part II; Matley (1976); Chubb and Chubb (1981) Chapter 3; and both Foster (1985) and Murphy's (1985) first chapters. Ideas for practical exercises in tourism and recreation geography are found in Bull and Daniel (1981).

Works dealing with aspects of tourist flows are less common but Matley (1976) gives a readable account written from a geographical viewpoint, whilst the measurement of flows is comprehensively dealt with in Burkart and Medlik (1981), Part III; and is also covered in Holloway (1983) pages 13–17. Capacity issues are dealt with in most texts covering destination development, particularly Patmore (1983), Chapter 7; Mathieson and Wall (1982) Chapter 2; and Murphy (1985) Chapter 5.

Chapter 2

The approach to tourist demand adopted in this book leans heavily on Chubb and Chubb's (1981) encyclopaedic account of demand for recreation and tourism worldwide. This is found in Part 2, particularly Chapters 4, 6, and 7. General concepts of demand for tourism are clearly expounded in Lavery's (1971) Chapter 1, and in Mercer (1980) where Chapter 3 deals with concepts of demand and Chapter 4 covers participation, but from a refreshingly Australian perspective. Aside from these all the major tourism texts deal with demand – Burkart and Medlik's (1981) Parts II and VII are characteristically thorough; Holloway's (1983) Chapter 3 is a readable account; Wahab's (1975) Chapter 8 is from an economist's viewpoint; Ashworth's (1984) Chapter 2 is more geographical; and Foster (1985) gives demand a marketing application in Chapter 3. More specialized aspects of demand are covered by Pearce (1982) whose book is concerned with social psychology; while McIntosh and Goeldner (1984) deal at length with the sociology and psychology of tourist demand (Chapters 4 and 5) – as does Foster in his chapters on marketing (particularly pages 31–7 and 251–6).

Chapter 3

There are a number of texts dealing with tourist supply. Good general accounts are found in Chubb and Chubb's (1981) Part 3 with its North American viewpoint; Patmore's (1972) and (1983) lively and readable accounts of the British experience; Burkart and Medlik's (1981) Part VIII; and Mercer's (1980) general account with an Australian flavour. Issues of supply are also covered in Ashworth's (1984) Chapters 3 and 4 where case studies are given. More advanced accounts of tourist development and its impact are found in Mathieson and Wall's (1982) thorough book, in Pearce's (1981) briefer account, and McIntosh and Goeldner's (1984) Chapter 11. Resource classification and evaluation are dealt with in Pigram's (1983) Chapter 3, and examined comprehensively in Coppock and Duffield (1975), though Lavery's (1972) Chapter 11 covers the same material in a more digestible form. The more specialized topic of resort development is covered in Lavery's (1971) Chapter 8; weather and tourism in Lundberg's (1985) Chapter 12; and destination planning and development in Lundberg's (1985) Chapters 9 and 10, Gee's (1984) Part 3, and Foster (1985) in pages 37–47. Murphy's (1985) Chapters 4 and 5 give a refreshingly different, and well-illustrated view of tourist resources with relevant examples. Issues of the impact of tourist development on developing countries are dealt with in de Kadt (1979).

Chapters 4 and 5

Tourism and transport are dealt with in many of the standard texts, particularly Burkart and Medlik's (1981) Part IV; Holloway's (1983) Chapters 5 and 6; Gee's (1984) Part 5; Robinson's (1976) Chapter 8; and Foster's (1985) Chapter 5. Chubb and Chubb (1981) give a well-illustrated basic account of transport for tourism and recreation. Faulks (1982) deals with transport from a professional transport planner's point of view. The geography of transport worldwide is well covered in Robinson and Bamford (1978) with sections on the elements of transport, the contemporary world transport network, and a chapter on transport and tourism.

Chapters 6 to 20

Robinson (1976) and Hurdman (1980) are the only English texts dealing with the geography of tourism worldwide, aside from Cosgrove and Jackson's (1972) highly selective accounts in Chapter 3. Robinson's Part 5 covers tourism in selected countries throughout the world, though with an emphasis on European destinations and those in the Americas. Hurdman's (1980) account of world tourism is less detailed, providing thumbnail sketches of the state of tourism in the major countries in Part VI, and a more comprehensive view of tourism in the USA in Chapter 11. Aside from these two books, there is no one English source which gives an account of tourism in the world on a country by country basis. Even regional geography texts often omit tourism completely; this was certainly the case until 1970 but since then tourism and recreation have been recognized as an activity worthy of mention in some regional texts. A notable leader in this field has been texts on France beginning with Clout's (1972) book with its sections on recreation and tourism planning, and later House's (1978) text where tourism is given full treatment (pages 286–98). Ardagh (1977) and (1982) gives lengthy everyday details of French leisure, recreation, and holiday patterns and has fascinating insights into the political background to the regional planning developments such as Languedoc-Roussillon. Aside from this French example extensive treatment of tourism at the regional level is only found in the geographical journals. Particularly useful sources are *Geography* (especially 'This Changing World'); the *Geographical Magazine*; and occasional articles in the *Geographical Review*. In fact, for regional coverage of tourism it is necessary to look beyond the geographical literature to the specialist tourism journals. *International Tourism Quarterly* (relaunched as *International Tourism Reports* in 1986) is invaluable here with its country and regional profiles of tourism. Other sources include *Tourism Management* which is taking on an increasingly international stance; *The Tourist Review* published in Switzerland; and the more descriptive *Holiday Which* and *ABTA Travel News*. For more general accounts of the role of tourism within countries the Bank Reports (National Westminster, Barclays, and Lloyds) are useful, as are the country profiles in the *Financial Times*, and the OECD country reports. The British Tourist Authority also publish travel market profiles, mainly from the point of view of inbound tourism to the UK but containing useful data on leisure time, holiday entitlement, and other aspects of various countries. Another useful, but sometimes superficial, source is the country profiles published in the *Travel Trade Gazette* (TTG) and *TTG Europa*. Finally national tourist organizations and embassies are an important source of information, particularly if they know exactly what is required by students.

There is a plethora of sources of data on countries throughout the world but perhaps the most useful are the *World Bank Atlas* (annual) with its maps and data on population and economies of every country in the world. Paxton's (annual) *Statesman's Yearbook*, and Europa Publications' (annual) *Europa Yearbook* give accounts of the economy, population, government, geography, and other aspects of virtually every country in the world. Pearce and Smith's (1984) *World Weather Guide* is an invaluable country by country guide to weather conditions throughout the world.

The basic sources for international tourism statistics are the OECD's annual 'Blue Book' – *Tourism Policy and International Tourism in OECD Member Countries*, and the series of statistical reports produced by the World Tourism Organization (WTO). Of the latter their annual *World Travel and Tourism Statistics* and biennial *Tourism Compendium* are perhaps the most useful. Withyman (1985) has written a definitive guide to these and other sources of tourism statistics. Edwards (1985) and Cleverdon (1985) give very detailed accounts and forecasts of various sectors of the tourist market, backed by extensive statistics and commentary.

Selected bibliography

Ardagh, J., *The New France*, Penguin, 1977.

Ardagh, J., *France in the 1980s*, Secker and Warburg, 1982.

Ashworth, G., *Recreation and Tourism*, Bell and Hyman, 1984.

Bull, C. J. and Daniel, P. A., *The Geography of Outdoor Recreation: Suggestions for Practical Exercises and Fieldwork*, Geographical Association Occasional Paper 23, 1981.

Burkart, A. J. and Medlik, S. (eds), *The Management of Tourism*, Heinemann, 1975.

Burkart, A. J. and Medlik, S., *Tourism, Past, Present, and Future*, Heinemann, 1981.

Chubb, M. and Chubb, H. R., *One Third of Our Time*, Wiley, New York, 1981.

Clawson, M. and Knetsch, J., *The Economics of Outdoor Recreation*, Johns Hopkins University Press, Baltimore, 1966.

Cleverdon, R., *International Business Travel: a New Megamarket*, Economist Intelligence Unit, 1985.

Clout, H. D., *The Geography of Post–war France*, Pergamon, 1972.

Cohen, E., 'Toward a Sociology of International Tourism', *Social Research*, Vol. 39, No. 1, pp. 164–83, 1972.

Coppock, J. T. and Duffield, B. S., *Recreation and the Countryside*, Macmillan, 1975.

Cosgrove, I. and Jackson, R., *The Geography of Recreation and Leisure*, Hutchinson, 1972.

de Kadt, E. (ed), *Tourism – Passport to Development?* Oxford University Press, 1979.

Edwards, A., *International Tourism Forecasts to 1995*, Economist Intelligence Unit, 1985.

Europa Publication, *The Europa Yearbook: A World Survey*, Europa, (annual).

Faulks, R. W. *Principles of Transport*, Allan, 1982.

Foster, D. *Travel and Tourism Management*, Macmillan, 1985.

Gee, C. Y., Choy, D. J. L., Makens, J. C., *The Travel Industry*, AVI, 1984.

Holloway, J. C., *The Business of Tourism*, Macdonald and Evans, 1983.

House, J. W., *France: An Applied Geography*, Methuen, 1978.

Hurdman, L. E., *Tourism: A Shrinking World*, Wiley, New York, 1980.

Lavery, P. (ed), *Recreational Geography*, David and Charles, 1971.

Leiper, N. 'The Framework of Tourism', *Annals of Tourism Research*, Vol. 6, No. 4, pp. 390–407, 1979.

Lundberg, D. E. *The Tourist Business*, Van Nostrand Reinhold, New York, 1975.

McIntosh, R. W. and Goeldner, C. R., *Tourism: Principles, Practices, and Philosophies*, Wiley, New York, 1984.

Mathieson, A. and Wall, G., *Tourism: Economic, Physical and Social Impacts*, Longman, 1982.

Matley, I. M., *The Geography of International Tourism*, Association of American Geographers

Resource Paper 76 1, Washington, 1976.

Mercer, D., *In Pursuit of Leisure*, Sorret, 1980.

Murphy, P. E., *Tourism. A Community Approach*, Methuen, 1985.

Organisation for Economic Co-operation and Development, *Tourism Policy and International Tourism in OECD Member Countries*, OECD, Paris, (annual).

Patmore, J. A., *Land and Leisure*, Penguin, 1972.

Patmore, J. A., *Recreation and Resources*, Blackwell, 1983.

Paxton, J. (ed), *The Statesman's Yearbook*, Macmillan (annual).

Pearce, D., *Tourist Development*, Longman, 1981.

Pearce, E. A., and Smith, C. G., *The World Weather Guide*, Hutchinson, 1984.

Pearce, P. L., *The Social Psychology of Tourist Behaviour*, Pergamon, 1982.

Peters, M., *International Tourism*, Hutchinson, 1969.

Pigram, J., *Outdoor Recreation and Resource Management*, Croom Helm, 1983.

Robinson, H., *A Geography of Tourism*, Macdonald and Evans, 1976.

Robinson, H. and Bamford, G., *Geography of Transport*, Macdonald and Evans, 1978.

Smith, S. L. J., *Recreation Geography*, Longman, 1983.

Smith, V. L. (ed), *Hosts and Guests: The Anthropology of Tourism*, Blackwell, 1978.

Turner, L. and Ash, J., *The Golden Hordes. International Tourism and the Pleasure Periphery*, Constable, 1975.

Wahab, S. A., *Tourism Management*, Tourism International Press, 1975.

Williams, A. V. and Zelinsky, W., 'On Some Patterns in International Tourist Flows' *Economic Geography*, Vol. 46, No. 4, pp. 549–67, 1970.

Withyman, M., 'The Ins and Outs of Tourism Data', *International Tourism Quarterly* No. 4, pp. 61–76, 1985.

World Bank, *The World Bank Atlas*, World Bank, Washington, (annual).

World Tourism Organization, *Economic Review of World Tourism*, WTO, Madrid, (biennial).

World Tourism Organization, *Tourism Compendium*, WTO, Madrid, (biennial).

World Tourism Organization, *World Travel and Tourism Statistics*, WTO, Madrid, (annual).

Appendices

APPENDIX 1

The gravity model

The gravity model is based on Newton's law of universal gravitation which states that two bodies attract each other in proportion to the product of their masses and inversely by the square of their distance apart. In other words, flows between two regions can be predicted by multiplying together their mass (for example population) and dividing it by the square of some measure of their distance apart. Simply, the model states that flows decrease as you move further away from their origin and increase to, or from, large locations. Distance can be measured as simple linear distance, or time, or cost. In the case of tourism, the model assumes that flows decrease as distance from the origin increases. This may be so after a certain distance, but tourists actually 'desire' to travel and the model may therefore need to be adjusted to accommodate this. Similarly, the model assumes two-way flow, but tourist flows tend to be one-way, from generating areas to destination areas, with fewer flows in the opposite direction.

The diagram shows the interaction between three countries. By using a measure of their 'mass' (the figures in circles) and the 'distance' between them, the two-way flow between the countries can be calculated. It must be noted that the gravity model predicts relative flows rather than absolutes (i.e. it can be said that the flow between B and C is twice that of the flow between A and C).

The gravity model predicts flows using the formula:

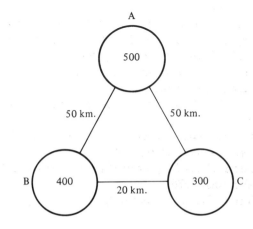

$$T_{AB} = K \frac{P_{op_A} \times P_{op_B}}{Dist_{AB}}$$

where T_{AB} is the estimated number of trips between countries A and B, P_{op_A} and P_{op_B} are measures of 'mass' (in this case population), $Dist_{AB}$ is the distance between countries A and B, and K is a scaling factor to ensure that the predicted number of trips is of the same order of magnitude as the actual trips.

so, $T_{AB} = \frac{1}{3} \dfrac{500 \times 400}{50} = 1,333;$

$T_{BC} = \frac{1}{3} \dfrac{400 \times 300}{20} = 2,000$

and $T_{AC} = \frac{1}{3} \dfrac{500 \times 300}{50} = 1,000$

APPENDIX 2

Defert's Tourist Function Index (T_f)

$$T_f = \frac{N \times 100}{P}$$

where N is the total number of tourist beds in a region, and P is the total number of residents in the region. Defert's Tourist Function Index can be calculated for the Channel Island of Jersey:

N = 25,000
P = 75,000

therefore, $T_f = \dfrac{25,000 \times 100}{75,000} = 33\frac{1}{3}$ per cent

APPENDIX 3

Calculation of travel propensity and travel frequency

Out of a population of 10 million inhabitants:

3.0 million inhabitants take one trip of one night or more   i.e. $3 \times 1 = 3.0\text{m trips}$
1.5 million inhabitants take two trips of one night or more   i.e. $1.5 \times 2 = 3.0\text{m trips}$
0.4 million inhabitants take three trips of one night or more   i.e. $0.4 \times 3 = 1.2\text{m trips}$
0.2 million inhabitants take four trips of one night or more   i.e. $0.2 \times 4 = 0.8\text{m trips}$

5.1 million inhabitants take at least one trip   8.0m trips

therefore:

Net travel propensity = $\dfrac{\text{Numbers of population taking at least one trip}}{\text{Total population}} \times 100 = \dfrac{5.1}{10} \times 100 = 51\%$

Gross travel propensity = $\dfrac{\text{Number of total trips}}{\text{Total population}} \times 100 = \dfrac{8}{10} \times 100 = 80\%$

Travel frequency = $\dfrac{\text{Gross travel propensity}}{\text{Net travel propensity}} = \dfrac{80\%}{51\%} = 1.57$

A further refinement to the above calculations is to assess the capability of a country to generate trips. This involves three stages. Firstly, the number of trips originating in the country is divided by the total number of trips taken in the world. This gives an index of the ability of each country to generate travellers. Secondly, the population of the country is divided by the total population of the world, thus ranking each country by relative importance in relation to world population. By dividing the result of the first stage by the result of the second the 'country potential generation index' (CPGI) is produced (Hurdman, 1979).

$$CPGI = \frac{\dfrac{N_e}{N_w}}{\dfrac{P_e}{P_w}}$$

where N_e = number of trips generated by country
N_w = number of trips generated in world
P_e = population of country
P_w = population of world

An index of 1.0 indicates an average generation capability. Countries with an index greater than unity are generating more tourists than expected by their population. Countries with an index below 1.0 generate fewer trips than average.

Adapted from: Schmidhauser, H., 'Travel Propensity and Travel Frequency', pp. 53–60 in Burkart, A. J. and Medlik, S., *The Management of Tourism*, Heinemann, 1975; and Hurdman, L. E., 'Origin Regions of International Tourism' *Wiener Geographische Schriften*, 53/54, pp. 43–9 1979.

APPENDIX 4

Domestic and abroad tourism in selected Western European countries

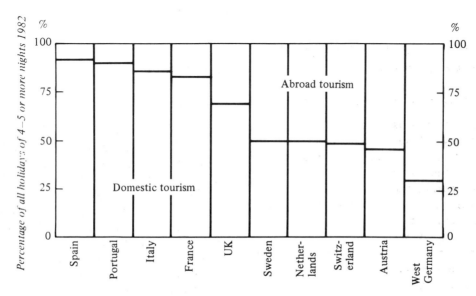

Adapted from *The Economist*, no. 192, 1984, pp. 53–4.

APPENDIX 5

Social and economic indicators of selected countries, 1980

Country	Population			Gross National Product	Per 1000 population numbers of:			Typical leisure		
	Total (millions)	Density per sq. km.	Urban % of total	Per capita US $ thousands	TVs	Tele-phones	Cars	Working week (hours)	Public holidays (days)	Annual leave (weeks)
Australia	14.6	2	89	10.0	378	489	478 [2]	40	9	4+
Austria	7.5	90	54	9.4	296	401	292	35–40	13	4+
Belgium	9.9	323	72	11.1	296	369	318	35–40	10	4+
Canada	23.9	2	80	10.2	471	686	428	35–40	9	3+
Denmark	5.1	119	84	12.0	368	641	322	35–40	12	5+
Finland	4.8	14	62	9.7	322	496	289	40+	16	5+
France	53.7	98	78	11.2	297	459	402	35–40	10	5+
Germany (FDR)	61.6	248	85	12.3	337	464	392	40	14	5+
Greece	9.6	73	n/a	4.2	156 [4]	289	90	40+	12	4
Ireland	3.3	47	58	4.9	190	187	226	40+	9	4
Japan	116.8	314	78	9.0	539	460	203	40	12	4
Italy	56.2	186	69	6.4	238	337	334	35–40	10	4+
Luxembourg	0.4	140	78	15.1	248	547 [1]	430	40	13	5
Netherlands	14.1	415	76	11.0	294	509	322	35–40	8	4+
New Zealand	3.3	12	85	6.7	278	550	399 [3]	35–40	11	3
Norway	4.1	13	53	12.8	293	452	340	40	10	4+
Spain	37.4	74	74	5.2	238	315	203	40+	14	6
Sweden	8.3	19	87	13.7	381	796	370	35–40	11	5+
Switzerland	6.3	154	58	16.0	310	727	373	40+	10	4+
UK	56.1	229	91	8.5	331	477	280	40	8	4+
USA	227.7	24	77	11.6	624	788	673	35–40	9	3+

Notes

n/a   not available

1   1979

2   1978

3   1977

4   licences

Sources: British Tourist Authority, *Travel Market Profiles* BTA; Edwards, A., *International Tourism Forecasts to 1995*, EIU, 1985; *The Europa Yearbook 1984*, Europa, 1984; United Nations, *UN Statistical Yearbook 1981*, UN 1983; World Bank, *World Bank Atlas 1984*, World Bank, Washington, 1983; Miscellaneous National Sources

APPENDIX 6

World international tourist arrivals by WTO region

WTO Region[1]	International tourist arrivals at frontiers (millions)				
	1979	1980	1981	1982	1983[P]
Africa	5.9	6.4	7.2	6.8	6.7
Americas	51.4	54.2	53.9	51.1	50.1
East Asia/Pacific	16.3	18.7	21.7	23.0	23.2
Europe	192.0	196.9	196.5	195.0	196.1
Middle East	5.1	5.8	6.1	7.0	7.0
South Asia	2.2	2.3	2.4	2.4	2.4
Total	272.9	284.3	287.8	285.3	285.5

Note: (P) Provisional
(1) See Appendix 12
Source: WTO, *Breakdown of World Tourism Statistics 1979–82*, WTO, Madrid, 1983.

APPENDIX 7

International tourist arrivals for selected countries, 1979, and 1983

Country	Notes		Tourist arrivals		Tourist nights	
			1979	1983	1979	1983
Austria	AH	TA	8.9	10.2	84.8	87.4
Belgium		TA	n/a	n/a	6.5	8.4
Bulgaria	V	A	5.1	5.8	16.8	16.8
Denmark		TA	n/a	n/a	8.3	9.5
Egypt	V	H	1.1	1.0	7.1	8.8
Finland		H	n/a	n/a	1.7	2.0
France	T	H	28.8	33.2	n/a	16.6
Hungary		A	n/a	n/a	11.3	14.0
Israel	T	H	1.1	1.0	7.1	6.0
Italy	V	H	48.7	46.6	66.3	63.2
Korea (Republic of)	V	A	1.1	1.2	3.1	3.7
Morocco	T	A	1.4	1.9	5.8	7.2
Netherlands	AH	H	2.7	3.0	6.0	6.1
Norway	NSV	H	0.5	0.5	2.3	2.3
Portugal	T	TA	2.2	3.7	9.2	11.9
Sri Lanka	T	A	0.2	0.3	2.7	3.2
Sweden		H	n/a	n/a	2.8	3.0
Switzerland	AH	H	5.8	6.9	16.9	19.8
Thailand	V	H	1.6	2.2	7.9	10.7
Tunisia	T	H	1.5	1.4	11.2	10.3
United Kingdom	V	TA	12.5	12.5	154.6	145.4
West Germany	ATA	H	8.9	9.8	17.1	19.1
Yugoslavia	V	TA	18.7	19.7	33.5	35.3
Argentina	T		1.0	1.3		
Australia		V	0.8	0.9		
Bahamas		T	1.1	1.2		
Bermuda		T	0.5	0.5		
Brazil		T	1.1	1.4		
Canada		T	12.6	12.5		
Chile		T	0.3	0.3		
Colombia		T	1.2	1.1		
Greece		T	5.2	4.8		
Guatemala		T	0.5	0.2		
Hong Kong		V	2.2	2.8		
India		T	0.8	1.3		

Iraq	V	1.2	1.5
Ireland	T	1.7	2.2
Japan	V	1.1	1.9
Jordan	V	1.3	1.7
Malta	T	0.6	0.5
Mexico	T	4.1	4.7
New Zealand	V	0.4	0.5
Philippines	V	1.1	0.9
Romania	V	6.0	5.8
Singapore	T	2.2	2.8
Spain	V	38.9	41.3
Syria	V	0.9	0.8
Turkey	Tr	1.0	1.6
USA	T	20.3	21.6

Notes

V   Foreign visitor arrivals at frontiers
T   International tourist arrivals at frontiers
AH Arrivals in hotel accommodation
NSV Non-Scandinavian visitor arrivals by air and sea
ATA Arrivals in tourist accommodation
Tr Travellers at frontiers
TA Nights spent in registered tourist accommodation
A   Nights spent in tourist accommodation
H   Nights spent in hotels
All figures are in millions

Sources: OECD, *Tourism Policy and International Tourism in OECD Member Countries*, OECD, Paris, (annual); United Nations, *UN Statistical Yearbook 1981*, UN, Washington, 1983; World Tourism Organization, *World Tourism Statistics*, WTO, Madrid, (annual).

APPENDIX 8

The Psychrometric Chart – Humidity and Effective Temperature

Relative humidity measures the moisture content of the air as a percentage of the total amount that it could contain at a given temperature. It is usually determined by using a psychrometer, which consists of two thermometers. One of these has damp cloth wrapped around its bulb and the reading taken from the thermometer is called the '*wet bulb*' *temperature*. This is always lower than the 'dry bulb' or air temperature due to cooling by evaporation, except when the air is saturated (100% relative humidity). Once both temperatures are known the relative humidity can be derived from the Psychrometric Chart. The right hand scale of the chart indicates the amount of water vapour actually present; it will be seen that tropical air at 35°C can carry nine times more moisture than cold air at 0°C.

Relative humidity will decrease as the temperature rises, and vice-versa; generally speaking the minimum will occur in early afternoon at the same time as the maximum air temperature. If in summer air at 35°C with 20% relative humidity is cooled to a comfortable room temperature of 22°C its relative humidity will increase to 40% without any moisture being added. Conversely, if in winter cold outside air at 0°C with 80% relative humidity is warmed to 22°C its relative humidity will fall to 20%, which is too dry for comfort.

An example of the importance of relative humidity is to compare the climate in June of Athens with Freetown, West Africa. Both places have the same average maximum temperature – 30°C, but the climate of Athens in summer is much drier, with a wet bulb temperature of 20°C and a relative humidity of 39%. Freetown on the other hand has a wet bulb temperature of 26.5°C and a relative humidity of 76%. The relatively dry air of Athens allows evaporation of moisture to take place rapidly from the skin, whereas in Freetown the body's natural cooling mechanism is inhibited by the high humidity, although sweating may be profuse over the skin surface.

Effective temperature combines air temperature and relative humidity in a way that can be applied to measure human comfort/discomfort. A similar concept is the Temperature-Humidity Index (THI) used by the United States Weather Bureau. An effective temperature of 26°C means that under actual conditions of temperature and humidity the sensation of warmth would be the same as in motionless saturated air at 26°C. This would occur at 29°C with 50% relative humidity but at a much higher temperature – 36°C in dry desert air with only 10% relative humidity. In June Athens and Freetown have daytime effective temperatures of 25°C and 28° respectively.

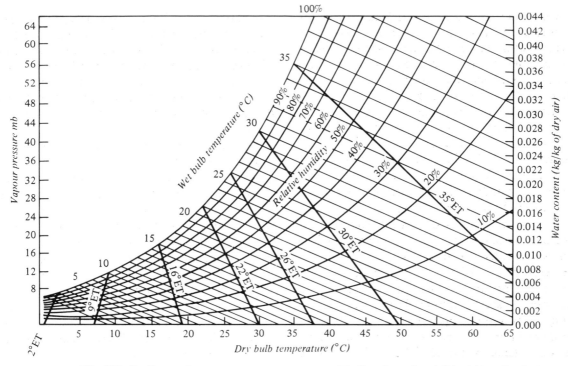

ET – Effective Temperature

35°ET – Probable heatstroke

30°ET – Outdoor activities severely restricted

26°ET – Everyone feels discomfort

22°ET – 50 per cent of people feel discomfort

Most people feel comfortable between 16°ET and 22°ET

The lines drawn from left to right on the chart show the wet-bulb temperature

APPENDIX 9

The ORRRC classification of recreation resources

High density recreation areas A wide variety of uses and substantial development using all available resources. Intensive development of resort hotels and facilities managed for mass use (e.g. Disneyland, theme parks, and amusement parks).

General outdoor recreation areas A wide variety of use with substantial development. More choice of resources exercised. Some distance from population centres (e.g. ski fields and centres).

Natural environment areas Multiple use frequent with a variety of uses according to area (e.g. national parks).

Unique natural areas Areas of scenic splendour, natural wonder, or scientific importance. Main activity is sightseeing.

Primitive areas Undisturbed wilderness and road-less areas where natural, wild conditions prevail.

Historic and cultural sites Local, regional, or national sites. Historic buildings and artifacts, archaeological sites, spas, health resorts, shrines, and pilgrimage sites.

Adapted from: Outdoor Recreation Resources Review Commission, *Outdoor Recreation for America*, pp. 96–120, US Government Printing Office, Washington, 1962.

APPENDIX 10

Duffield and Owen's resource evaluation technique (1970)

The technique uses four separate assessments of resource capability and then combines them into a single assessment for two-kilometre grid squares. The assessments used are suitability for land-based recreation activities, suitability for water-based recreation activities, scenic quality, and ecological significance. Minimal criteria are established for six groups of land-based recreation activities and five groups of water-based activities. The criteria for land-based recreation suitability are:

(a) Camping, caravanning, picnicking: all countryside within 400 metres of a metalled road;
(b) Pony-trekking: all upland areas above 300 metres with rights of way, or established footpaths and bridleways;
(c) Walking and hiking: all upland areas above 450 metres with rights of way, or established footpaths and bridleways;
(d) Game-shooting: all areas assessed as shooting on valuation rolls;
(e) Rock-climbing: all cliff faces over 30 metres in height;
(f) Skiing: available relief over 280 metres with an average snowholding period of more than three months.

Each time a criterion is satisfied for a grid square a point is scored by the square. The scores are then weighted, with 100 representing the highest possible score on each component, giving a possible top score of 400 when the assessments are combined. These totals are mapped and used to identify a range of recreation environments.

The method is not free of problems. Choice of activities and criteria is arbitrary and no account of access or management is included. However, the technique is readily handled by computers and it does allow the identification of areas of recreation and tourism potential.

Source: Duffield, B. S. and Owen, M. L., *Leisure and Countryside – A Geographical Appraisal of Countryside Recreation in Lanarkshire*, University of Edinburgh, 1970.

APPENDIX 11

A typology of tourist resorts

Capital cities High standard of accommodation located around transport links and adjacent to tourist attractions. High standard of retailing, tourist facilities, and services. Concentrations of 'national culture' in museums and art galleries. Tourism is only one of many functions. Business tourism is important. Tourists are typically short-stay, with a high percentage of international visitors (e.g. Paris, Rome, London, Tokyo, New York).

Select resorts Concentration of high standard accommodation with some lower standard accommodation. Located away from large population centres, often in scenically attractive settings. Extensive visitor hinterlands (e.g. Cannes, San Remo).

Popular resorts Wide range of accommodation, attracting large numbers of holiday visitors. Purpose-built, modern accommodation and facilities are common. Typically very seasonal (e.g. Benidorm, Blackpool, Acapulco).

Minor resorts Absence of commercialism and organized tourism. Small towns in rural or coastal settings attracting a limited, but loyal clientele, located in less accessible, less popular holiday areas (e.g. Tenby, Granville).

Cultural/historic centres Attract a high proportion of overseas visitors because of the nature of their facilities, including museums, art galleries, and theatres (e.g. Florence, Stratford-upon-Avon).

Winter sports resorts   Typically in mountainous location with resort facilities often purpose-built and geared to skiing, skating, and snowmobiling. Now expanding into all-year-round provision. (e.g. Grenoble, St Moritz, Aviemore, Aspen).

Spas/watering places   A growing category in Western Europe, but with long-stay visitors (e.g. Vichy, Baden Baden).

Day-trip resorts   Located close to major population concentrations. Day visitors dominate and this is reflected in the facilities and services provided. Highly seasonal and weather sensitive visiting patterns (e.g. Atlantic City, Southsea, Ostend, Brighton, Zandvoort).

Adapted from: Lavery P. *Recreational Geography*, pp. 188–90, David and Charles, 1971.

APPENDIX 12

Time zones and elapsed flying times

The world's time zones are shown on the map. These correspond to political units rather than strictly following the meridians (for example Paris one hour ahead of GMT despite having the same longitude as London). A number of countries are too large for one standard time to be conveniently acceptable. The Soviet Union has the greatest east to west spread of any country, with no less than eleven time zones; when the sun sets on the Baltic coast at Leningrad the new day is already breaking on the Pacific shore 11,000 kilometres to the east. In the continental United States there are four time zones – Eastern, Central, Mountain, and Pacific.

Time differences can be illustrated by a case study. Take an aircraft flying from London to Singapore. Assuming the time of departure to be 0700 GMT on November 30 it would arrive at its destination at 0600 on the morning of December 1, a timetable difference of 23 hours. To calculate the elapsed time – how long the journey actually takes – it is necessary to find out the time zone designation for Singapore and convert local time to GMT as follows:

	0600	Arrival time Singapore (local time = GMT + 7 hr 30 minutes)
Deduct	0730	to convert to GMT
	2230	the previous day, equivalent time in London GMT
	0700	departure time in London GMT
	1530	

The difference is the actual journey time, 15 hours 30 minutes.

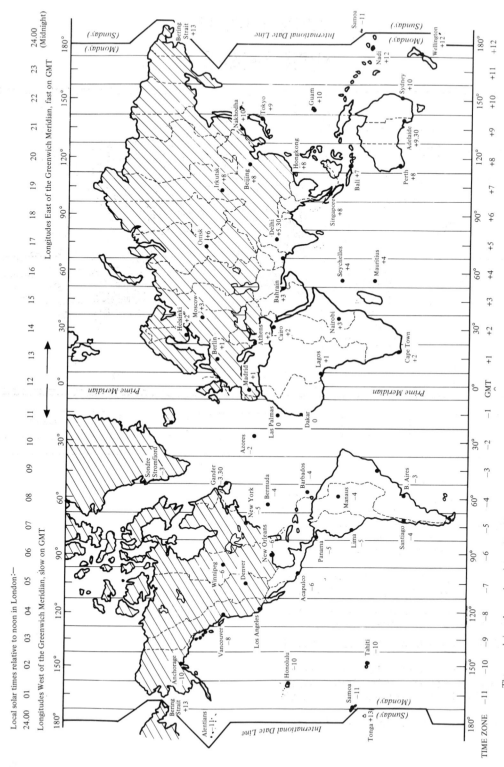

The numerals in each zone show the number of hours to be added to, or subtracted from, Greenwich Mean Time (GMT = 0) Thus Sydney in Time Zone + 10 is ten hours fast or ahead of GMT. The shaded areas on the map use Daylight Saving Time during the Summer months, thus New York in July is GMT − 4, in January GMT − 5 (Daylight saving time is also used by some Southern Hemisphere countries during their summer.)

APPENDIX 13

IATA AREAS

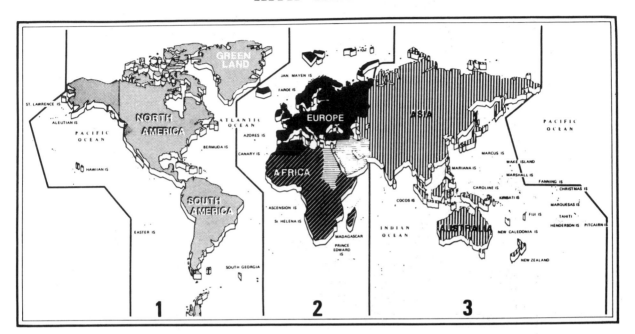

AREA 1
North. Central and South America and environs.

AREA 2		
Europe	Middle East	Africa

AREA 3
Far East, Australia, New Zealand and Pacific Islands.

IATA traffic conference areas

For organizational purposes, the world is divided into three main IATA traffic conference areas, each with geographical subdivisions (see map).

No. 1 (TC1) For the Western Hemisphere (North, Central and South America, including Hawaii and the Caribbean)

No. 2 (TC2) For Europe, Africa and the Middle East

No. 3 (TC3) For Asia and the South West Pacific

There are also four traffic conferences covering routes between the various conference areas:

Nos. 1 and 2 (TC12) North, Mid and South Atlantic Routes

Nos. 2 and 3 (TC23) Routes between Europe/Africa/Middle East and South West Pacific

Nos. 3 and 1 (TC31) North, Central and South Pacific Regions

Nos. 1, 2 and 3 (TC123) Round the World Routes

Indexes

Subject

Accessibility, 28
Aeroflot, 122
Air Algerie, 130
Air transport, 35, 38–40
    airports, 39–40
    routes, 38–9
Aircraft:
    jet, 37
    STOL, 39
Airports, 38–40
    location, 39
    needs, 39–40
Albergues, 96
Albtourist, 121
Algerian Ministry of Tourism, 130
Altitude, see Climate; Relief
Andean Pact countries, 191
ASEAN, 152
Attitudes, 13
Australian Tourist Commission, 161
Australian Transcontinental
   Railway, 42
Austrian National Tourist
   Organisation, 72
Avianca, 193
Aviogenex, 112

Balkan Tourist, 120
Belgian National Tourist Office, 83
Berlin Wall, 120
Berolina, 121
Blue Train, 135
Bord Failte Eireann, 55
British National Travel Survey, 5
British Tourism Survey, 5
British Tourist Authority, 55
Bulgarian Association for

   Recreation and Tourism, 120
Bullet train, 156
Business tourism, 3, 11

Canadian Government Office of
   Tourism, 179
Canadian National Railroad, 179
Canadian Pacific Railroad, 42, 179
Car ownership, 42, 45
Caribbean Tourism Association,
   186, 190, 191
CARICOM, 184, 190
Carpati, 119
Carrying capacity, 6
   environmental, 7
   physical, 6
   psychological, 7
Carrying unit, 33
Cedok, 118
Central American Common Market,
   190
Centros de Iniciativas, 97
Ceylon Tourist Board, 152
Chicago Convention, 38
Chinese General Administration of
   Travel and Tourism, 157
CIT, 106
Clarksons, 48
Clawson's classification of recreation
   resources, 26–7
Climate, 18–25, 53, 62, 71, 80, 86,
   99, 111, 121, 127, 131, 134, 137,
   141, 149, 162, 165, 166, 170, 179,
   186, 189, 193–4
Climographs, 19
Club Mediterranée, 127

Coaching, 42
Coastal resource, 26
Colonies des Vacances, 87
Common interest tourism, 3
Communism, 115
   planned economies, 12
   in Southeast Asia, 155
Complementarity, 31
Copesco, 194
Corporacion Nacional de Turismo,
   193
Cruising, 40–1
   destinations, 41
Currency controls, 12
Cyprus Tourism Organisation, 145

Dachas, 122
Danish Tourist Board, 64
Demographic transition, 11
Destination surveys, 5
DFDS, 64
Domestic tourism, 2
   patterns of, 12

East Asia Travel Association, 149
Economic development, 9
ECOWAS, 137
Educational attainment, 13
EGAPT, 143
EI AL, 143
Elapsed time, 213
Embratur, 194
Employment, 13
English Tourist Board, 55
ENIT, 106
Enturperu, 194

Ferries, 41
Finnish Tourist Board, 67
Föhn wind, 21, 71
FONATUR, 189
Forestry Commission, 53
Freedoms of the air, 38–9
French Secretary of State for
    Tourism, 88
Friction of distance, 5, 31
FUNAI, 195

Gambling, 136, 177
GARUDA, 54
German Convention Bureau, 76
German National Tourist
    Organisation, 76
German Reise-analyse, 5
German Tourist Federation, 76
Gîtes, 87
Grand Tour, 105
Gravity model, 5
Great circle routes, 38
Greenwich Mean Time, 38

Haj, 146
HIDB, 60
Holiday tourism, 3
Hovercraft, 35
Humidity, 19
Hungarian Ministry of Tourism, 118
Hydrofoil, 25

IATA, 39
Icelandair, 68
Income, 12
    discretionary, 13
    disposable, 12
    gross, 12
Indian Ministry of Aviation and
    Tourism, 150
Indian Tourism Development
    Corporation, 150
Indonesian Directorate General of
    Tourism, 154
Inex Adria Airways, 112
Infrastructure, 28
Inland water resources, 26
International Date Line, 38
International Passenger Survey, 6
International tourism, 2
    patterns of, 12
Intervening opportunity, 31
Intourist, 122
Israeli Ministry of Tourism, 143
Israeli occupation of the West Bank,
    144

JAT, 112
Japanese National Tourism
    Organisation, 156
Jet lag, 38
Jet stream 38
Jordanian Tourism Board, 144

Kenyan Tourist Development
    Corporation, 133

Landforms, 22
Land surface:
    influence on climate, 19
Latitude, 19
Leisure, definition, 1
Life cycle, 13
Life product, 28–9
Life zones, 189
Load factor, 33
London Visitor and Convention
    Bureau, 57
Long-haul tourism, 3
Luxembourg Ministry of Tourism,
    84

Malaysian Airline System, 154
Malta Government Tourist Board,
    109
Mardi Gras, 175
Marginal cost, 33
Mass tourism, 15
Migration, 2
Mobility, 13
Motive power, 32
Motorways, 42

National parks:
    France, 90, 92
    East Africa, 131, 133
    North America, 171, 176, 177,
        181
    South Africa, 135
National travel surveys, 5
National Trust (UK), 54
Netherlands National Tourist
    Office, 83
Northern Ireland Tourist Board, 55
Norwegian State Railways, 67

Oceans, 22
Orbis, 120
Organisation of East Caribbean
    States, 186
ORRRC, 27

Paid holiday entitlement, 13
Paradors, 96
PATA, 160
Perceptions, 13
Petroleum, 37
Philippines Ministry of Tourism,
    155
Philippines Tourism Authority, 155
Pleasure periphery, 29
Political administrations, 11
    Conservative, 11
    Socialist, 11
Polish General Committee for
    Tourism, 120
Political influences on demand, 11
Population:
    growth and development, 11
    density, 11
    distribution, 11
Portuguese Secretary of State for
    Tourism, 102
Pousadas, 102
Precipitation, 19
Pull factors, 4
Push factors, 4

Rail transport, 41–2
    decline of, 42
    track, 35
Recreation, definition, 1
Recreational business district, 28
Regional nature parks (in France),
    92
Relief, influence on weather, 19, 23,
    25, 71, 189, 193–4
Resorts, 28
    classification, 28
    cycle, 28
    landscapes, 28
Resource evaluation, 27
Road transport, 33, 42
Ryokan, 156

Safaris, 131
SAS, 68
Scale, 3
SCNM, 130
Scottish Tourist Board, 55
Sea transport, 35, 40–1
    routes, 40–1
    sea ports, 41
Seasonality, 18
SETUR, 189
Shanty towns, 184

Falkland Islands, 196
Fano, 64
Fiji, 167
Finland, 62, *65*, 67–8
Flanders, 83
Florence, 105, 106
Florida, 171, 175
France, 48, 85–93, *89*
Frankfurt, 76–7
Fraser River, 181
French Riviera, 88, 90
Fuerteventura, 100
Funchal, 101, 103

Galapagos Islands, 194
Galicia, 97
Gambia, 137, 138
Garden Route (Cape Province), 135
Georgia, USA, 174
Georgia, USSR, 124
Germany, East (GDR), 70, 120–1
Germany, West, 70, 71, *73*, 75–7
Gibraltar, 95, 101
Goa, 150
Gold Coast (Ghana), 138
Gold Coast (Queensland), 163
Gota Canal, 67
Gotland, 67
Gran Canaria, 100
Great Barrier Reef, 163
Great Lakes, 176
Greece, 109–11, *110*
Greenland, 38, 182
Greenwich Meridian, 38
Grenada, 187
Gross Glockner, 72
Guatamala, 191
Guianas, 191, 193
Gulf of Mexico, 170, 175
Gulf States (Arabia), 146

Haifa, 143
Haiti, 188
Halkidiki, 111
Hamburg, 76, 77
Hammamet, 129
Hanover, 77
Harz Mountains, 77, 121
Hawaii, 166, 177–8
Helsinki, 67
Hesse, 77
Himalayas, 149, 150, 152
Hokkaido, 155, 157
Holland, *see* Netherlands
Holy Land, 141
Hong Kong, 39, 158

Honolulu, 178
Hungary, 116–18

IATA Conference Areas, 39, *215*
Ibiza, 100
Iceland, 62, 68–9
India, Republic of, 149–51
Indian Subcontinent, 149–52, *151*
Indian Ocean, 136–7, 138, 152, 163
Indo China, 152
Indonesia, 154–5
Inland Sea, 157
Innsbruck, 72
International Dateline, 38
Iran, 146–7
Iraq, 147
Ireland, Republic of, *see* Eire
Isle of Man, 61
Isle of Wight, 58
Israel, 143
Istria, 112
Italy, 104–8, *107*
Italian Lakes, 108
Italian Riviera, 106, 108
Ivory Coast, 137, 138

Jaipur, 150
Jamaica, 187
Japan, 12, 37, 42, 155–7
Java, 154
Jerusalem, 143
Johannesburg, 135
Jordan, 143, 144
Jura Mountains, 75

Kalahari, 135
Karakorum Highway, 152
Kashmir, 150
Keflavik, 68
Kent, 58
Kentucky, 174
Kenya, 131, 132
Kilimanjaro, 131, 133
Kjolen Mountains, 62
Knokke-Heist, 83
Korea, 157
Kruger National Park, 135

Labrador, 40, 179, 181
Lake District (England), 59
La Mancha, 100
Langkawi Islands, 154
Languedoc-Roussillon, 90, *91*, 92
Lanzarote, 100
Lappland, 67, 68
Las Vegas, 176

Latin America, 96, 183–97
Laurentian Mountains, 181
Leningrad, 122
Lebanon, 144
Lesotho, 136
Libya, 126
Liguria, 106, 108
Lima, 194
Loire Valley, 90
Lombardy, 104
London, 38, 39, 51, 54, 57
Los Angeles, 177
Luxembourg, 79, 83–4

Macau, 158
Machu Piccheu, 194
Madagascar, 136, 137
Madeira, 101, 103
Madras, 151
Madrid, 96, 100
Maine, 173
Majorca (Mallorca), 19, 99, 100
Malawi, 136
Malaysia, 154
Maldives, 152
Malta, 108–9
Manaus, 195
Manila, 155
Marrakesh, 127
Martinique, 188
Massif Central, 90
Maui, 178
Mauritius, 137
Mecca, 146
Melanesia, 167
Melbourne, 163
Meseta (Spain), 95, 100
Mexico, *185*, 188–90
Miami, 175, 186
Michigan, 176
Micronesia, 166
Mid West, 175–6
Middle East, 37, 141, *142*, 145–7
Minorca, 100
Mississippi, 170, 174
Mittelge-birge, 71, 76
Moldavia, 119
Mombasa, 133
Mongolia, 155
Montenegro, 113
Montreal, 179, 181
Moravia, 118
Morocco, 101, 126, 127, *128*
Moscow, 122
Moselle, 77
Mozambique, 136

Munich, 77
M'zab, 131

Nairobi, 131, 133
Naples, 105, 108
Narita Airport, 39
Nassau, 186
Natal, 134, 135
Nepal, 152
Netherlands, 3, 12, *81*, 80–2
Nevada, 176
New Caledonia, 167
New England, 173
New Mexico, 176
New Orleans, 174, 175
New South Wales, 162
New York, 173
New Zealand, 35, 165–6
Newfoundland, 181
Ngorongoro Crater, 131
Nigeria, 138
Nile Valley, 141, 143
Norfolk Broads, 54, 58
North Africa, 126–31, *128*
North America, 26, 33, 39, 41, 42, 169–82
North Cyprus, 145
North Frisian Islands, 76–7
North Island, *see* New Zealand
North Korea, 157
North West Territories, 182
Northern Hemisphere, 18, 19, 22
Northern Ireland, 53, 54, 55, 60
Northern Territory, 162, 165
Norway, 41, 62, 64–6, *65*
Nova Scotia, 181

Oahu, 178
Okanagan, 181
Okinawa, 155
Oman, 146
Oregon, 177
Oslo, 66
Ostend, 83

Pakistan, 152
Pan-American Highway, 42, 190, 191
Panama, 191
Panama Canal, 40, 191
Papua-New Guinea, 167
Paraguay, 195
Paris, 87, 88, 90
Patagonia, 196
Peak District, 59
Penang, 154

Pennine Way, 7
Pennsylvania, 174
Peru, 193, 194
Philadelphia, 174
Philippines, 155
Piedmont, Italy, 106
Piedmont, USA, 174
Poland, 120
Polynesia, 167, 178
Portugal, 94, *98*, 100–3
Prague, 119
Prince Edward Island, 181
Puerto Rico, 188
Pusztas, 118
Pyrenees, 90, 95, 96, 100

Quebec, 179, 181
Queensland, 162, 163

Red Sea, 134, 143
Reykjavik, 69
Rhine, 76–7
Rift Valley, 131, 134
Rio de Janeiro, 194–5
Rockies, 21, 170, 176, 181–2
Rome, 108
Rotorua, 166
Ruanda, 131
Rumania, 119
Russia, *see* Soviet Union

Sahara, 126, 129, 130, 131
Sahel (West Africa), 137
Saimaa, 68
St Lawrence River, 41, 170, 179, 181
St Lucia, 181
St Moritz, 74, 75
St Pierre and Miquelon, 181
Salvador (Bahia), 195
Salzburg, 74
Samoa, 167
San Francisco, 35, 177
San Sebastian, 95, 99
Santander, 95, 97
Santiago de Chile, 196
Santiago de Compostela, 97
Sao Paulo, 194
Sardinia, 108
Saudi Arabia, 146
Scandinavia, 62–9
Scheveningen, 82
Scotland, 47, 53, 60
Senegal, 138
Serbia, 113
Serengeti, 133

Seville, 101
Seychelles, 137
Siberia, 39, 123
Sicily, 108
Silk Road, 158
Singapore, 152, 154
Slovakia, 118
Slovenia, 112–13
'Snowbelt', 170
Snowdonia, 59
Somalia, 134
Sousse, 129
South Africa (RSA), 134–6
South America, 191–6, *192*
South Asia, *see* Indian Sub-Continent
South Australia, 163
South East Asia, 11, 152–5, *153*
South Island, *see* New Zealand
Southern Alps, 165–6
Southern Hemisphere, 19, 22
Soviet Union (USSR), 39, 41, 121–4, *123*, 213
Spain, 48, 94–101, *98*
Sri Lanka (Ceylon), 152
Stockholm, 67
Sudan, 134
Suez Canal, 40
Sun City, 136
'Sunbelt', 170
Swaziland (Ngwane), 136
Sweden, 62, *65*, 66–7
Switzerland, 42, 71, 74–5
Sydney, 163
Syria, 144

Tahiti (French Polynesia), 167
Taiwan, 157
Takoradi, 35
Tangier, 101, 127
Tanzania, 131, 133
Tasmania, 162, 163
Tatra Mountains, 118
Tenerife, 100
Tennessee, 174
Texas, 176
Thailand, 155
Tibet, 158
Tijuana, 190
Tobago, 187
Togo, 137
Tonga, 167
Toronto, 179
Trans-African Highway, 138
Trans-Canadian Highway, 179
Trans-Siberian Railway, 42, 123

Transylvania, 119
Trinidad, 186, 187
Tropic of Cancer, 18
Tropic of Capricorn, 19
Tunisia, 129
Turkey, 109, 144–5
Tuscany, 108
Tyrol, 72

Uganda, 131, 133
Ulvik, 66
Umbria, 108
United Arab Emirates, 146
United States of America, 3, 9, 12,
    27, 28, 31, 37, 39, 42, 48, 169,
    170–8, *172*, 213
Uruguay, 196
USSR, *see* Soviet Union

Valais, 75

Valparaiso, 196
Vancouver, 181
Veneto, 106
Venezuela, 191, 193
Venice, 105, 108
Vermont, 173
Victoria, Australia, 163
Victoria Falls, 136
Victoria, Lake, 133
Vienna, 71, 72
Virgin Islands, 188
Virginia, 174
Volga, 122
Vorarlberg, 72

Wadden (Frisian) Islands, 82
Wales, 47, 59–60
Washington DC, 174
Washington, State, 177
West Africa, 137–8

West Bank (of Jordan), 143
Western Australia, 163
Western Hemisphere, 38
Winnipeg, 181

Xian, 158

Yellowstone, 176
Yemen, 146
Yorkshire, 59
Yosemite, 177
Yugoslavia, 111–14, *113*
Yukon, 182

Zaire (Congo), 126, 138
Zambezi, 126
Zambia, 136
Zimbabwe, 136
Zululand, 135
Zurich, 71, 74, 75